Dynamics of Asian Development

The series situates contemporary development processes and outcomes in Asia in a global context. State intervention as well as neoliberal policies has created unusual economic and social development opportunities. There are also serious setbacks for marginalized communities, workers, the environment, and social justice. The rise of China, India, and new dynamism of South Korea, Indonesia, and Vietnam in East and South East Asia have given a new meaning to Asian development dynamics. Japan's energetic ties with India and Vietnam, Korea joining the OECD's Development Assistance Committee, and China and India's investments and foreign aid in Africa and Latin America are some of the new processes of development whose impact transcends the vast Asian region. Globalization compounds uneven development, affecting macroeconomic stability, internal and international migration, class and caste dynamics, gender relations, regional parity, education and health, agriculture and rural employment, informal sector, innovation possibilities, and equity. Thus the series views development studies as an unfinished agenda of economic, social, political, and cultural interactions in a fluid policy and global contexts. The editor, with the assistance of a distinguished group of development scholars from Asia and elsewhere specializing in a variety of disciplinary and thematic areas, welcomes proposals that critically assess the above-mentioned wide-ranging developing issues facing Asian societies. With Asia's contemporary transformation, the series promotes the understanding of Asia's influence on the prospects of development elsewhere. The editor encourages interdisciplinary, heterodox approaches within the social sciences, and comparative work with solid theoretically informed empirical research. Critical development policy debates in Asia and regional governance issues that have a bearing on development outcomes are also sought.

More information about this series at http://www.springer.com/series/13342

Nandini Ghosh
Editor

Interrogating Disability in India

Theory and Practice

Springer

Editor
Nandini Ghosh
Institute of Development Studies Kolkata
Kolkata
India

ISSN 2198-9923 ISSN 2198-9931 (electronic)
Dynamics of Asian Development
ISBN 978-81-322-3593-4 ISBN 978-81-322-3595-8 (eBook)
DOI 10.1007/978-81-322-3595-8

Library of Congress Control Number: 2016945108

Printed on acid-free paper

This Springer imprint is published by Springer Nature
The registered company is Springer (India) Pvt. Ltd.

Acknowledgements

The chapters published in this volume are revised and updated editions of papers presented in a two-day multidisciplinary conference titled "Interrogating Disability: Theory and Practice", held on 27 and 28 September 2012 at the Institute of Development Studies Kolkata. The conference was the first of its kind in India. As the convener of the conference, I appreciate the encouragement provided by Prof. Amiya Kumar Bagchi, Emeritus Professor of the Institute. Dr. Ramkrishna Chatterji provided the critical support for organizing the conference. I would like to thank all my colleagues and staff at IDSK who have been with me through the process of publishing this book.

A big thanks to all the contributors who have painstakingly reworked their papers and waited patiently for the publication of this book.

Kolkata Nandini Ghosh

Contents

Editor and Contributors

About the Editor

Nandini Ghosh is an assistant professor of sociology at the Institute of Development Studies, Kolkata. She has a bachelor's degree in sociology from Presidency College Kolkata, a master's degree from the University of Calcutta, and a Ph.D. from the Tata Institute of Social Sciences, Mumbai. Her areas of interest are qualitative research methodology, sociology of gender, marginalization and social exclusion and social movements. She has coedited a book titled *Pratyaha Everyday Lifeworlds: Dilemmas, Contestations and Negotiations* (Primus 2015). Her other publications include "Bhalo Meye: Cultural Construction of Gender and Disability in Bengal", in Renu Adlakha (ed.), *Disability Studies in India: Global Discourses, Local Realities* (Routledge India, 2013) and "Sites of oppression: Dominant ideologies and women with disabilities in India", in Tom Shakespeare (ed.), *The Disability Research Reader: New Voices* (Routledge UK, 2015). (nandinighosh@gmail.com)

Contributors

Shilpaa Anand is an assistant professor, Department of English, Maulana Azad National Urdu University. Her research interests are disability history, culture and corporeality, disability studies and the humanities. (shilpaaanand@gmail.com)

Tanmoy Bhattacharya is associate professor in linguistics at the Centre for Advanced Studies in Linguistics, University of Delhi. He was the coordinator, Equal Opportunity Cell of the University of Delhi, and was the convenor of the UGC Committee on Higher Education and Disability. His core areas of interest are language and disability, disability and education, sign linguistics and deaf education. (tanmoy1@gmail.com)

Achin Chakraborty is professor of economics at the Institute of Development Studies, Kolkata. His research interests include welfare economics, human development, health economics and microeconomic issues in development economics. (achinchak@gmail.com)

Jagdish Chander teaches political science at Hindu College in New Delhi. He has a Ph.D. degree in disability studies from Syracuse University, and his interests include research on different aspects of lives of disabled people. (jagdish100@gmail.com)

Srilatha Juvva is an associate professor, Centre for Disability Studies and Action, School of Social Work, Tata Institute of Social Sciences, Mumbai. Her research interests include mental health, disability, family therapy and disaster and mental health issues. (juvvas@tiss.edu)

Subrata Mukherjee is an associate professor at the Institute of Development Studies, Kolkata, and actively engaged in teaching M.Phil. courses and research. He has a Ph.D. in Economics from Jawaharlal Nehru University, Delhi, through the Centre for Development Studies (Kerala). His areas of research interests are quality, inequality and financing-related issues in health and health care issues of the elderly. He is a founder member and former joint secretary of the Indian Health Economics and Policy Association. (msubrata100@gmail.com)

Madhura Nagchoudhuri is an assistant professor, Centre for Equity and Justice for Children and Families, School of Social Work, Tata Institute of Social Sciences, Mumbai. Her areas of interest include gender, disability and education. (madhuranag@tiss.edu)

Ipsita Sapra is an associate professor, School of Livelihoods and Development, Tata Institute of Social Sciences, Hyderabad. She has a Ph.D. degree in social sciences from TISS, Mumbai, and has undertaken research in the area of disability and livelihoods and disability policies. (ipsita.sapra@tiss.edu)

Rukmini Sen is an associate professor, School of Liberal Studies, Ambedkar University Delhi. She teaches courses on law and society, relationships and affinities, women's movements and researching the rural. She is currently working on her manuscript, *Exploring the Everyday, (Re)-constructing the Social: Smriti-katha as Sociological Sites* (forthcoming, Cambridge University Press, India). She is the coeditor of a special issue of the *Journal of Indian Law and Society* (January 2016) "Indian Feminisms, Law Reform and the Law Commission of India: Special Issue in Honour of Lotika Sarkar". (senrukmini18@gmail.com)

Shubhangi Vaidya is an assistant professor at the School of Inter-Disciplinary and Trans-Disciplinary Studies, Indira Gandhi National Open University, Delhi. She is a sociologist with current research interests in the interdisciplinary areas of disability studies, gender studies, labour and development and education. Her doctoral thesis is an ethnographic exploration of families of children with autism spectrum disorder, and she has presented and published research papers in the area of gender and disability. She has also written self-learning instruction materials for IGNOU's M.A. programmes in anthropology, sociology and women and gender studies. (svaidya2404@gmail.com)

Chapter 1
Introduction: Interrogating Disability in India

Nandini Ghosh

Abstract The academic discipline of disability studies resulted in the establishment of a new paradigm, with Western scholars problematizing disability as discrimination rooted in personal, interpersonal and institutional processes of exclusion and oppression, which is endemic to any society. Theoretical approaches to disability have engaged in critically unpacking structures of categorical exclusion in the form of ableism, normalcy and construction of disabled people as the other. Thus, interdisciplinary disability studies continuously attempts to unravel different ways in which disability is conceptualized and its impact on the daily lived experiences of disabled people at the community level. The introduction to this volume endeavours to lay out the debates around disability and the ways in which disability studies as an academic discipline have addressed the concerns of disabled people. Further the chapter tries to weave together the papers in this volume by examining the relevance of the Western perspectives on disability in contextualizing the concept of disability from the vantage point of social, cultural, political and legal discourses in India that have an impact on the way in which disability is defined, interpreted and experienced.

Keywords Disability studies · Defining disability · Quality of life · Disability policy

Disability studies emerged as an academic discipline in the Western countries in the 1960s and 1970s mainly through the efforts of disabled people and their organizations whose voices emerged in the 1960s (Roulstone et al., 2012). This new field of study was multidisciplinary and resulted in the establishment of a new paradigm around disability, shifting the focus from a personal medical problem to a social and political one, where social discrimination and prejudice dominated. The disability

---

N. Ghosh (✉)
Institute of Development Studies Kolkata, Kolkata, West Bengal, India
e-mail: nandinighosh@gmail.com

N. Ghosh (ed.), *Interrogating Disability in India*,
Dynamics of Asian Development, DOI 10.1007/978-81-322-3595-8_1

rights movement that emerged in the 1960s provided an impetus to highlight issues that were relevant to persons with disabilities, as a challenge to the gatekeeping role of medical and rehabilitation professionals who had the power to decide the interventions required for disabled people and who qualified for benefits (Snyder, 2006). The demand for civil rights for disabled people emerged mainly out of the engagement of disabled scholars with the issue of disability and the ways in which it may be interrogated advocated for a change in the way in which disability was understood. With the broadening of the field of disability, there emerged many strands of theories that problematized disability as discrimination rooted in personal, interpersonal and institutional processes of exclusion and oppression, which are endemic to any society. The broad array of theoretical approaches to disability forwarded by activist scholars has engaged in critically unpacking structures of categorical exclusion in the form of ableism, normalcy and construction of disabled people as the other. These approaches include the strict social model, the minority group model (where persons with disabilities are a distinct oppressed minority), disability as culture (where particular groups especially the deaf constitute a discrete culture and possess unique cultural heritage) and the idea that disability is diversity such as gender, race, ethnicity. Thus, interdisciplinary disability studies ask the following questions—(a) How is disability best defined or conceptualized? (b) What impact does disability have on persons with disabilities in terms of quality of life? (c) How we ought to respond to disability at individual and social level?

The articles in this volume reflect a multidisciplinary approach to the issue of disability and lives of disabled people. The contributors come from varied backgrounds across the social sciences and humanities, from sociology to political science, social work, economics, to English and linguistics. Almost all disability studies scholars emphasize the need to contextualize the concept of disability within particular social cultural contexts, recognizing the fact that different social, cultural, political and legal discourses have a differential impact on the way in which disability is defined, interpreted and experienced.

1.1 Defining Disability

One of the major barriers to the analysis of disability stems from the confusion over the nature or meaning of disability. The term disability has become a contentious one, mainly due to the fact that different conditions, physical, mental, psycho-social and sensory impairments are considered disabilities. Historically, "disability" has been used either as a synonym for "inability" or as a reference to legally imposed limitations on rights and powers. It is only in the past century that the term "disability" has been used to refer to a distinct class of people. Theories of disability have problematized the concept of disability differently based on their philosophical and disciplinary stances, ranging from moral/religious definitions to more dominant medicalized explanations to radical sociopolitical negotiations in the last few decades. All these definitions have had a significant impact on the state's formulation of the concept of disability and its resultant impact on policies and programmes tries to blend these approaches together, leading to different sets of solutions to issues raised by disabled people and the most effective means of allocating resources.

Perhaps the strongest claim to the definition of disability in present days is made by the field of medicine, which emphasizes limitation in functioning. With the spurt of development of the medical sciences in the early nineteenth century and the initial focus on disability acquired as a result of the world wars, the concept of disability came to be defined as a deficit or lack in terms of human functioning, which privileges a notion of the normal. The definitions of disability came to include a range of physical, sensory and mental conditions labelled as abnormal or disabling. Disability, thus, became a negative variation from the physical norm that impaired the functional capacities of the physically disabled person (Shakespeare, 1996). The medical approach raises the question of normality, both in the sense of performing and conforming to a certain standard from which disabled people deviate. Medical interventions aim at restoring the disabled person to normality, as reduction of the ability to perform in the "normal" modes and at "normal" levels needs to be remedied. There is a power play between the doctor and the disabled person or the patient, who is ascribed a clinical label and sought to be normalized through preventive or curative medical technology. Such clinical definitions of disability also become administrative tags for controlling disabled people's access to financial and other assistance as well as attaching a stigma to the labelled person by suggesting a physical imperfection or deviance from the norm.

Defining disability and providing facilities for the disabled people are the main supports of the medical model of disability, which aggravates the dependence of the disabled person on the "professional" caregivers. Thus, in most disability and rehabilitation programmes, a medical determination usually is an essential prerequisite for participation. The medical model completely ignores the crucial role of obstructive environments in creating dysfunctionality by treating the built and arranged environment as an invariable and hence disabled persons must adapt and adjust to their surroundings. There is a denial of common social experiences, which unite disabled people and the focus is only on the medical dimensions of difference (Shakespeare, 1996). The prevalence of a medical approach to disability may be one aspect of what Illich (1976) has termed "the medicalization of life". A medical definition not only imposes a presumption of biological or physiological inferiority upon disabled persons, but it also inhibits recognition of the social and structural sources of disability. From this perspective, the problems of disability arise from physical flaws within a person rather than from an unadaptive environment or society, and solutions to these difficulties must be sought primarily through individual rather than collective efforts. The medical perspective implies a demand that disabled persons must adapt and adjust to their surroundings without imposing a corresponding obligation on policy-makers to create an environment which can accommodate the needs and desires of citizens with disabilities.

The medical model was subjected to criticism by disabled people themselves because of its biologically deterministic stress on physical or sensory deficits and ignoring the lived experiences of disabled people. The application of a clinical label obscures the ubiquity of physical disability, i.e. the experience of stigma, exclusion, discrimination and dependency—all of which deprive people with disabilities from having control over their lives (Lonsdale, 1990; Marks 1999). There is a denial of common social experiences, which unite disabled people and the focus is only on the medical dimensions of difference (Shakespeare, 1996). Disabled people have been critical of the normalizing medical programmes that aim to refashion bodies of individuals to conform to "naturally" desirable standards. Normalizing programmes imposed to force anomalous individuals to adjust to environments suited to dominant social classes totally ignore the role of obstructive environments in creating "dysfunctionality". Moreover, as disability is contextual and variable over time and circumstance, any individual can become impaired at any point of time. Impairment is simply a bodily state, characterized by absence or altered physiology, which defines the physicality of people.

The social model of disability developed out of the disabled people's movement both in Europe and in the USA in the 1970s and 1980s. The social model recognizes that disability is not the outcome of bodily pathology but is socially produced by systematic patterns of exclusion that are built into the social fabric (Shakespeare, 1994; Hughes and Paterson, 1997). One strand of the social constructionist paradigm suggests that society creates a negative social identity for people with disabilities, which is characterized as deviant or abnormal (Asch and Fine, 1988). The able-bodied community uses prototypical portrayals of disability for legitimizing the social exclusion of the disabled people. The disabled identity exists as mutually exclusive identity from all other identities because the cultural and media discourses on disability are influenced by the personal tragedy principle or by images of the super-cripple or the emotionally stunted disabled stereotypes (Oliver, 1990). Another strand of the social constructionist paradigm posits disability as both a socially and historically relative social relation that is conditioned by political–economic dynamics (Finkelstein 1980 cited in Oliver, 1990). Attitudes, discourses and symbolic representations are critical to the reproduction of disablement, but are themselves the product of the social practices which society undertakes in order to meet its basic material needs (Oliver, 1996; Gleeson, 1997). The material conditions that produce the attitudes and meaning systems about disability have a great influence on the concrete experience of, and attitude towards impairment, which may vary between different modes of production. The social construction of physically impaired people as disabled people arises from the specific ways in which society organizes its basic material activities.

The social model of disability has served as an effective tool for remedying the injustices faced by disabled people and relocating efforts of service providers from individual solutions to removal of barriers to participation in the mainstream activities. While the social model recognized the importance of appropriate individually based interventions in the lives of disabled people, it chose to focus on their limitations in terms of furthering their inclusion and empowerment within a society constructed by non-disabled people for non-disabled people (Barnes and Mercer, 2003). The social model was able to bring about structural changes in the developed countries in which it had been developed by insisting on citizenship rights and anti-discrimination legislation. At the same time, the social model argued for a strong minority identity and demanded better services and facilities for the disabled, like higher benefits, more provisions for education and employment and increased access to all public facilities.

However, even though the social model shifted the focus from the disabled individual to societal structures, it has failed to take into account subjective and bodily experiences of people with disabilities (Morris 1991; French, 1993; Tregaskis, 2002). This rejection of the lived experience of impairment in favour of the social barriers to disability denies the pain of impairment, both physical and psychological. Thus, the social model perspective is seen as the rejection of impairment as well as the denial of the value of appropriate individually based interventions for rehabilitation, education or livelihood. The social model attempts to shift attention away from functional limitations of individuals to problems causes by disabling environments, barriers and cultures, moving away from materialist conceptions of disability. The social model of disability proposes an untenable separation between the body and culture, impairment and disability, and in spite of its critique of the medical model, actually concedes the body to medicine and understands impairment in terms of medical discourse. The impaired and dysfunctional body is seen as devoid of meaning and history, a fixed, material entity subject to the empirical rules of biological science, existing prior to the mutability and flux of cultural change and diversity and characterized by unchangeable inner necessities (Csordas, 1994; Shakespeare, 1994). As a consequence, the body disappeared from disability discourse (Hughes and Patterson, 1997; Asch, 2001; Shakespeare, 2004).

Despite the acceptance and promotion of the social model by disability activists and theorists, the medical model remains very powerful in influencing the international definitions of disability. The influence of medical ideas on disability is also reflected international documents like the United Nations Standard Rules on the Equalization of Opportunities for Persons with Disabilities (1991) which views disability in terms of physical, intellectual or sensory impairment, medical conditions or mental illness, which may be permanent or transitory in nature. The World Health Organization (WHO) developed the International Classification of Functioning, Disability and Health (2001) refers to disability as an umbrella term for impairments, activity limitations and participation restrictions. The concept of impairment retains a focus on biological systems, thus reiterating a supposed biological norm as the standard against which individuals are judged to be impaired. Participation and restrictions are defined in terms of the individual rather than in more social structural or even environmental terms.

On the other hand, the United Nations Convention on the Rights of Persons with Disabilities 2007 spells out clearly and unconditionally that states have a positive and prominent role in promoting, protecting and ensuring the full and equal enjoyment of all human rights and fundamental freedoms by all persons with disabilities, and to promote respect for their inherent dignity. Persons with disabilities include those who have long-term physical, mental, intellectual or sensory impairments, which in interaction with various barriers may hinder their full and effective participation in society on an equal basis with others. Based on the premise that all human beings have inherent dignity, which entails the enjoyment of all human rights, persons with disabilities are unconditional (human) rights-holders. Subsequently the focus is not on the possible impairment(s) but rather on the constraints that the social fabric builds into accessing the enjoyment of rights. In addition to the more obvious physical barriers, this approach focuses on the manifold social, behavioural, stereotype-based barriers that lead to and potentially sustain the exclusion of persons with disabilities.

Thus, defining disability remains tenuous and tentative at best, as both practitioners and disability scholars debate the ways in which disability and impairment may best be understood and thus addressed. While the (medical) condition or impairment remains the basis on which is constructed an entire range of social interpretations regarding the impairment, there is an increasing focus on the context and how the contextual sociocultural, religious and linguistic influences construct a person with impairment/disability. The alternate social model that is proposed needs to incorporate aspects of medical interventions that impact the life of a person with disability in terms of the effect it has on the experience of impairment within a particular context. These contextual forces interact to give rise to varying degrees and types of deprivations and social disabilities that influence the daily lives of disabled persons. Disability can thus be conceived as being embedded in a particular social context and must then be interpreted in terms of oppression, keeping in mind other identity markers such as caste, class, gender, sexuality, religion, ethnicity, etc. There needs to emerge a focus on exclusionary societies and its impact on persons with disabilities in pluralistic societies in which we increasingly find ourselves.

Chapters 2, 3, 4 attempt to illuminate theoretical discourses within disability and endeavour to contextualize it in an Indian context. Shilpaa Anand draws attention to the ways in which disability studies in India has adopted the models approach to disability in academic research, which has in turn provided suggestions to improve services like rehabilitation, education, policy-making and law. However, such a stance has exposed the limitations of the disability studies models approach and indicates the need to develop theoretical and methodological tools that are context-sensitive, as the idea of the individual is conceptualized very differently in different contexts. Tanmoy Bhattacharya points out that the difference between inclusion as the notion that everybody is the same regardless of race, gender, disability or sexual orientation, and recognition, which demands a change in the basic norms by which a society is governed actually determines the way in which disabled people are viewed by society and the state at large. He argues that inclusion of disabled people in education and employment has remained a token gesture and advocates for recognition of difference and protection of cultural diversity in order to ensure preservation of rights of disabled persons. The legal discourses on disability individualize definitions veiling the concerns of solidarity within the community. Rukmini Sen's paper highlights the way in which the Rights of Persons with Disabilities Bill 2012 addresses the gender question in the light of few contemporary incidents of harassment/violence on persons with disability in their everyday lives.

1.2 State Policies, Disability Discourse and Quality of Life of Disabled People in India

In India, the attitude of the state has always been one of charity and welfare. From the colonial period, schools and residential institutions mainly for visually and orthopaedically impaired people were started mainly in towns with religious shrines (like Benares and Lucknow), where there was a preponderance of disabled people, living off the charity of visiting pilgrims. After Independence, the Constitution of India guaranteed through the Directive Principles of State Policy and Fundamental Rights, equality before the law and equal protection of law for all its citizens, and prohibited discrimination on the grounds of "religion, race, caste, sex, place of birth". The state in India accepted social welfare as a responsibility, seeking to promote the welfare of the weaker sections of society, defined as groups of individuals in need of special considerations like children, women, people from certain scheduled castes and tribes and disabled people (Billimoria, 1985). However, people with disabilities were considered to be different, as is evident from Article 41 which stipulates, "The state shall, within the limits of its economic capacity and development make effective provision for securing the right to work, to education and to public assistance in cases of unemployment, old age, sickness and disablement" (Advani, 1997).

The reluctance of the government in formulating and implementing a coherent disability policy reflects the sociocultural assumptions about the disabled in India, where a religio-moral-medical model of disability is still prevailing. While the welfare approach towards other disadvantaged sections of the population such as women, children and the Scheduled Castes/Tribes led to comprehensive state-initiated policies and programmes, the attitude towards disabled people was of token inclusion and general neglect and apathy for their concerns. The Planning Commission, entrusted with the responsibility for allocating funds and planning programmes for different sections of the populace, sought to define during the first Plan period (1951–1956) the physically disabled as those lacking in one or more physical senses like blindness, deafness, those suffering from movement difficulties, mainly orthopaedic, and lepers and epileptics (Mehta, 1983). This definition of disability, with its strong medical bias, has since then influenced the state's attitude and orientation towards disabled people and their concerns. The allocation of funds for the disabled during the first few plan periods followed an arbitrary and skewed pattern, with the medical rehabilitation of the disabled receiving top priority, as the state had by then, adopted the medical model of disability as the key paradigm for service delivery. A large part of the financial allocation for welfare and rehabilitation of disabled people was channelized into providing facilities for medical treatment and management of people with different orthopaedic and sensory disabilities, such as restorative surgery, provision for assistive aids and appliances and different therapeutic interventions (Mohit and Rungta, 2000). The major responsibility for providing medical and support services to the disabled still remains with the local non-governmental organizations (NGOs), who cater mostly to the needs of the disabled in the urban areas.

But the problems of disabled people were not addressed in a comprehensive manner (Mani, 1988). One of the reasons for this was the lack of adequate data about the persons with disabilities in India. Although the British rulers had initiated the collection of accurate information about disabled people during census operations in India from 1872 to 1931, the collection of statistics on disability in independent India was first initiated in 1981, as a result of developments in the international arena such as the United Nations General Assembly's Declaration on the Rights of the Disabled Persons in 1975 and the declaration of 1981 as the International Year for Disabled Persons. However, the biased terminology used in the census operations (totally crippled, totally blind and totally dumb) rendered the data inadequate, as only 0.16 % of the total Indian population was found to be disabled, leaving out two major categories, people with hearing impairments and mental disabilities. The category of disability was dropped from the 1991 census without any explanation and then re-included in 2001 and further delineated in Census 2011 due the advocacy efforts of disability activists in India. According to Census 2011, the disabled population in India is 26,810,557, which is about 2.21 % of the total population of India (Census of India, 2011).

The state in India has displayed reluctance in developing a comprehensive equitable policy for persons with disabilities, despite sporadic efforts initially in 1970–71 and later in 1980–1981 (Abidi, 1996; Advani, 1997). With the framing of the United Nations' Rules on the Equalization of Opportunities for Disabled Persons in 1993 and increasing pressure from disability activists in India, the Government of India hurriedly enacted the Persons with Disabilities (Equal Opportunities, Protection of Rights and Full Participation) Act in 1995, which came into force in February 1996 (Mohit, 2000). This forestalled the drafting of a comprehensive National Policy on Persons with Disabilities which would clarify the government's stance on the issue of disability by outlining initiatives, priorities or guidelines that would then lead to the passage of laws necessary for fulfilling the directives mentioned in the policy. The Persons with Disabilities Act 1995 thus became the first policy statement in India, which recognized the rights of people with various impairments to equal opportunity to participate fully in social, cultural, economic and educational programmes of the country.

The PwD Act has defined disability primarily in medical terms, proceeding from the medical model of disability that ignores the social perceptions about disability (Mohit and Rungta, 2000). Thus, the categories of disability-blindness and low vision, leprosy cured, hearing impairment, locomotor disability, mental retardation and mental illness—are all dependent on certification by medical professionals. This highlights and legitimizes the control of the medical professionals over the diagnosis, management and interventions for the disabled. Moreover, many disabilities are conditions that may not need medical interventions or management, but a more inclusive attitude towards the disabled person and his/her needs. The main thrust of the Act has been to spell out the State's responsibility towards prevention of impairments and protection of disabled people's rights in health, education, training, employment and rehabilitation. The Act treats disability as a civil right, and lays down provisions for creating a barrier-free environment for disabled people as well as removing discrimination and abuse against people with disabilities. There are extensive strategies laid down for development of comprehensive programmes and services for equalization of opportunities for disabled people and provisions for the integration of disabled people into mainstream society. The Act also emphasized the need for supporting institutions for persons with disabilities as well as social security provisions for the disabled (Advani, 1997; Mohit and Rungta, 2000).

The National Policy for Persons with Disabilities in India 2006 is a state response to the United Nations' Convention on the Rights of Persons with Disabilities, which was passed in 2007 and became an international law in 2008 (Government of India 2006). In an attempt to clarify the framework under which the state, civil society and private sector must operate in order to ensure a dignified life for persons with disability, the National Policy for Persons with Disability recognizes the need to replace the earlier emphasis on *medical rehabilitation* with an emphasis on *social rehabilitation*. Although the National Policy "recognizes that persons with disabilities are valuable human resource for the country and seeks to create an environment that provides them with equal opportunities, protection of their rights and full participation in society", it limits itself to only reiterating the provisions enlisted in the already existing laws for persons with disabilities in India. This "forward looking" policy thus ends up endorsing the medical model of disability by keeping intact the process of identification of disabled people, requiring certification by panels of medical doctors in order to access policies and entitlements.

1.2.1 Programmatic Interventions for Persons with Disabilities in India

In spite of focusing on different aspects of the lives of disabled people, the Act has sustained its inclination towards the medical model of disability, by projecting disability as an individual problem that can be remedied through different interventions and specialized services. The Act has ignored the definitions of disability advocated by the social model, which lay more stress on the disabling barriers faced by people with impairments and press for structural changes within society. Thus, both the state and most of the NGOs working in the field have tacitly adopted the medical model of disability. The Indian Human Development report states "physical disabilities are genetic, biological and even birth defects and future research must focus on the medical causes of such disabilities" (Shariff 1999). As the recognition of a category of disability depends on its inclusion in the Act, people belonging to categories that have been overlooked are being sidelined and refused access to services. The stipulation that the disabled people will receive benefits according to the degree of their disability totally ignores the impact of social, psychological or political factors on individual disability. As the provisions of the State depend on the medical certificate indicating the percentage of impairment issued by State Medical Boards, there have been reports of gross discrepancies in the awarding of the disability certificates.

The implementation of the policy programmes and various schemes for the disabled people both before and after the Persons with Disabilities Act 1995 has been characterized by ad hoc and sporadic efforts on part of the state. The disabled person has usually been treated as a compartmentalized being, with different aspects of his/her existence coming under the purview of different wings of the State apparatus, with little or no coordination among themselves. For example, education and employment concerns of persons with disabilities are looked after by the Ministry of Social Justice and Empowerment, and the Ministry of Human Resource Development runs parallel systems resulting in a conceptual fragmentation of the core concerns (Alur 1997 cited in Ramanujam, 2000). This kind of segregation and individual intervention is reminiscent of the medical model where the affected part of the body becomes the focus of attention and subjective experiences of the disabled person are negated. The primary focus of the rehabilitation services continues to stress the medical aspects of disability: prevention and early detection of disabilities as well as the management of disabilities through corrective surgery, supply and fitment of aids and appliances and assistive devices, etc. State approach towards implementation of programmes has varied from benign neglect to complete dependence on non-governmental organizations for delivering different services in remote parts of the country, which has reached only 2 % of the disabled population.

The Census of India 2011 has enumerated 26,20,974 children and young adults in the age group of 0–19 years. Yet in India the fact remains that a majority of children with disabilities do not have access to education. A World Bank Report (2007) highlighted that 38 % of the children with disabilities in the age group 6–13 years are out of school. The PwD Act 1995 stipulates that every child with disability is entitled to a free education up to the age of 18 years (Government of India 1996). However, the act reposes the responsibility for integration of students with disabilities in regular schools in local authorities. Alur (2003) observed that in India there is a dichotomy between policy and practice; the government promotes the "inclusionist" philosophy through its schemes and extends a parallel support to the "segregationist" policy by promoting the idea of special schools through their assistance to voluntary organization schemes. Programmes such as Integrated Education of Disabled Children Scheme (IEDC) in 1974 and the Project Integrated Education for the Disabled (PIED) in 1987, which existed even before disability legislation was enacted in India, met with limited success as exclusionary policies and practices prevalent all over regular schools in India. The Universal Primary Education (1997) programme and lately the District Primary Education Programme

(DPEP) has had an impact on integrating disabled children as it addressed core issues related to curriculum. Most schools have not been able to remove even architectural barriers and hence still refuse admission to disabled children (Zachariah, 2001). The provision of only three resource teachers per block under the DPEP pattern has proved inadequate, as schools are spread over vast geographical stretches, limiting interactions between the teachers and students. Thus, education of people with disabilities has remained confined mostly to special schools in urban areas.

The Right to Education Act 2009, which came into force in 2010, guarantees right to free and compulsory education to all children between ages six to fourteen. However, there is very little awareness about the provisions of the act among school personnel, parents and disabled people themselves. Some educators and parents who are knowledgeable about government policies and laws concerning integrated education are found to have positive attitudes towards implementing such programs (Sharma, 2001). The majority of school personnel in India are not trained to design and implement educational programs for students with disabilities in regular schools. Most teacher training programs in India do not have a module on teaching children with disabilities (Myreddi and Narayan, 2000). Also, placement of pre-service teachers in special or integrated schools is rarely given consideration (Jangira et al., 1995).

According to Census 2011, there are around 17,070,608 unemployed persons with disabilities. Although the government has established 47 Special Employment Exchanges and 41 Special Cells in the regular Employment Exchanges, the scheme has provided employment to only 49,000 disabled persons, most of whom had orthopaedic impairments. The special employment exchanges have achieved limited success even though most of those registered had received vocational training (NCPEDP-NAB, 1999). The placement of disabled people in various private institutions has also been only partially successful. In a survey conducted by the National Centre for the Promotion of Employment of Disabled Persons (NCPEDP) and National Association of the Blind (NAB) in 1999, it was found that 50 % of disabled people were self-employed as both public and private sector companies were found to be employing very few disabled people. The reservation of jobs in identified government departments also has not been implemented properly, and the posts filled are mostly in the lowest ranks. The concept of identified jobs is itself questionable as it may not take into account the actual capacities of people with disabilities (Rajalakshmi, 2002). The National Handicapped Finance and Development Corporation (NHFDC), which finances a wide range of activities such as self-employment ventures and loans for education to disabled people, has also met with limited success because of the lengthy and cumbersome procedures for accessing its services.

A serious lacuna in the Persons with Disabilities Act is that there are very few penal provisions for non-implementation of its measures. The Act stipulates that in most cases programmes would be initiated and implemented subject to the economic capacity and development of the state. There are no time-bound programmes of action or obligations by the state for the initiation and implementation of the provisions of the Act. The enforcement of its provisions has been left to courts of law without specifying procedures to be followed in case of violations of the recommendations. This makes the enforcement of the provisions of the law very debatable and totally dependent on the magnanimity of the State (Advani, 1997; Mohit, 2000). Consequently, many state governments and local authorities have cited lack of funds as a reason for non-implementation of the provisions, especially those concerning access to public buildings and utilities. Campaigns for providing access to public buildings by disability organizations have been sporadic and limited to urban areas, yielding very little results. Although air travel has been made more accessible for people with disabilities following a Supreme Court directive, the more commonly used modes of public transport such as buses and trains continue to be inaccessible to the disabled (Rajalakshmi, 2002).

A group of papers (Chakraborty and Mukherjee, Vaidya, Nagchoudhuri and Juvva, Ghosh and Sapra) in this volume explore the quality of life of people with disabilities in terms of their individual attainments, within families and cultural contexts, in social encounters and workspaces. Achin Chakraborty and Subrata Mukherjee use NSS 58th Round, 2002, and Census 2001 data to illustrate connections between the gender, living arrangements and marital status, which reveal the fact that the nature and extent of disadvantage follow distinct patterns among men and women and influence very important functionings that constitute the well-being of persons with disabilities. Nandini Ghosh discusses about the gender socialization of women with disabilities and the ways in which they negotiate their femininity and gender identity by positing a different yet acceptable feminine conduct which takes into account their physical limitations yet stays in tune with the larger gendered contexts. Shubhangi Vaidya argues for the need of a social security net that will address the long-term needs of vulnerable populations as the language of rights and the emphasis on autonomy, agency and independence that has underpinned the disability rights discourse finds itself on shaky ground in this context. As Rights alone cannot guarantee a humane society until they are backed by caring practices, there is need for a model based upon an acknowledgement of mutual dependence as the common human condition, the creation of ethical caring communities where individual worth is not measured in utilitarian terms and the right to live and die with dignity is guaranteed to all irrespective of the way their minds and bodies work. Madhura Nagchoudhuri and Srilatha Juvva argue that developing an understanding of disability as "socially constructed" is essential to realizing personal power for persons with disability. Many people with disabilities skilfully use to their image as a "powerless" and helpless person as a tool to gain power and to have influence. Drawing on case studies from different groups of disabled people, the authors illustrate how this dynamic of use of power by subordinate groups operates through the leveraging of their vulnerable status. Ipsita Sapra highlights the struggles of persons with disabilities in rural 24 Parganas South of West Bengal in terms of livelihood pursuits that enable them to combat ideologies of dependence and yet leave them economically dependent on families and communities. This paper demonstrates that the livelihood insecurities that disabled people face as a result of the impairment rarely takes into account their range of capabilities, functioning and conversion handicaps in their pursuit for livelihood.

1.3 Emerging Discourse on Disability: Contradictions and Contestations

The Persons with Disabilities Act, 1995, has been criticized severely for overtly privileging medical definitions of disability. The UNCRPD, the first human rights treaty of this millennium, came into force in May 2008. India signed this convention on the very first day and ratified it without any reservations in October 2007. With the signing and ratifying of the UNCRPD by India, disability activists across the country rallied to demand for a new legislation to fulfil the commitments under the UNCRPD. This process of amendment had been initiated many times even before the UNCRPD but with no concrete results. The Ministry of Social Justice and Welfare, Government of India, constituted a New Law Committee in April 2010 under the chairpersonship of Dr.(Mrs) Sudha Kaul, who has decades of experiences of working in the field of disability in India. The other members of the committee comprised representatives of Central ministries, state governments, disability rights activists, parents of persons with disabilities, civil society organizations and persons with disabilities along with the Chairpersons of the National Trust and the Rehabilitation Council of India. In view of the legal expertise required to draft the new law, the Committee appointed the Centre for Disability Studies (CDS), NALSAR University of Law, to support and assist the Committee in putting together a working legal draft. The mandate of the committee was to draft a comprehensive rights-based law in accordance with the provisions of the United Nations Convention on the Rights of Persons with Disabilities (UNCRPD).

The UNCRPD introduces a paradigm shift in the realm of disability rights from the welfare approach to a rights-based approach. This means that persons with disabilities are seen as subjects rather than as mere objects of social welfare. The new Rights of Persons with Disabilities Bill 2011 focuses on legal capacity, equality and dignity of the disabled. Drawn after open and transparent consultations with key disability groups and members of civil society, the new Act is guided by the principles of inherent dignity, individual autonomy, equal opportunity, accessibility, respecting differences, acceptance for all, and evolving capacities of children with disabilities among others. While outlining a list of rights that persons with disabilities are entitled to, the Bill also elaborates on the role of the state and Central government with regard to implementation. The Bill is different from the previous PwD Act 1995 as it moves away from the purely medical model to incorporate the social and medico-legal approaches. Disability is no longer seen as a purely personal "problem" but rather a challenge that has to be met by the State and society through suitable provisions. The Bill also takes into cognizance the autonomy of persons with disability and the freedom to make choices. The Bill is a shift from the charity paradigm to a more rights-based approach.

The law-making process has proved to be challenging primarily because of the competing demands of a large and diverse sector. However, in a society that has systematically discriminated against persons with disabilities and has rarely considered their rights; the new law will be the first step in a long-drawn movement.

The new law offers an outstanding opportunity to bring about a change in societal perception as persons with disabilities ask the world around them to be rebuilt in acknowledgement of their existence and not in ignorance of it. However, the dialogue on the new law for persons with disabilities in India has been fraught with several debates, with different groups of people claiming different vantage points for rallying and establishing their own demands. On the one hand, it has been the old and time-tested lobbies of specific disabilities such as the visually impaired and the locomotor disabled dominating the dialogue and shaping the debates. Silenced voices like that of people with hearing impairments, people with intellectual impairments and people living with mental illness remain in the margins even though some groups advocated strongly for their inclusion. The issues around accessibility tended to focus more on needs of the dominant groups, with more attention being paid to accessibility to buildings, transport systems and public spaces. Framing of such detailed provisions for physical access often ignores the role of social disability in form of discrimination and oppression.

One of the major debates revolved around the issue of defining disability in the new law, in consonance with the way in which it has been done in the UNCRPD. However, since many of the members of the drafting committee were government officials, still rooted in the medical model which is more concrete and allows for a rigid categorization of disability, the definitions were still sought to be in the medical mode. This is because historically the definition of disability in India has been linked to welfare and disabled people have been seen as recipients of charity through different schemes. A medical definition of persons with disability is therefore more amenable first for identification and then for doling out support based on degree of disability, ignoring thereby the social oppression and discrimination faced by disabled people on an everyday basis. But as oppression is difficult to express in quantifiable terms, which is relatively easier to standardize and clearly understood by people who are implementing the schemes, the pressure to revert to medical visible quantifiable definitions of impairments is high. The new law has tried to blend both view points, by combining a generic definition of disability in tune with UNCRPD with an impairment-specific additional definition, which is to be reviewed by competent authority from time to time. However, the politics behind recognizing and constituting competent authority may well be dominated by the medical and specialist lobby.

The lobby of the specialist professionals, almost all of whom are non-disabled, emerged even strongly in the first few drafts of the new bill. Hence, the chapter on education, which should have focussed on inclusive education, was titled Education and Educator Training, with major focus being on special education and protection of the interests of the special educators. The provisions in the law seemed to be intending to provide legitimacy to these people who are more rooted in medicalized and technical interventions rather building inclusive education systems for all children, including the disabled children. As most of the members of the drafting committee were either professionals themselves or run institutions of special education, the thrust on specialized services would ensure their survival. Leading blind disability activists also favoured continuous existence of special education in conjunction with so-called inclusive education, as their community has most benefitted from these provisions. The debate on inclusive education was limited by the special education professionals by citing the specialist nature of the interventions required for each type of impairment, which established the hegemony of different groups of professionals over domains of knowledge and rejected the possibility of creating systems of learning that cater to difference, not just of so-called ability but also to other dimensions such as gender, caste, religion, ethnicity and language.

Another major debate was around legal capacity which has been recognized as a right in the UNCRPD. Legal capacity has been defined as the right to recognition everywhere as persons before the law and interpreted as the right of every person with disability to exercise their own will, preferences and choices in all decisions that concern them. Thus, the UNCRPD recognizes that persons with disabilities enjoy legal capacity on an equal basis with others in all aspects of life, especially in the matters of managing finances, holding and selling property and making decisions about their lives. Debates around legal capacity have been very important for people with dominant disabilities in India as impairment has been associated with inability to make decisions about their own lives. However, the clause of legal capacity is much more significant for people with severe impairments, intellectual disabilities and mental illness. During the process of framing the bill, parents of persons with intellectual impairments whose wards are protected through guardianship under the present National Trust Act 1999 completely rejected the according of legal capacity to their wards. Most parents felt that their wards would never be in a position to make choices about themselves and their lives and ran the high risk of causing harm both to themselves and to their finances and property. Parents also could not envisage a system where people with intellectual impairments had support for decision-making, moving them slowly towards degrees of independence. However, voices that came out loud and clear were also going to be affected by the loss of power and autonomy that the National Trust Act had provided. On the other hand, the lobby of persons with mental illness was strongest on the point of legal capacity, as they have been historically denied of it, causing much bodily harm, financial loss and mental anguish. The clamour over inclusion and recognition of legal capacity also led some parents of persons with intellectual disability to claim that persons with mental illness were not actually disabled.

Thus, the debate around the issue of whether India should have one comprehensive law for persons with disabilities or a range of laws addressing concerns of different groups of disabled people has been interpreted in different ways by different activists and other stakeholders. Some groups of disabled people and their caregivers felt threatened by the inclusion of all disabilities in the scope of care and protection of particular groups of severely disabled people. The special protection offered by the National Trust Act to specific groups of people would, they felt, be removed if a comprehensive law came into force and the National Trust would lose its efficacy and prominence. This debate, however, has focussed more on what these specific groups of people would lose rather than how the entire disabled population could gain with the bringing of all authorities and bodies concerning issues of disabled people under one umbrella. On the other hand, blind and locomotor disabled activists argued for a comprehensive Disability Code that would help to strengthen existing structures, where the primary document would spell out the major provisions, while specific laws within it could address specific concerns of different groups of people with disabilities. The main focus of this line of argument was to point out that disabled people are a homogenous category, but varied groups of people claiming commonalities are based on the experiences of discrimination and oppression.

Disability activists, however, have claimed that the new disability law does not seem to reflect the principles and provisions of UNCRPD in its entirety. They have critiqued the process of drafting the law as one that has repeatedly insulted and sidelined persons with disabilities in India during the entire process of drafting the New Law. The process, which was meant to ensure the voice of persons with disabilities unfortunately, became a barrier to their participation. The process, which was meant to contextualize UNCRPD for India has led to the dilution of what the UNCRPD offers. The process has failed in initiating, facilitating and closing debates; this should have been done by bringing in the multiple dimensions and nuances of the issues like legal capacity, civil political rights, multiple discriminations, processes of ensuring inclusion, processes of establishing the social model of disability and the convergence in the structures of state's authorities and their obligations.

The final articles (Chandar, Ghosh) problematize collective action by disabled people in the form of social movements to highlight their deprivation and the denial of their rights. Jagdish Chandar analyses the emerging trends and issues covered as a part of the disability rights movement as well as the methods of advocacy adopted by the activists of this movement in the post-1995 period after the enactment of the PwD Act. He argues that the rights-based perspective is now widely embraced by the current generation of disability rights activists from cross sections of disability and the non-governmental organizations. Nandini Ghosh's paper explores the different dimensions of the grass-roots-level mobilization in disability in the form of rural disabled people's organizations (DPOs), which have experienced success at local levels but have never managed to become a strong force at the state or national level.

1.4 Conclusion

Interrogating Disability thus begins and continuously engages with the struggle to define and redefine disability. This process is ongoing for the last few decades with academicians and activists on the one hand evolving definitions that reflect social reality while policy-makers and administrators choosing to adhere to more concrete definitions that can be linked to schemes and entitlements. Academic and activist engagement has traced the trajectory in the conceptualization of disability, varied notions of which coexists with and is often conflated with one another. While the dominant functional perspective focuses on a person's functional limitation

(Abberley, 1987), thereby placing onus on the impaired person to make additional efforts to be acceptable and accepted within society, the social model stresses that disability is an interaction between an individual with an impairment and an environment that lacks adaptations. Thus, disability might appear in some situations but not in others and is thus relational as disability is seen as a relation between a person and her/his environment (Söder 1987). The social constructionist approaches to problematizing categorization attempts to reveal the inequalities and oppressions that have resulted from such categorization, which includes limitations on civil rights of the negatively identified group. The role of language in constructing meanings and thus determining life worlds often gives rise to medically decoded categories that do not reflect disabled people's experiences. Mairs (1986) feels that the term "differently abled" conveys the hopefulness that transformed countries from "undeveloped" to "underdeveloped", then to "less developed", and finally to "developing" nations, while ground realities remained unchanged.

Policy-makers worldwide and in individual nation states, however, have been greatly influenced by the concrete definitions offered by the dominant medical paradigm which ensures measurement of disability and disabled people. Leading international agencies like the World Health Organization and Disabled People's International have based their definitional schemas on the concept of normality and the assumption that disabled people want to achieve this normality. While the World Health Organization stresses normal social roles, Disabled People's International highlights the normal life of the community. Increasingly, these international agencies, influenced by the global disability movement, have come to acknowledge the sociopolitical understanding of disability that recognizes that the physical, built and social environment are fundamentally shaped by public policies that reflect attitudes and social values, which contain many aversive or prejudicial perceptions of persons with disabilities. The achievement of the disability movement has been to break the link between physical bodies and the social situation and to focus on the real cause of disability, i.e. discrimination and prejudice (Shakespeare, 1994).

State policies have started to reflect this consciousness of discrimination existing in the attitudinal environment of society, despite being pegged on the medical notions of normality for categorization of persons with disabilities. So, while globally disability activists have been increasingly calling for the celebration of difference rather than on restoration of normality, the persistence of the idea of normality demonstrates how ingrained and deep-rooted the ideology of normality is within social consciousness. States are concerned with the measurement of disability and disabled persons as allocations for welfare are usually decided based on the categories and numbers that correspond to them. Hence, censuses and surveys, aimed at serving administrative purposes and indicating distributive responsibilities of the welfare state (Stone 1985), primarily use functional definitions (United Nations, 1991, 1996, 2006). The welfare state, fighting the rising costs of social security uses such definitions to allocate resources to support particular categories of people, while denying the same to others.

Thus, two important agents of the administrative definition are politicians and welfare authorities. In recognizing that disability is finally whatever public officials say it is, both social scientists and decision-makers must also be aware that understandings are shaped primarily by the concepts inherited from previous research. Any approach to the formulation of disability policy that fails to encompass the political aspects of this problem, therefore, may be inadequate. Thus, the multiplicity of conceptual paradigms that define disability, the disabled person and disabling social structures present a challenge to the measurement of disability as definitions used by researchers and practitioners need to be adapted to various cultural and social contexts (Baylies, 2002; Groce, 2006). Over the last decade, however, there have been major steps taken to reconcile these various views by looking at the disabling condition, or the interplay between the individual situation and the collective resources (and limitations) that may make an individual impairment a social disability.

Here, Sen's capability approach (1999) offers an alternative approach by defining disability as a lack of capability, thereby placing disability within a wide spectrum of human development. Sen's (1999) conceptualization of the individual's capability set, that is, the substantive freedoms s/he enjoys to lead the kind of life s/he has reason to value, which influences both what a person is able to do and to be effectively, through realized functioning and achievements, such as travelling, feeding, accessing education and health centres, and all that a person is potentially capable of if opportunities are provided (Bakshi and Trani, 2006). Such a view provides broader insights into the issues related to disability since it proposes to look not only at what a person actually does (his/her functioning) but also at the range of possibilities from which s/he chooses that specific functioning (Sen, 1999). Under the capability approach, disability may be understood as being the result of a combination of different factors. It may result from (a) the nature of an impairment and other personal characteristics (e.g. age, gender, race), (b) the resources available to the individual and (c) the environment. Thus, at one level, deprivation can result from the very nature of the impairment, irrespective of other personal characteristics, the amount of resources available to the individual, and the environment. On another level, deprivation can be the result of barriers in the environment, in its physical, economic, social, political and cultural aspects. At a third level, deprivation can result from the economic constraints that impairment may place on the availability of, and demand for, resources, or may induce higher costs to achieve a given level of advantage or well-being (Mitra, 2006). Following the capability approach, the full range of the disability experience can be covered, shifting the focus away from the restricted view of identifying types of impairment.

As Terzi (2003) posits, using the capability approach entails examining the full set of capability one person can choose from and assessing the value an impairment has on this set of freedoms. Focusing on developing potentialities means to look at the adaptability of the individual to an ever-changing social context, the ability to tackle and even change the elements of the context that make a situation disabling for a given person. This approach stresses the interplay between characteristics of the individual and the social groups that s/he belongs to, as well as the institutional factors that may influence or even hinder his/her choices (Bakshi and Trani, 2006). This approach also takes into account the agency of the individual in terms of the extent to which extent the person considers him/herself as the main actor and decision-maker in his/her own life. It is the "ability to form goals, commitments, values, etc." It is recognizing a person as "someone who acts and brings about change, and whose achievements can be judged in terms of her/his own values and objectives, whether or not we assess them in terms of some external criteria as well" (Sen, 1999). By taking the view of the individual, we look at the interaction between the person, with his/her limitations in functioning (which may or may not be permanent), and the context, which consists of a number of resources as well as expectations, stereotypes and often prejudice and discrimination. While defining disability at the level of individual functioning and taking into consideration the sociocultural barriers, one hopes to create an affirmative purpose of rehabilitation, which impacts individual functioning. Measuring needs of disabled people and thus planning for their medical and rehabilitation needs in terms of enhancing functions necessitates this kind of definition. As a result, the policies that would be set up would aim at establishing an equality of activity and participation.

Yet there is need to understand the importance of a subjective understanding of disability (Morris, 1993; Thomas 1999; Wendell 2001) as stressed by intersectionality and identity studies has led to redefining of disability as a positive aspect of a person's identity. Disabled people have multiple identities and contemporary (social scientific) definitions of disability have been criticized for not being sensitive to the intersection between disability and gender. Such criticisms consider that a "proper" definition must recognize disability as a multifaceted phenomenon (Thomas 1999). Construction of the body and impairment-related experiences determined by access to a range of social and material resources and disabled people face oppression due to pursuit of profit over inequality and social justice. The need to shift away from structural analysis becomes particularly important with inequality increasing in all capitalist countries and global economic crises. The struggle for a fairer and inclusive global society is difficult. Hence, there is a need for more active political activism and scholarship to generate a shift in perception of disability in order to bring about a change in the way in which both disability and disabled people are viewed globally and in local contexts. The attempt of this volume is to highlight the ways in which valued social attributes of personhood such as autonomy, agency including rationality, control over one's body and life links up with concepts of difference and interdependence in the lives of disabled people in India.

References

Abberley, P. (1987). The concept of oppression and the development of a social theory of disability. In M. J. Deegan & N. A. Brooks (Eds.), *Disability studies: Past present and future*. Leeds: The Disability Press.

Abidi, J. (1996). The advent of an advocacy age. *Dipsikha* (December).

Advani, L. (1997). *Rights by law*. Paper presented at the National Consultation Meet on Rights of Disabled Children.

Alur, M. (2003). *Invisible children—A study of policy exclusion*. New Delhi: Viva Books Private Limited.

Asch, A. (2001). *Critical race theory, feminism and disability: Reflections on social justice and personal identity*, http://moritzlaw.osu.edu/lawjournal. Accessed 18 June 2003.

Asch, A., & Fine, M. (1988). Introduction: Beyond pedestals. In M. Fine & A. Asch (Eds.), *Women with Disabilities: Essays in psychology, culture and politics*. Philadelphia: Temple University Press.

Bakshi, P., & Trani, J. F. (2006). *The capability approach to understanding disability: Increasing comparability, defining efficient programs*. Source: http://www.ucl.ac.uk/lc-ccr/lccstaff/jean-francois-trani/BakshiTraniAFD060306.pdf

Barnes, C., & Mercer, G. (2003). *Disability*. Cambridge: Polity.

Baylies, C. (2002). Disability and the Notion of Human Development: questions of rights and capabilities. *Disability & Society, 17*(7), 725–739.

Billimoria, R. B. (1985). *Educating the mentally retarded: A study of special schools in Bombay.* Ph.D. Thesis, Tata Institute of Social Sciences, Mumbai.

Census of India. (2011). *Tables on disability*. New Delhi: Registrar General and Census Commissioner. http://www.censusindia.net/disability/disabled.html. Accessed 19 Sept 2004.

Csordas, T. (1994). Words from the holy people: a case study in cultural phenomenology. In T. Csordas (Ed.), *Embodiment and experience: The existential ground of culture and self.* Cambridge: Cambridge University Press.

French, S. (1993). Disability, impairment or something in between. In John Swain, et al. (Eds.), *Disabling Barriers, Enabling Environments* (pp. 17–25). London: Sage.

Gleeson, B. J. (1997). Disability studies: a historical materialist view. *Disability and Society, 12* (2), 179–202.

Government of India. (1996). *The persons with disabilities (equal opportunities, protection of rights and full participation) act 1995*.

Government of India. (2006). *National policy for persons with disabilities*. Ministry of social justice and empowerment.

Groce, N. (2006). Cultural beliefs and practices that influence the type and nature of data collected on individuals with disability through national census. *Research in Social Science and Disability, 29*(4), 41–55.

Hughes, B., & Patterson, K. (1997). The social model of disability and the disappearing body: Towards a sociology of impairment. *Disability and Society, 12*(3), 325–340.

Illich, I. (1976). *Medical nemesis: The expropriation of health*. New York: Pantheon Books.

Jangira, N. K., Singh, A., & Yadav, S. K. (1995). Teacher policy, training needs and perceived status of teachers. *Indian Educational Review, 30*(1), 113–122.

Lonsdale, S. (1990). *Women and disability*. London: Macmillan.

Mairs, N. (1986). On Being a Cripple. *Plaintext: Essays* (pp. 9–20). Tucson, AZ: University of Arizona Press.

Mani, D. Rama. (1988). *The physically handicapped in India: Policy and programme*. New Delhi: Ashish Publishing House.

Marks, D. (1999). Dimensions of oppression: Theorizing the embodied society. *Disability and Society, 14*(5), 611–626.

Mehta, D. S. (1983). *Handbook of the disabled in India*. Allied: New Delhi.

Mitra, S. (2006). The capability approach and disability. *Journal of Disability Policy Studies, 16* (4), 236–247.

Mohit, A. (2000). Governance and legislation: Initiatives of government of India to advance asia & pacific decade of disabled persons. *Disability World, 2* (Apr–May).

Mohit, A., & Rungta, S. K. (2000). *Regional experiences: Legal protection for persons with disabilities in India.*

Morris, J. (1991). Pride against prejudice: Transforming attitudes towards disability. London: The Women's Press. http://disability-studies.leeds.ac.uk/files/library/morris-Pride-and-Prejudice.pdf. Accessed 14 June 2014.

Morris, J. (1993). Prejudice. In J. Swain, V. Finkelstein, S. French & M. Oliver (Eds.), *Disabling barriers—Enabling environments*. London: Sage.

Myreddi, V., & Narayan, J. (2000). Preparation of special education teachers: Present status and future trends. *Asia Pacific Disability Rehabilitation Journal, 10*(1), 1–8.

National Centre for Promotion of Employment for Disabled People and National Association for the Blind. (1999). *The employment scenario in India with reference to people with disabilities.* NCPEDP-NAB. New Delhi. Source: www.dpa.org.sg/DPA/publication/dpipub/fall99. Aug 2004.

Oliver, M. (1990). *The politics of disablement.* Houndmills: Macmillan.

Oliver, M. (1996). *Understanding disability: From theory to practice.* Basingstoke: Macmillan.

Rajalakshmi, T. K. (2002). A law on paper. *Frontline* (Apr 12).

Ramanujam, P. R. (2000). Social policies on disability in India. *International Journal of Disability Studies, 1*(1), 3–15.

Roulstone, A., Watson, N., & Thomas, C. (2012). Introduction. In N. Watson, A. Roulstone, & C. Thomas (Eds.), *Routledge handbook of disability studies*. Routledge: London, UK.

Sen, A. K. (1999). Development as freedom. Oxford Indian paperbacks, seventh impression, 2004.

Shakespeare, T. (1994). Cultural representation of disabled people: Dustbins for disavowal? *Disability and Society, 9*(3), 283–299.

Shakespeare, T. (1996). Disability, identity and difference. In C. Barnes & G. Mercer (Eds.), *Exploring the divide*. Leeds: The Disability Press.

Shakespeare, T. (2004). Social models of disability and other life strategies. *Scandinavian Journal of Disability Research, 6*(1), 8–21.

Sharma, U. (2001). *The attitudes and concerns of school principals and teachers regarding the integration of students with disabilities into regular schools in India.* Unpublished Ph.D. Thesis, University of Melbourne, Melbourne.

Shariff, A. (1999). *India: Human Development report: A profile of Indian states in the 1990s*. New Delhi: Oxford University Press.

Snyder, S. L. (2006). Disability studies. In Gary Albrecht (Ed.), *Encyclopaedia of disability* (pp. 478–490). Thousand Oaks, CA: Sage Publications, Inc.

Söder, M. (1987). Relative definition of handicap: Implications for research. *Upsala Journal of Medical Sciences,* (Suppl. 44), 24–29.

Stone, D. (1985). *The disabled state*. Basingstoke: Macmillan.

Terzi, L. (2003). A capability perspective on impairment, disability and special needs: Towards social justice in education, capabilities and freedom. In *3rd International Conference on the Capability Approach*. Pavia University, 7–12 Sept 2003.

Thomas, C. (1999). *Female forms: Experiencing and understanding disability*. Buckingham: Open University Press.

Tregaskis, C. (2002). Social model theory: The story so far. *Disability and Society, 17*(4), 457–470.

United Nations Organisation. (1991). *United Nations standard rules on the equalization of opportunities for persons with disabilities*.

United Nations Organisation. (2006). *Convention on the rights of persons with disabilities.*

Wendell, S. (2001). Unhealthy disabled: Treating chronic illnesses as disabilities. *Hypatia, 16*(4), 17–33.

World Bank Report. (2007). *People with disabilities in India: from commitments to outcomes*. Washington DC: Human Development Unit, South Asia Region, World Bank.

World Health Organisation. (2001). *International classification of functioning, disability and health.* Source: www3.who.int/onlinebrowser/icf.cfm. Feb 2004.

Zachariah, J. (2001). *Universal light of knowledge: Opening new doors*. Source: www.un.org.in/JANSHALA/march2001/educdisb.htm. June 2004.

Chapter 2
The Models Approach in Disability Scholarship: An Assessment of Its Failings

Shilpaa Anand

Abstract The present chapter contends that the models approach to studying disability, when used in India, has little descriptive or explanatory ability and has become a way of evaluating research studies and judging them. While critiques of medical models approaches to framing disability have facilitated aspirations and demands of disability rights movements the world over, its present use in the Indian academic context requires critical examination. What is known as a medical model framing of disability cannot as conveniently describe or explain disability in the Indian context for multiple reasons. One, the social role of biomedicine in India is a complex one because of the prevalence of different kinds of treatment traditions that are accessed variously and whose conceptualization of treatment, object of treatment and corporeality are different in different ways from those of biomedicine. Additionally, the models approach intrinsically affirms a progressive historiography; the progression is from a moral or religious model to a medical model and then to a social–contextual model. Such a historiography is inadequate while tracing the genealogy of disabling conditions such as leprosy in the Indian context.

Keywords Models approach · Medical model · Social model · Alternative medical traditions · Leprosy history

2.1 Introduction

Disability studies conferences and seminars in India usually bring together a set group of scholars who are fairly well acquainted with the major debates of disability studies (DS), which is dominated by Western scholarship. But every event also

S. Anand (✉)
Department of English, Maulana Azad National Urdu University,
Hyderabad, Telangana, India
e-mail: shilpaa.anand@gmail.com

N. Ghosh (ed.), *Interrogating Disability in India*,
Dynamics of Asian Development, DOI 10.1007/978-81-322-3595-8_2

brings newer researchers working on disability to the fore and face to face with the more established scholars. Often, such exchanges turn into tense encounters where an "established" scholar, in the discussion that follows the presentation of the "new" scholar, characterizes the latter's work as bearing strong resemblances to the "medical model". This subjection to a trial where judgement is made on the "new" scholar influences the participation of the person in future disability studies conferences and scholarship. The "medical model crime", if one may use that term, refers to research pertaining to rehabilitation of a certain category of disability or the use of terminology that draws heavily upon the biomedical framing of a disability, or even focuses on the individuality of the disabled person and not on the social environment. The "crime" may be that the findings presented belong to the perspective of a rehabilitation or educational professional, one that does not adequately or fairly represent the "voice/s" or perspective/s of the disabled informants. Such kind of moral labelling forecloses the examination of the data presented or an analysis of why or how it might be "medical". Such research may in fact contain important disclosures about the culturally[1] specific context that we belong to and research in. The present chapter critiques the "models" approach to studying disability, that is the use of the "medical model", the "moral or religious model" and the "social model", which has become a way of evaluating research studies. This chapter may also be seen as a status report on the way the models approach has been adopted in research on disability related to India. It discusses the practice of using the "medical model" and "social model" to judge and evaluate a piece of research which occludes the use of these categories as heuristic tools. In order to use these categories as heuristic tools, scholarly research would also have to test the efficacy of the categories themselves while employing them to describe or explain their research data; if not, these categories stand out as Holy Grails that limit critical advances in disability studies. This chapter investigates the role played by the models approach in research related to disability in and outside of the Indian context. In order to do so, the chapter examines recent scholarship that draws on field studies and research in social medicine and medical anthropology that attempts to historicize disability. A second intent of this chapter is to present a close reading of critiques of the models approach that have received lesser recognition in disability studies scholarship as the more prominent research, and scholarship has wholeheartedly embraced the models approach. Such a reading becomes essential for researchers and scholars so that they may engage with the models approach more critically while not denying that its adoption has facilitated a necessary corrective to the erstwhile one-sided conceptualizing of disability as a medical phenomenon and experience.

[1]The term culture, for the purposes of this chapter, may be understood as "configuration of learning" and as a way of going about the world.

2.2 Elaborating the "Models" Approach

What is the "medical model"? And what does charging a type of research as being medical model entail? Medicalization of disability has been identified as presenting a restrictive understanding of disability. All practices that address disability as disease or as deficit conditions that can be cured or fixed in some way are considered to medicalize disability. This charge of medicalization in theoretical terms is called "the medical model" within disability studies which is primarily driven by the disability rights movements in the UK, and the corrective is supplied in the "social model" framework. Variations of the models approach include the "strong social model" that emerged in Marxist-style disability studies discipline in the UK in the 1970s as well as critiques of the "individual model" or the "deficit model" that were widely used in the American context a little later. These theories of medicalization and efforts to practice the social model as a corrective have served several purposes over the decades:

(a) To enable disability as a category of politics—disability rights movements in different parts of the world have embraced the social model of disability as an attempt to demedicalize and depathologize disability and thereby enter the identity politics paradigm. The medical model has played an important role in putting disability on the social movement map. Tom Shakespeare refers to this as a "political strategy" in the UK context. In the American situation, critiques of medical or individual approach—that resulted in various systems of dependence such as institutionalization—were used to enable the "independent living movement".
(b) To change law and policy from an orientation that focused on addressing only the individual with disability to a focus that would address the structural factors such as physical and social barriers and restrictions. The UNCRPD is a good instance of such an initiative. The Americans with Disabilities Act (1990) in the USA and the Disability Discrimination Act in the UK (1995) are both legislations that are based on social models approaches. They refrain from defining disability on the basis of biomedical characteristics (which address only the individual) and turn the onus on treatment of disabled people as well as physical and social barriers that hinder independent living. These laws emphasize the improvement of social factors that enable a better quality of life for disabled people alongside rehabilitation measures that focus on correcting the impairment in the disabled person. Similar features are the mainstay of the UNCRPD which is to guide future disability laws the world over. The Rights of Persons with Disabilities Bill that is still being debated in India, a bill that seeks to be in compliance with the UNCRPD, upon being passed, will replace the fairly medically oriented existing disability law in India, the Persons with Disabilities Act 1995.
(c) The models approach has played an important role in furthering the rights-based approach and enabling disabled people as participants in decision-making related to education, employment, law and policy related to

access to public spaces over the last few decades in India. As a result of this, disability has emerged both as a sociopolitical and as an identity category within disability rights articulations. Participation of disabled people in all forms of public life has become a reality in many parts of the world over the last three decades. The rights-based approach has been able to effectively check the advance of different eugenic practices, bring about the termination of dehumanizing practices of psychiatric institutions and introduce the practice of ethical medical procedures.

(d) The models approach has facilitated the emergence of disability as a non-negative category or as one that does not predominantly indicate a "state of injury". Disability as a category of diversity is being forwarded by several disability activist groups in the West in imitation of the civil rights movement in the USA. This argument has also been used by identity movements by other minority and marginalized groups such as the LGBT and Dalit (socially and economically marginalized) communities. This emergence of disability minority identity has aimed to move beyond the rights-based framework to one that demands a sociocultural identity, i.e. a move towards an identity politics framework, a good example of which is the deaf community's assertion of deafness as a linguistic minority.

While the models approach has facilitated a strong social movement framework in policy making and governance, how can we appraise its role within academic research? Tom Shakespeare, an important voice in the disability movement in the UK as well as disability studies scholarship makes an important assessment of the models approach. Shakespeare argues that one of the problems with the social models approach in disability studies over the decades is that it has been posited as "unchanging", as if its fundamental ideas are "correct and indispensable" (Shakespeare 2014, p. 20). The British social model, he says, is probably "one of the only areas in academia that still proudly maintains allegiance to Marxist orthodoxy" (2014, p. 20) that it persists as an outdated ideology-based academic framework. Shakespeare's primary move is to pronounce that the distinction between impairment and disability, as forwarded by the models approach scholars, is an artificial one. He argues that the distinction between "biological/individual impairment and social/structural disability is conceptually and empirically very difficult to sustain" (2014, p. 21–22). Social circumstances and biology are inextricably twined in cases where the impairment is caused by social conditions. He cites cases of impairments generated by poverty and malnutrition and in situations where pain-alleviating treatment may not be available easily because of controls placed on distribution of drugs or poor income. In the latter case, the social restriction combines with the impairment in such a way that we cannot argue that the mere lifting of the social restriction would reduce the effect of the impairment, because the social restriction is brought into play by the very existence of the impairment. Further, Shakespeare argues that impairments are socially constituted as well and not only biologically. In the case of mild intellectual disability, the level of IQ that determines the having or not of impairment is determined socially. He explains that "dyslexia may not become a problem until society demands literacy of its citizens" (2014, p. 23). He elaborates on social expectations that cause or exacerbate impairments and therefore impact the psycho-emotional well-being of a person with a physical impairment such as a spinal cord injury or a person diagnosed with a degenerative disease like multiple sclerosis. In such situations, removing the physical barrier or an economic barrier may not facilitate well-being because of emotionally distressing factors such as negative reactions from family members or colleagues at work or even the hyper-visibility of media representations of multiple sclerosis. Shakespeare cites this situation as one where we may not be able to distinguish between the impact caused by disablement and the impact caused by impairment.

A more recent critique of the models approach comes from Aimi Hamraie. She criticizes disability studies (hereafter, DS) scholarship for not adequately theorizing the "models framework" (Hamraie 2015, p. 110) as an "epistemic apparatus that the field of DS constructs" (2015) which enables the field to make truth claims about histories and epistemologies of disability. She argues, adopting insights from Foucault's method of archaeology, that DS scholarship does not go beyond articulating situated knowledge. Hamraie, then, is interested in placing "the models framework within broader conversations in the history and philosophy of science in order to foreground the constructed, contested and contingent nature of systems of knowledge about disability" (2015, p. 111). The "models framework", according to her, is not critical or self-conscious of its adoption of the progressive historicizing of disability which it assumes to be true, i.e. the progression from a moral model to a medical model and then on to a social model. The assumption that this progression is true limits DS scholarship from investigating messy contexts that show evidence of a mixing of moral and medical factors. The framework also tends to mischaracterize non-biomedical medical technologies as belonging to a premedical moral realm. She proposes the method of historical epistemology to be incorporated within DS research so that this field of inquiry may also reveal "the material effects of knowledge upon bodies, techniques and systems and analyse the systems of formation of knowledge (savoir) that make bodies intelligible" (2015, p. 115).

Both Shakespeare and Hamraie's analyses have important implications for the present chapter as well as for the changes it seeks in contemporary disability research in India. They demonstrate the limits of the models approach within the Anglo-American Western context but do not grasp the complexity of cultural situatedness of the models approach and the problems that arise when we try to study disability in contexts that are as distinct as the Indian one. While Shakespeare's critique casts the non-West as socio-economically different, Hamraie dismisses the cultural approach to studying disability as just another social–contextual approach that is invested in the ideology of situated knowledge. There appears to be an assumption that culturally different contexts can be described and known in terms of concepts that are native to Western epistemology. For instance, the use of the term "global South" is adopted and it succeeds in marking out the regions labelled thus in terms of socio-economic difference or in terms of religion and sociocultural practices. The category "global South" however misses the point that culturally different contexts may be so because their ways of knowing about and going about the world are peculiarly constituted. We may be researching a context that may not be at all intelligible through concepts such as "moral", "medical" and "social" and may therefore require us to develop a set of methodological and theoretical tools that will reveal what those concepts are. A culturally contextual way of theorizing would have to consider not just culturally situated knowledge but how that knowledge is conceptually and methodologically different. The scholarship reviewed here offers insights into these conceptual and methodological differences that disability scholarship pertaining to the Indian context would have to take cognizance of.

If we are to take the Indian context as culturally different in its engagement with concepts affiliated to the disability cluster—impairment, illness, medical diagnosis, family, development of institutions, social practices, notions of the individual, plural treatment practices—then it becomes relevant to critically investigate the relations between cultural context and disability theory carefully. In due course, precaution will be taken not to settle for categories of cultural difference that have been posited by the West with which to study India, in other words Orientalist categories. Harish Naraindas warns against the tendency to succumb to viewing and studying India as exclusively "religious" when compared to other cultural contexts (2001). Another instance is the use of karma, supposedly a category of fatalism that is peculiar to India, as an explanatory frame with which to comprehend all notions of and attitudes towards disabled people. The chapter will conclude with a reflection on issues pertaining to theorizing disability in the Indian context and what this review of the models approach can bring to such a theorizing.

2.3 Formulating a Cultural Critique of the Models Approach

Medical model research is classified as such by virtue of certain determining factors: one, the dependence of the research on biomedical categories that are treated as fixed and treatable; two, that the affected person exists (within the realm of the research study) as an individual entity whose voice is undervalued and to whom the treatment is administered after verifying that he or she requires a certain procedure established through objective methods of enquiry. Three, that there is a notion of "deficit" or "tragedy" associated with the individual affected which presents disability as a burden, flaw or negative aspect of the individual's personality. Given that these are the criteria for determining aspects and phenomena in the research field as medical model, what are some of the concerns they raise when collecting disability-related data?

Insights from disability-related fieldwork: Sociological and anthropological ethnographic fieldwork undertaken by disability researchers has revealed that it is not easy to identify and classify phenomena as being part of a medical model; it is not a useful way of classifying responses. Respondents do not use biomedical categories to identify themselves as disabled (Staples, 2012; Mehrotra, 2013). James

Staples's ethnographic research in Hyderabad is about "how and when notions of 'disability' were invoked" (Staples 2012, p. 558) and why they were being invoked. His interest was in finding how disability is constituted discursively and in everyday practices. Significantly, his essay, "Culture and Carelessness: Constituting Disability in South India", begins with an affirmation that the official discourse of disability in his field area is definitively set within the medical framework, be it the government's categorizing of disability or NGO approaches to addressing disabled people's needs. He observed the ways in which disability is invoked rhetorically in the context he studies to identify the distinctions between the official discourse and people's use of the concept. Like Shakespeare, he finds categories of impairment and disability limiting, as there is a far more complex interaction between notions of the individual that are grounded in moral practices of individual selves and families. While interviewing medical practitioners and rehabilitation experts, he finds that they are quick to morally judge their patients who come to them for disability-related treatment by calling them "careless". They attribute "carelessness" as the cause of disability and the "carelessness", usually a euphemism for actions resulting from being poorly educated or being poorly informed, ranges from the patients' faith in non-medical cures such as visiting shamans or offering sacrifices at places of worship, to their inability to care for the disabled family members by accessing timely health care. Social structural factors such as poverty, unemployment or the hardships experienced because of poor lifestyle of migrant labourers were hardly ever identified as causing disability, factors that were highlighted by the social model. These medical practitioners who were themselves not in favour of the patients espousing religious remedies for their disabling conditions did not hesitate to assume a god-like position in dismissing patients' lifestyles as being immoral.

In his informal conversations with lay people in Hyderabad in southern India, such as auto-rickshaw drivers, street vendors, shopkeepers, students and other people he may have met in waiting rooms of clinics, Staples finds that the rhetoric is not very different from that of the medical practitioners. They identified poverty, inability to take care of oneself, improper sexual relations, not accessing reproductive health care and as individual failings of the disabled person or as failings of the disabled person's family. What is important to note here is that social structural problems are identified as personal failings of disabled individuals. These responses then trouble standard DS notions of "medical", "moral" and "social". The medical model, which is also known as the individual model, is almost absent in these exchanges where it seems to be an individual's moral responsibility to ensure a proper upholding of social structures.

Further, Staples finds that his respondents' "stated views about disability were frequently strongly at odds with their relationships with actual disabled people" (2012, p. 566). In their personal interactions with disabled people, the sense of personal responsibility attached to people not accessing timely health care vanished and was replaced by an attribution of their disability to fate, god's will or not having the resources to access timely medical care. Staples also adds that attribution to fatalism was rhetorical in nature and respondents seemed somehow aware of using fatalism rhetorically to respond to certain questions. Staples qualifies the fatalism as a rhetoric because of his awareness of the types of treatment that the affected person had sought out in the hope of a cure before deploying such fatalism. He also finds that the fatalism serves as a rhetoric that is part of being in a disability context, rather than being indicative of what the person really thought of their condition, or of someone they knew or lived with. The significant finding here is that causes of disability in disabled people known to the respondents were differently attributed when compared to causes attributed to "disabled people" as a more general and abstract, third-person category. It would be inappropriate to categorize these responses that invoke fatalism routinely as being purely of a "moral" variety.

Fieldwork conducted by Veena Das and Renu Addlakha in Delhi also has significant implications for an assessment of the models approach. Das and Addlakha (2001) find that notions of personhood are located not at the individual level but at the intersections of the family and the state. They adopt the method of listening in on rumour, gossip and other talk around the family of the disabled individual instead of a method of collecting data drawn from interviews where the word disability is enunciated explicitly. They find using the names of disabilities or impairment limiting in trying to understand the social relations of women with facial disfigurement and those diagnosed with psychiatric illnesses. They study the daily practice of kinship and domesticity within the familial context in relation to disability and impairment. With regard to one of their case studies, they find that the parents of a woman with facial disfigurement, in their attempt to give her as "normal" a life as possible, forgo kinship relations and social interactions with their extended friends and family (Das and Addlakha, 2001). In relation to this particular study of a woman with a facial disfigurement, in a post-Partition Punjabi family, the authors find that within that specific context, there appears to be the presence of "connected body-selves" (Das and Addlakha 2001, p. 520) and no evidence of the individual as we standardly know it, as a constituent of the "medical model".

In Staples's work as well, we find that there is a dependence on talk about disabling conditions by the affected individual and people around them (2012). Neither of these studies focuses on how well-versed affected individuals, their families and health practitioners are in the medical definitions and rhetoric of their conditions, and so they do not lend themselves to conclusions about the ineptitude of people when it comes to being informed about medical notions. These studies point to the uselessness of categories used within official discourses to relate to the way that affected individuals and their families know themselves. Both these studies destabilise the significance attributed to disabled people's agency by indicating that this agency is not located at the individual level but at the level of social interaction. While a key method of the models approach is to give primacy to the 'voice of the disabled person', these studies emphasise that acts of speech are to be acknowledged and comprehended in the context of and alongside social interaction. The constitution of disability is found at the interstices of interacting voices of disabled persons, their family, their kin[2] and people around them. Based on the observations of their respondents' actions, these researchers have shown that the social responses to disabled people may only be recorded through observation of their actions and not through a record of their opinions, which may be formulated in a particular manner to be in sync with popular discourses.

Historical research and the medical model: Attempts to study the history of disability in the Indian context show that categorizing something within a medical model occludes rather than explicates an occurrence or a phenomenon. Leprosy serves as an illustration. A disabling disease with a long history of moral stigma attached to it, the only way leprosy could be made more socially acceptable was through a process of medicalizing by emphasizing its disease status. The case of leprosy is an important one as it demonstrates a more complex relationship between disability and the medical realm than what is understood as the medical model. It would be necessary to examine briefly the sequence of events and ideas that led to the moment when the medicalization of leprosy or its establishment as bacterial infection lent it a more tolerated social identity.

Buckingham's (2002) study of leprosy in colonial south India, particularly the Madras Presidency, shows that the earliest responses to leprosy in India, prior to missionary involvement, were governmental and medical in the early 1800s. Her study of responses to leprosy in the colonial Indian context complicates the DS models approach of a historical progression from a more moral framework to medical framework in knowing and treating disabling conditions. Her work focuses on the extensive research that was undertaken by authorities in the colonies when they encountered leprosy. This research, in the first half of the nineteenth century, arrived at findings that were similar to those of experts researching leprosy in Europe. Buckingham also documents that medical systems indigenous to the Madras context such as Siddha and the more pan-Indian Ayurveda had identified and distinguished between as many as 18 types of leprosy of varying kinds and degrees.

Leprosy discourses in India took a more moral turn later, in the mid to late nineteenth century, and became contextualized in a religious realm, most likely because of the West's experience of leprosy as a strongly moralized condition at an earlier period. When the missionaries took over leprosy governance in India, it became increasingly a matter of the "moral model". The leper's body was an important site where the contest between religions was dramatically played out. Christian missions that settled in India brought with them a story of leprosy that was plotted within a narrative that typified the leper as the innocent sinner, a reprobate

[2]Shakespeare's critique of the distinction between disability and impairment cited earlier in this chapter assumes that the voices of people around the disabled person, in the multiple sclerosis instance that he describes, may be negative, thus adding to the emotional aspect of the impairment of the disabled individual. This kind of an assessment of the voices of people surrounding the disabled person is difficult to make in the contexts studied by Staples (2012) as well as Das and Addlakha (2001). For one, the reactions of the people surrounding these individuals lead them to take actions of different kinds in Das and Addlakha's study. Two, what these "voices" say has to be understood in context and weighed as being rhetorical or not, as Staples's study demonstrates.

who had no role in being cast as such. It was projected that Christianity would save the leper through a programme of salvation that would ultimately become an important tool for conversion of natives into the new religion. What is significant about this emplotment, something that is often forgotten, is that leprosy was presented as a "problem" that needed solving, an idea that may or may not have been present prior to missionary intervention. Another significant aspect of the plot was the casting of other religions and their customs as being villainous to those affected by leprosy. A third feature of the leprosy story is that leprosy served as the stage on which the presentation of Christianity as a reformed and continually reforming religion could be performed. Medieval/early Christian characterization of leprosy as an evil condition and the leper as one who was despised and ostracized was shunned in the later Christian rendition that was prevalent in colonial India. The link between the missionary approach to the disease and the (then) new public health discourse was strong. Hospitals and asylums run by the Mission to Lepers received funding from the British government in India, thus supporting wholeheartedly the missionary initiatives. Significant actors of the BELRA (British Empire Leprosy Relief Association), such as Rev. R.G. Cochrane, were invested in Biblical notions of leprosy and applauded the transition the religion had made from severe Old Testament beliefs to the New Testament practices of bringing salvation to the leper:

> It has happened that God in His mercy has overruled the mediaeval misunderstanding regarding leprosy and used it for His glory. Through it He has wrought a marvellous work, leading His Church into fresh avenues of service among people who, the world over, were utterly despised and rejected. … God reveals to men from time to time human injustices which must be put right, and through His servants He issues the challenge that these things must not be (Cochrane, 1961, p. 22).

The public health view of leprosy, in its attempt to provide a rational aetiology of the disease, presented an orientalized picture of leprosy that succeeded in further moralizing the emergence and existence of the disease in India:

> Leprosy may be regarded as a malady of uncivilized or partially civilized races, and its chief predisposing causes comprise personal uncleanliness, overcrowded and dirty dwellings, combined with a dietary that is deficient in quality or insufficient in quantity.… The eradication of the native filthy habits and customs which predispose to, and assist in spreading, leprosy is recognised to be a matter attended with many difficulties; it would therefore seem that the hope for the future must lie in the education of the rising generation in the elements of personal and domestic hygiene. (The Lancet, 1913, p. 1557)

It is not hard to detect the moral tone that guards this seemingly scientific "public health" discourse in the report above. Evidently, the medical and moral had become so deeply intertwined that the more scientific of interventions had to be ushered in by those actors who were in fact working as social reformers and political activists. It was Gandhi and others who intervened around the 1940s, armed with up-to-date scientific knowledge about the disease so that measures such as sterilization of leprosy-affected persons and segregation based on sex would not be adopted. Gandhi was convinced that the procedures adopted to stall the spread of leprosy were under-researched. He demanded that efforts be concentrated on the medical aspects of leprosy so that information emerging from that field could be disseminated to all parts of India. When people came to him with questions about leprosy prevention and treatment of persons with leprosy in colonies and villages, he directed them to Dr. Ernest Muir's work on the diagnosis, prevention and treatment of leprosy. Interestingly, Muir's work on leprosy, in general, differed from previous as well as contemporary medical scholarship, in that it rigorously attended to scientific medical efforts at addressing the disease. It was during Muir's tenure with the BELRA that leprosy-related projects in the British colonies became invested in medical research that would thwart the disease's march. Muir's term in India also saw an increase in the use of *chaulmoogra* oil in treating leprosy.[3] The history of leprosy in India serves to show that the framing of disability historicizing that is inherent to the DS models approach cannot adequately describe histories of disabling conditions in the Indian context. Another challenge leprosy history throws up is that different forms of treatment persisted through the centuries whose epistemology varied drastically from the biomedical knowledge system. Can those modes of treatment be assigned the category of the "medical model"?[4] Or is the notion of the "medical model" inherently related to biomedical forms of treatment?

A plural medical context: A third area of research that enables a critical examination of what the medical model means in context would be the prevalence of multiple treatment conceptualizations which challenge the very criteria that constitute the "medical" as per the models approach. Unlike American or European contexts where the turn to alternative systems of medicine is more recent, India has a long history of plural medical practices. Thus, it becomes important for us to examine the links between certain underlying conceptual and epistemic frames of these practices, be it text-based ones like Ayurveda, Unani and Siddha or others like bone-setting and indigenous birthing practices. These practices are not only systems of knowledge or methods of medical practices that are different from biomedicine but also systems that are grounded in epistemological bases that vary from that of biomedicine in the Anglo-European American West.

Ayurveda and Siddha conceptualize the human body as "a system of relationships defining functions which manifest themselves through the structures" (Jayasundar, 2012, p. 42). In Ayurveda, a function is constituted by collective effort of various factors, including structures (as in biomedicine), biochemistry, electric and magnetic activities and the mental and emotional status of a person. For instance, these systems do not assume the duality of mind and body or conceive of the body in terms of separate systems such as the skeletal system, the endocrine

---

[3]*Chaulmoogra* oil was used in Ayurvedic treatment of skin diseases for a long time prior to its emergence as an ointment expressly used for the treatment of leprosy. Its use in China and Burma at the same time is also variously recorded.

[4]The question this chapter raises is at a tangent from Hamraie's (2015) research question that points to the problems of designating only biomedical forms of treatment as "medical" and not other forms of medicine that were based in humoral systems.

system and so on. A function, in Ayurvedic terms, reflects the whole system of a human being where a variety of components work together to constitute it (Jayasundar, 2012). Siddha practice does not regard disease in terms of organs affected, so the concept of organ is not a useful entity within the Siddha tradition. In Siddha, different substrata of the body are composed by substances that nourish them, be they items such as food and water that nurture the earthly or gross parts of the body as well as subtle substances like *prana* (the concept of air circulating through hollow channels of the body) and thoughts and intellect (Sujatha, 2012).

Ayurveda uses the concepts of *vata*, *pitta* and *kapha*,[5] the *tridosha*s (three elements), that refer to "a set of parameters which include functions like movement, transformation and support and growth, respectively, and other physico-chemical and physiological parameters contributing to these functions" (2012, p. 43). The *dosha*s, however, literally mean "that which can become impaired and also [have] the potential to impair other tissues" (2012, p. 43). These *dosha*s include physiological as well as psychological functions. The concept of health within this system of medicine is not linear (as in biomedicine) and refers to a homeostatis or fine balance among the *dosha*s.[6] Thus, "disease"[7] as well is a result of imbalance in the *dosha*s.

"Diagnosis" in Ayurveda consists of an assessment of any deviation from the state of equilibrium of *dosha*s; the impaired *dosha* has to be identified. "Diagnosis" here includes the evaluation of the inherent mental and physical constitution of the patient, age, occupation, the season in which the "disease" has manifested itself, the immediate living environment of the patient including the weather, the food habits of the patient and so on. Ayurvedic "diagnosis" is aimed at knowing the root cause of the disease condition. As the method of treatment is tailor-made for a specific patient, it is important to know all these factors; sensitivity to context is of prime importance (Jayasundar, 2012). Ayurvedic diagnosis also pays keen attention to cause of the "disease", why something is happening to the patient, rather than merely knowing the symptoms or what is happening to the patient. These treatment traditions provide personalized treatment to each patient, thus not repeating the same method of treatment even for two people who may have the same symptoms and, in the DS framework, the same impairment. Given this, it would be impossible to have a common diagnostic category and thus follow an objective system of naming and labelling diseases. Contemporary DS, framed within the models approach, discredits attention paid to the individual in biomedical treatment procedures because this attention locates the "problem" within the person of the

[5]*Vata* refers to air, *pitta* refers to fire or heat, and *kapha* refers to characteristics of fluid or fluidity such as unctuousness, coldness, heaviness, sluggishness and so on.

[6]For instance, if there is a variation in one of the *dosha*s, the components of the other two *dosha*s are automatically affected. If the dryness of *vata* increases, there is a decrease in the oiliness of *pitta* and *kapha*.

[7]The quotation marks around a word/concept in this discussion indicate that the concept is not native to the system of medicine being discussed and is a placeholder term that refers to a somewhat similar notion.

individual affected. But it is important to consider that the critique here is of the objective nature of biomedical knowledge that decontextualizes the person by treating him or her as representative of an infected body. The other systems being surveyed here depend on subjective experiences and the narratives of those experiences as *sui generis*.

Siddha tradition believes that the only source of knowledge for treating the living human being is the living human being; "one can never study the flow of *prana* in a body that is devoid of *prana*" (Sujatha 2012, p. 86) . Siddha practitioners believe that cognition is something that everyone is capable of because they include perception and inference (2012). So also, as in Ayurveda, knowledge of the "disease" is based on how the patient experiences their ailment (Bode, 2012). The context is important to "diagnose" the disease as well as the information given by the patient; both contribute to this process of diagnosing in ways that are different from the biomedical system. These systems then deploy narratives of the patients to develop the treatment. In a volume titled *Multiple Voices and Stories: Narratives of Health and Illness* (Mishra and Chatterjee, 2013), the editors discuss the significance of narratives in non-biomedical treatment practices. The volume of essays draws on studies of narratives of practitioners of different medical and treatment systems as well as the patients. Though the introduction to the book acknowledges its debt to the emergence of illness narratives within biomedical practices as a guiding framework (Mishra and Chatterjee, 2013), it becomes clear as one reads through the essays how and why narratives are intrinsically part of these treatment traditions.

Ayurveda and Siddha systems, as also bone-setting traditions, depend heavily on the knowledge that a person has of themselves and their bodily functions; therefore, the narratives of patients play an important role in developing the treatment. Treatment in Ayurveda is denoted as *chikitsa*, which includes procedures "aimed at removal of disease-causing factors" (Jayasundar 2012, p. 51) as well as repair of imbalances (2012). The root causes and not surface-level symptoms are the focus of treatment—another reason that the narratives of patients form the corpus of knowledge which also forms part of the treatment. Siddha and Ayurvedic practices address the patient in context. In order to know the context of the patient, these systems need the active participation of the patient to inform them of their contexts in terms of environmental factors, daily activities and bodily functions. This gives the practitioners a sense of minute changes in the routines of the person, including why they may have done something differently on a particular day. Details like this invariably involve a narrative that describes the social context of the person being treated. Treatment in turn is developed to address the specificities of the individual's condition in context, thereby giving us a different theory of individuality, one where the treatment is individuated, not the person. What this demonstrates is that the context and the individual are contiguous; the separation between the two does not exist in the conceptualization of "patient", "disease" and "treatment". In disability terms, this translates to knowing the individual lesion or condition as well as the social context of that condition. The "social" then is not separate from the "medical"; it is intrinsic to it.

With regard to these complementary and alternative medical practices, it is important to engage with the charge that is often levelled against practices such as bone-setting and the *dai* (midwife) tradition, not so much Ayurveda, Siddha and Unani, that they belong to unscientific or premedical and therefore irrational practice systems. Within the DS framework, these practices may also be characterized as evidence of the "moral model" or the "religious model".[8] In her study of bone doctors in Rajasthan in 2009–2010, Helen Lambert finds that the practitioners describe their work in terms of "moral" practices (2013). On observing the narratives she compiles, it is clear that her use of the word "moral" indicates "ethics" and is therefore descriptive, to convey the sense of appropriate action, and not be confused with the evaluative use of the word "moral" in the "moral model" of the DS framework. These bone doctors commenting on the ethics of their practice claim that they provide "decent, affordable" (Lambert 2013, p. 35) treatment to their clients and do not make a profit by exploiting them. Lambert records that on occasion these practitioners provided free treatment as well to clients who could visibly not afford the fees. A few respondents also characterized their work as a form of "public service". This kind of discourse of providing affordable treatment and service could easily be typecast as belonging to the "moral" or "charity model" in the DS framework. However, it is significant to note that the bone doctors' narratives of themselves match the narratives of their clients who state that they prefer them to government hospitals that charge exorbitant amounts as fees, for medicines and tests as well as for the plastering procedure. The characterization of their work as public service is a reaction to the doubts expressed about the rationality or viability of their profession by biomedical practitioners. The rhetoric of charity, then, appears to be a way of establishing themselves as ethical practitioners in the face of threats from biomedical institutions that are supposedly manifesting unethical practices.

In case of the "bone doctors", they are also *pahalwan*s, or wrestlers, who belong to a community in which the tradition of *pahalwani* and bone setting is passed on from generation to generation (Lambert, 2013). This was also true of Siddha *vaidya*s (medics) and Ayurvedic practitioners before the governement's support of these traditional medical systems, through AYUSH, gave a fillip to more widespread teaching and imparting of these systems. Their knowledge of the "art" is not textually acquired but gained through a lived practice of an "ethics of the self", to use a Foucauldian formulation. In a sense, it is through knowledge and practices related to one's own corporeality that they have the expertise to treat others who approach them to treat joint dislocation or broken joints. If one were to cast this information in terms of the DS models approach, these systems run the risk of being identified as belonging to the "moral model", which is many times a euphemism for methods and practices that are pre-Enlightenment.

[8]Hamraie (2015) also makes this point in her chapter with regard to the West that humoral medical practices have been relegated to the moral model because of the progressivist framing of DS, which necessitates that the medical, in the sense of the biomedical, be regarded as an improvement on the "moral" (implying humoral) practices.

These systems are also community based, meaning that one has to be born into a certain community or caste group to be able to continue a certain practice. This is also true of Ayurveda and the *dai* tradition of midwifery. Chawla's (2013) research group in the Jharkhand area examines the epistemic aspects of the *dai* tradition and argues that it is one instance of subjugated knowledge or subaltern knowledge that is suppressed by the development discourse which gives primacy to propositional forms of knowledge and not practical forms of knowledge. While this line of argumentation belongs to a larger set of discourses on subalternity and development, this chapter is concerned with how the disregard of certain kinds of knowledge that are intrinsic to a specific cultural context demonstrates a kind of cognitive enslavement (Dhareshwar, 1998) to not just Western epistemic frames, but also to the indifference that Western epistemic frames bear towards non-theoretical forms of knowledge.

2.4 Conclusion

If studies of disability are undertaken to reveal insights about this phenomenon that we call disability, then we would have to retool our theoretical and methodological toolboxes so that they serve our purposes appropriately if not adequately. It is time to recognize the limitations of the DS models approach and develop theoretical and methodological tools that are context-sensitive. Insights from existing research, reviewed in this chapter, strongly suggest that the very notion of the individual as distinct from the "social" that is intrinsic to the critique of the medical model is conceptually unavailable in certain contexts. Second, the progressivist routine that DS scholarship is imbued with runs the risk of turning disability research in all contexts into a primarily moral discourse that is more invested in fulfilling its reformist function than developing a knowledge base. In wanting to adhere to the agenda of a "transformative scholarship" that "serves a remedial function", researchers should not forget that it is "necessary to correct omissions, inaccuracies and faulty logic" (Linton 1998, p. 531), even if it means that these "inaccuracies and faulty logic" (1998) are created by what may be considered the founding ideas of DS scholarship. A theoretical retooling would enable research that is not restricted by temporally and culturally specific conceptual frames such as 'moral', 'medical' and 'social'. Methodologically, disability research would require that we not assume that "voices" of disabled people are available to us just because we are able to conduct interviews with them. Conversely, speaking to persons related to or known to the disabled person, about them, or a health practitioner who treats them does not mean that the concerned research study would fail to reveal significant insights about the conceptualization of disability. This chapter does not propose that another more appropriate set of models replace the existing models framework or that a new model that is more sensitive to diverse cultural contexts be formulated; rather, it has tried to critique the use of models as limiting and looks forward to a scholarly practice that is more critical of the theoretical and methodological tools it adopts.

References

Bode, M. (2012). Ayurveda in the twenty-first century: Logic, practice and ethics. In V. Sujatha & L. Abraham (Eds.), *Medical pluralism in contemporary India*. Orient Blackswan: New Delhi.

Buckingham, J. (2002). *Leprosy in colonial South India: Medicine in confinement*. Palgrave: Basingstoke.

Chawla, J. (2013). Outcaste women, cast-out birth knowledge. In A. Mishra & S. C. Chatterjee (Eds.), *Multiple voices and stories: Narratives of health and illness*. Orient Blackswan: Hyderabad.

Cochrane, R. G. (1961). *Biblical leprosy: A suggested interpretation*. Retrieved Jan 27, 2008, from http://www.biblicalstudies.org.uk/article_leprosy_cochrane.html

Das, V., & Addlakha, R. (2001). Disability and domestic citizenship: Voice, gender, and the making of the subject. *Public Culture, 13*(3), 511–532.

Dhareshwar, V. (1998). Valorizing the present: Orientalism, postcoloniality and the human sciences. *Cultural Dynamics, 10*(2), 211–231.

Hamraie, A. (2015). Historical epistemology as disability studies methodology: From the models framework to Foucault's archaeology of cure. *Foucault Studies, 19*, 108–134.

Jayasundar, R. (2012). Contrasting approaches to health and disease: Ayurveda and biomedicine. In V. Sujatha & L. Abraham (Eds.), *Medical pluralism in contemporary India*. Orient Blackswan: New Delhi.

Lambert, H. (2013). Moral narratives and biomedical critiques in the accounts of bone doctors and their clients. In A. Mishra & S. C. Chatterjee (Eds.), *Multiple voices and stories: Narratives of health and illness*. Orient Blackswan: Hyderabad.

Linton, S. (1998). Disability studies/not disability studies. *Disability & Society, 13*(4), 525–540.

Mehrotra, N. (2013). *Disability, gender and state policy: Exploring margins*. Jaipur: Rawat Publications.

Mishra, A., & Chatterjee, S. C. (2013). *Multiple voices and stories: Narratives of health and illness*. Orient Blackswan: Hyderabad.

Naraindas, H. (2001). Of therapeutics and prophylactics: The exegesis of an eighteenth-century tract on smallpox. In D. Kumar (Ed.), *Disease and medicine in india: A historical overview*. New Delhi: Tulika Books.

Shakespeare, T. (2014). *Disability rights and wrongs revisited*. London: Routledge.

Staples, J. (2012). Culture and carelessness: Constituting disability in South India. *Medical Anthropology Quarterly, 26*(4), 557–574.

Sujatha, V. (2012). The patient as knower: Principle and practice in Siddha medicine. In V. Sujatha & L. Abraham (Eds.), *Medical pluralism in contemporary India*. Orient Blackswan: New Delhi.

The Lancet. (1913). *The leprosy problem* (pp. 1556–1557).

Chapter 3
Diversity at Workplace and in Education

Tanmoy Bhattacharya

Abstract There is a potential conflict between the value of diversity at workplace—a concept touted and encouraged since the mid-1990s in America among private business/corporates—and the findings of the rights-based disability movement, namely (i) a person with disability (PwD) does not need charity, and (ii) disability is not a spectacle. A PwD represents in some sense the "spectacle of diversity" to an extreme in the mainstream unconscious imagination: if a prospective employer encourages hiring an employee with disability solely for the reason of diversity, then there is a problem. However, there ought to be some value to a practical implementation of a policy; i.e., if an organization wishes to implement a policy that encourages diversity in the workplace/institution, it ought to be considered an affirmative action. This is equally true of any possible future attempt at designing an instrument to 'implement' a theoretical perspective, be it from within the humanities or the social sciences; that is, actually hiring/admitting people as per a policy requirement may eventually lead to designing of an "instrument" or a set of algorithms, or a programme, to follow in cases of any such implementations. Nonetheless, designing instruments can address some of the issues which are often projected as problems which differentiate the social sciences from the humanities, since it has been argued that "designing" or "instrumentation" per se leads to a mechanistic world where human values are neglected—a bone of contention between the humanities and social sciences. A return to humanistic studies seems to be the only sure way of arriving at the truth. This is true in education as well as in employment, where the mere reportage of managers'/teachers' or employees'/students' satisfaction over employing PwDs and ignoring the axis of domination to investigate such status of employment, i.e. whether the person was employed/admitted "only" because of his/her disability to add to the so-called spectacle for the institute or whether because the organization truly believed in doing a good thing like diversity, does not constitute an analysis. This chapter thus critically examines the construction of diversity at workplace and in education with a view to comprehending the underlying notions.

T. Bhattacharya (✉)
Centre for Advanced Studies in Linguistics, University of Delhi, New Delhi, India
e-mail: tanmoy1@gmail.com

N. Ghosh (ed.), *Interrogating Disability in India*,
Dynamics of Asian Development, DOI 10.1007/978-81-322-3595-8_3

Keywords Diversity · Social Capital · Centring · Employment · Inclusion

3.1 Setting the Theoretical Background

3.1.1 Introduction

Diversity is a good thing. Or is it? This is the debate that launches the main idea in this chapter. If disabled persons[1] are hired in a public or private sector company or admitted in a regular school, but are either kept at lower rungs of the office hierarchy, or removed periodically from regular schools, then disability is simply a spectacle. A disabled person represents in some sense the "spectacle of diversity" to an extreme in the mainstream unconscious imagination. So, if a prospective employer encourages hiring a person with disability (PwD) solely for the reason of diversity from such a perspective, then there is a problem.

However, it is not easy to sort this problem out. One, there ought to be some value to a practical implementation of a policy; i.e. designing an instrument that makes available a way of implementing a policy is a good thing—the instrument here being increased diversity at workplaces and institutions. In the realm of education, diversity has been shown to play a significant role by providing people an opportunity to interact in a meaningful way with individuals from diverse backgrounds, and the benefits that accrue from such exposure better prepare them to exist in a multicultural society. There is enough literature showing that diversity in the classroom and the curriculum adds to the quality of the educational experience for students and educators (Rudenstine, 2001).

However, typically "diversity" in either education or workplace refers to diversity in ethnicity and race. Persons with disabilities are marginalized once again and are not included in discussions on diversity, though it is clearly "one of many areas in which true equality requires not identical treatment, but rather differential treatment in order to accommodate differential social needs" (Kymlicka, 1992: 113). Throughout history, disabled persons have experienced similar attitudinal and architectural barriers in the society. Although "disability" can refer to a wide range and degree of physical and/or mental impairments and any social categorization on that basis is thus problematic, one can perceive the recognition of disability culture from the perspective of the social status of individual members of a group as full partners in social interactions; that is, the common thread running through persons with disabilities is the participation disparity they experience, which is often a result

[1]In this chapter, I deliberately switch between a person-first and a disability-first terminology, making in fact the claim that the tyranny of choosing one or the other must be overcome. Apart from the respective histories of the struggles, these different usages are also partly linguistic, as English being a subject–verb–object, and prepositional language allows nominal expressions with a prepositional phrase within it, such as "X with Y", which may not be allowed in a verb-final, postpositional language like most Indian languages.

of institutionalized cultural practices. This particular view with regard to disabled persons is advocated by Danermark and Gellerstedt (2010) on the basis of the status model of recognition proposed by Fraser (2000). Fraser is primarily interested in a view of social justice that is rooted in redistribution (of resources) and recognition, where "parity of participation" is considered to be the normative. She is thus able to integrate socio-economic as well as cultural injustices, where "remedies to socio-economic injustice would be redistribution of resources, while remedies to cultural injustice would be recognition" (Danermark and Gellerstedt, 2010: 343). Social status in this model is therefore tied to participation parity as a norm.

A mere reportage of managers'/teachers' or employees'/students' satisfaction over employing/being employed or admitting/being admitted disabled persons and ignoring the axis of domination to investigate such status (with respect to the reason for inclusion being mere "spectacle" or a genuine belief in diversity) is undesirable. If there was a way to "measure" (un)favourable reasons for the presence of disabled persons at workplace and institutions, then a truer picture might emerge. In short, in order to create an instrument that ensures diversity at workplace and institutions, we need to generate another instrument to "measure" the true characterization of diversity.

"Measuring" of course is a much-maligned word in the context of humanistic studies, but not always so in social sciences, which nonetheless is wrecked by the famous absence of the "subject" or its preference of structural systems over the human subject or agency; the "narrative turn" across social sciences (Plummer, 2001: 11) is a critique of this absence of agency. At the same time, if we go by Biklen's (2005: 3) comment that disability is not "knowable in any definitively objective sense … [it] can be studied and discussed, but it is not knowable as a truth. It must always be interpreted", then a return to humanistic studies seems to be the only sure way of understanding disability. In other words, studying disability seems to highlight a possible tension between the issue of the missing subject in the context of social sciences and the need for "measuring" in the context of humanistic studies. How do we resolve this tension?[2] I will come back to this question after a brief and relevant detour.

3.1.2 Centring Disability as Knowledge Empowerment

In this section, I will develop and outline my thesis of "centring disability" with respect to sign language, which I claim informs and augments our understanding of

[2]Although this question formed the background for the talk on which the present chapter is based (Bhattacharya, 2012), the question and the answer became clearer in my mind from another question posed by the (late) Prof. Jasodhara Bagchi present in the audience, whose untimely passing (in January 2015) has caused a lot of grief among the intelligentsia in the country; I wish to express my gratitude to her for asking the most relevant question that the chapter raises, which was, how is reducing the distance between humanities and social sciences an instance of centring disability?

language as such—the basis of much of human nature itself. On the face of it, it sounds like a rather tall claim, but I will show that not only is there a precedence for such a framework, but in fact, this might be the only desirable way to move forward for knowledge development and, specific to the concerns of this chapter, in thinking about disability.

To re-emphasize the title of the section further, by the phrase "centring disability", I mean the strategy of locating disability at the centre of studying other phenomena such as modernity (McCagg and Siegelbaum, 1989; Radford, 1994) or medicine (Zborowski, 1960; Gilman, 1985; Morris, 1991) and thereby obtaining an enlightened perspective on these other phenomena; this, I call the empowerment of knowledge in general. Although according to Linton (1998) the studies above do not exactly centre disability, Radford (1994: 22, emphasis in original), studying intellectual disability, says the following which defines what I mean by centring disability: "[M]odernity is a lens through which we can see that our culture has not only marginalized people with an intellectual disability, *it has also marginalized the study of intellectual disability as a phenomenon*".

A striking example of centring disability can be read into Keller's (1985) account of Nobel laureate but much neglected cytogeneticist Barbara McClintock's work on transposition. McClintock's philosophy can be understood from what she has to say about research in general and her own research on transposition in corn kernels in particular:

> If the material tells you, 'It may be this,' allow that. Don't turn it aside and call it an exception, an aberration, a contaminant.... That's what's happened all the way along the line with so many good clues. ... The important thing is to develop the capacity to see one kernel of maize that is different, and make that understandable. If something doesn't fit, there's a reason, and you find out what it is (quoted in Keller, 1985: 163, 1995).

McClintock's world view begins and rests with difference. Instead of viewing the world as constituted by dichotomy, in this view, difference gives rise to a radical reorganization of the world around us that finally resolves into multiplicity. The kernels of corn that did not appear to fit in revealed a larger world of multidimensional order irreducible to a single law.

My thesis of "centring disability" with respect to sign language is based on a conspicuous character of sign languages—the *multi-modal* nature of the language that achieves the impossible task of uttering two words at the same time in terms of a spoken language equivalent. Sound, as we know, is embedded in time; we can only utter Word_3 after Word_2 after Word_1, and so on. Sign language, on the other hand, being a visual language, makes use of both space and time to produce language. For example, producing a certain handshape for asking a question does not by itself mean a question unless also accompanied by facial expression or non-manual marking, like a raised eyebrow in this case. Producing a question with just a handshape will be taken as being inarticulate. In this example, thus, only the simultaneous production of handshape and raised eyebrow can be a meaningful question.

However, a more striking example of multi-modality of sign languages comes from the frequent employment of what is known as classifier constructions in sign languages. These are a set of handshape units that represent noun classes and/or characterizing spatial relations and motion events. However, a unique property of these classifiers is the non-dominant hand representing yet another classifier at the same time as the dominant hand. For example, if the dominant hand represents the classifier unit for a "vehicle", the non-dominant one might at the same time represent the classifier unit for a "tree". Furthermore, not only are the two handshapes meaningful, but the locations articulated by the hand(s) signify the space to represent the event. On top of this, different types of movements of the two hands within the signing space indicate existence, location, or motion (Supalla, 1986), a complexity that is beyond any known spoken language.

This multi-modal property of sign languages opens up dimensions otherwise invisible in spoken languages. Centring sign language in language studies can thus enable us to look at language—the pure representation of the human mind—in a new light (Bhattacharya and Hidam, 2011). Thus, the fact that more than one modality can be active simultaneously in sign language may indicate that "order" in spoken language may be an epiphenomenon. In sign language, a sign can co-occur with non-manual marking, mouthing, torso tilt, head tilt, etc., whereas in case of speech, each unit of sound must be produced at a time, generating a linear order of sounds, or words. It is, as if speech is tied to the time axis only because of the physical limitation of speech but not of sign.

As it so happens, a certain view of the evolution of language, namely the "non-evolutionary" view (which denies a gradual evolution of language), in fact, derives the consequence that linear order is irrelevant. The non-evolutionary view of language evolution (Hauser et al., 2002), or the *exaptation thesis*, is focussed towards the emergence of language as an internalized event that is optimally designed with respect to the communication between different components of the faculty of language. This internalized, language-as-thought object is externalized as speech much later in the evolutionary history of humans, when early humans migrating out of Africa realized that the new sensation arising out of the coming together of sound and meaning is also shared by other humans. Thus, speech came about as secondary, as an epiphenomenon of the prior internalized language-as-thought object. As has been pointed out above, the one-sound-at-a-time physical limitation of speech inflicts an order on speech, for example Word_1 preceding Word_2 preceding Word_3. Order, then, in this analysis, seems to be a property of speech but not language. This realization, independently arrived at by considering a particular theory of language evolution, matches with the actual realities of sign language, where the notion of order is highly complicated, and overlapping modalities are the norm.

In terms of practice, this implies that if adequate services are provided in the classroom with D/deaf[3] students in terms of teaching through sign language,

[3]As per convention, "Deaf" signifies deaf people who share a language (sign langauge) and cultural values which are distinct from the hearing society, whereas "deaf" denotes the audiological condition of deafness.

acquisition of this medium of communication will open up such an enriching experience for the hearing student that it may radically alter their understanding of the world around them. In this perspective, an inclusive education will transform the lives of the so-called non-disabled majority students in immeasurable ways.

In a recent book, Ghai (2015) repeatedly talks about the struggle between disabled persons and their diagnosis of disability by medical professionals. Diagnosis as a structural instrument is used culturally—in the sense of a shared system of labelling, explanation, and evaluation—to define disability and in many cases malign and devalue the disabled individual. As Ghai (2015: 77–78) notes, "it [diagnosis] can also lead to disrespectful and dehumanizing treatment, and a severe restriction of opportunities". However, Ghai considers diagnosis as a double-edged sword since unless there is diagnosis, access to services is not possible. Medical diagnosis therefore actively promotes medicalization of disability. However, if we locate disability as the site of our epistemology, then the perspective gained from understanding the role of diagnosis in disability will inform our general perspective on the role of diagnosis in various other domains, which at least cuts across gender and age, be it gynaecological or palliative care or dementia.

In terms of the questions raised at the end of the introductory section (*How do we resolve this tension?*), I imply in the discussion below that bridging the gap between the humanities and the social sciences is yet another example of centring disability.

3.1.3 Methodology: Humanities or Social Sciences?

I will show that these two problems/tensions referred to in the first section are related and a resolution of one may lead to the resolution of the other. That is, the tension between encouraging diversity and using diversity as a marker of spectacle, on the one hand, and one between the famous lament for the lack of agency and "measuring", on the other, may constitute two sides of the same coin, the latter more appropriately identified as the well-known tension between the humanities and the social sciences. To elaborate further, in the social sciences, it has been pointed out (Plummer, 2001, for example) time and again that the discipline has moved away from the subject. Instead of the human subject, social science lent itself too willingly to what Giddens (1986) calls *structuration*—the preference of system over agency. A similar tradition developed too in psychology and anthropology, from Skinner's behaviourism and Lacan's structuralism to the structural anthropology of Lévi-Strauss. It is the chasm between looking inside, exploring, feeling and imagining, and recording externals, measuring, generalizing, and theorizing; one "falls in love", and the other "observes love" (Plummer, 2001: 8). So much so that Lévi-Strauss (1966: 247) in fact announced the death of the subject thus: "the final goal of human sciences is not to constitute *hu*man, but to dissolve him *or her*" (the matter in italics added).

3.1.3.1 A Return to "Design"

The lament for subjectlessness in the social sciences was meant to reignite an appeal for a return to the narrative, thus bringing the two disciplines of social sciences and humanities closer to each other. The technique that is mentioned most often in this regard is different versions of reflexive or biographical *life story* projects, successfully employed in sociology and anthropology. However, there is another approach to the whole concern for bringing the two (i.e. humanities and social sciences) together; I will term this as a *return to design*. Let me explain.

If bringing the subject back in the social sciences is one way of bringing the two disciplines closer by changing the way social sciences are studied, then there must exist another approach—a push from the other direction, namely changing humanistic, interpretive studies in a way so that the two disciplines are brought closer. The push, I claim, can be achieved through a return to design in the humanities, or bringing back the much-hated concepts such as quantification and measuring within the perimeters of the humanities, in simplistic terms, *instrumentalizing* the humanities. But *what* and *how* do we measure?

The interesting and recent work on computational social science (see Lazer et al., 2009) that emphasizes personal reality mining through quantification of massive data is a step in this direction.

3.1.3.2 Social Capital

In order to understand the background to the theory of social capital, a somewhat forgotten past of sociology needs to be re-emphasized. When Coser (1978: 311) expresses the sentiment that "it seems no exaggeration to say that for roughly twenty years, from the First World War to the mid-1930s, the history of sociology in America can largely be written as history of the Department of Sociology at the University of Chicago", it only adds to the well-documented fact of the launching of sociology and ethnography in the 1920s Chicago, now famously identified as the Chicago School.

The distinct "Chicago voice" became synonymous with the methodology that urged the researcher to avoid chasing abstract systemic patterns instead of "the detailed, the particular, and the experiential" (Plummer, 2001: 114). According to Plummer, this further led to the importance of the need for a dual concern with the subjective and the objective that brought out the inevitability of a perspective, and not the Grand Absolute. It is no surprise therefore that the Chicago voice spoke of the marginal and the underdog. My interpretation is that the early Chicago school interests in the marginal and the underdog made a conscious political statement in addition to its anti-categorial (anti-Aristotelian) view of the world. In a way, the Chicago School sociologists were claiming this to be the nature of the society, and by talking about the marginal and the underdog, there was an attempt at integrating the marginal. It was a challenge to the then dominant positivism and social determinism, to existing social conditions and policies, and represented a dramatic epistemological, ontological, and normative shift (Thomas, 1983).

The normative of the Chicago School was to remove the conception of pathology from the description of culture: "Instead of pathology, the ideas of natural variation, cultural diversity, and normative deviation gradually emerged" (Matza, 1969: 44). Surprisingly, though, and rather tellingly for our present concerns, the deep interest in the marginal was also marked by a dilemma that led to some kind of social reformism, where deviant behaviours were considered "correctable"—this necessarily leads to a medicalized view. However, pitted against this dilemma, the contemporary ethnographic research is ironically only outwardly liberal, being sympathetic to deviants, but practising a rather uncritical methodology deriving a style of ethnography that is "subjectivist, superficial, and above all, devoid of the original critical programme of social concern that once guided the Chicago school" (Thomas, 1983: 483).

Ethnography as a method, however, was critiqued heavily on the grounds of it being qualitative, based more on little more than romantic tales, relying on subjective viewpoints arrived at through idle, unplanned observations, and due to its lack of predictability, it could not be deemed scientific. Consequently, there is no way to distinguish "good" from "bad" ethnographic research (Thomas, 1983: 477). Some of the criticism of the Chicago School, especially on its lack of scientific spirit and quantification, began early, as in Lundberg (1926) and Stouffer (1930); others can be found in Davis (1981) and Snodgrass (1976).

Against this background, Putnam's (2000) notion of social capital marks an important shift in focus, within Western political theory, away from either the state or citizen to the civic space in between. This notion also highlights the need for quantification within the humanities for the analysis of community, by evaluating large amount of collected data of individual behaviour and opinion. Social capital, according to Putnam, unlike the popular notion of "community", is "quantifiable". The quantifiability helps bridge the gap between more "scientifically" oriented disciplines of social science (like economics) and the more culturally bound study of politics, society, and community, within the social sciences.

Putnam (2000: 9) defines social capital as the "connections among individuals—social networks and the norms of reciprocity and trustworthiness that arise from them" that ultimately "enable participants to act together more effectively to pursue shared objectives". In this view, community becomes a repository of a common "civic culture", which unites citizens in a sphere distinct from the liberal state. The focus is largely on the *amount* of social connectedness rather than a detailed analysis of the *nature* of any past or present connections (Arneil, 2006).

However, this is a functional theory of social capital; that is, it works in an instrumental way, as a free-flowing and functional means of exchange either in the past or the present. Bourdieu (1986), on the other hand, focuses on networks and resources rather than trust and shared norms. Social capital is thus built up or accumulated over time in particular ways. This in turn implies that the opportunities for social capital accumulation are not equally open to all. That is, it cannot ameliorate the power hierarchies of the past. The functional view on the other hand encourages certain erasure of multicultural commitments to diversity and difference.

Thus, a more appropriate and context-specific measure of social capital must be found. Within the context of developing countries in general, informal rather than formal networks have been found to be more profuse and relevant. For example, the suggestion made in this chapter that a measure of social capital may provide us tools to understand diversity better may be harvested in a more appropriate manner if both structural and cognitive aspects of social capital are considered. Let us discuss an example in this connection.

Within this framework, Kudlick's (2001) comparison of the objectives of two organizations within the blind community, namely the American Blind People's Higher Education and General Improvement Association (ABPHEGIA), the membership of which consisted largely of blind people, and the American Association of Workers for the Blind (AAWB), made up largely of sighted professionals, attains importance. A study of their two respective magazines—*The Problem* and *The Outlook for the Blind*—indicates a shift in purpose in the second half of the twentieth century, from service to advocacy.

Thus, the advocacy-driven interactive space mitigated by organizations of disabled persons constitutes the social capital as the *what* of measure indicated in the earlier section. The *how* of measuring may require a reconsideration along the lines hinted above, where more informal aspects of social capital, which are also contextually richer, are more meaningful. Beliefs that people hold about their possible interactions with others in particular situations provide a networking pattern, which is a better indication of collective action in a marginalized sector than people's membership in a particular organization. Arneil (2006: 4), based on Coleman (1990), too states that social capital is "the set of resources that inhere in family relations and in community organizations".

Of course, not all activities may be considered as contextually specific measures of social capital. Activities may thus more or less indicate individual behaviour patterns; that is, there are activities that people typically undertake collectively or at least with other persons for mutual benefit. However, such a cognitive criterion based on norms, values and beliefs that people share but are facilitated by structural criteria such as social networks and roles, will strengthen the structural and cognitive aspects of social capital (Krishna and Uphoff, 1999). For example, the following may form a typical set of informal and relational social capital envisaged here:

- The extent of belief and expectation of students or workers with disability about their institution being an equal opportunity provider, structurally, academically, workspace-wise (cognitive);
- The kind of access the student/worker with disability would consider essential (cognitive);
- Situations where resolving crisis involving such students or workers are concerned (structural); and
- Situations of students/workers with disability during natural disasters or other emergencies (structural).

This is only an indicative list of criteria that can be "measured" as markers of social capital[4] and thus have the potential to contribute to identifying true diversity and distinguish it from diversity as a spectacle. However, the suitability of any of these or other indicators will depend on actual field-based studies that may reveal patterns of informal networking that influence and impact the lives of disabled persons.

3.2 The Empirical Evidence

3.2.1 Disability at the Workplace and in Educational Institutions

I now present empirical evidence of the true nature of diversity as practised and imagined at the workplace and in educational institutions. I mentioned earlier that the true nature of diversity can be understood if we have an instrument to measure job satisfaction at workplace and a sense of belonging in regular institutions. Both job satisfaction and sense of belonging, without an axis of domination, can also contribute positively towards a repository constituting the social capital of a group or community. Therefore, an instrument needs to be designed to measure such social capital of a group of disabled persons (at work and in educational institutes). We will see here that the rhetoric of diversity coming from both the state parties and private concerns actually discourages diversity.

3.2.1.1 A Typology of Employment

The National Policy for Persons with Disabilities (2006) (NPPD) and previous work in this domain (e.g. Mitra and Sambamoorthi, 2006) more or less identify the following five types of employment for disabled persons:

Government establishments: Reservation in various ministries/departments against identified posts for groups A, B, C, and D[5] jobs in the government sectors (central as well as states) is 3.07, 4.41, 3.76, and 3.18 % respectively as mentioned in NPPD (2006), Article II(c)(i). In public sector undertakings (PSUs),

---

[4]This list has been constructed roughly on the basis of Krishna and Uphoff's (1999) six questions in their study (p. 27).

[5]As per The Central Civil Services (Classification, Control and Appeal) Rules, 1965, classification of jobs broadly correspond to rank, status, and degree of responsibilities: Group A carries administrative and executive responsibilities, Group B is middle management level, Group C is supervisory, operative, and clerical work, and Group D involves routine duties. They are further differentiated in terms of pay scales, which are as follows: Group A Rs. 13,500 and above, Group B between Rs. 9000 and 13,500, Group C between Rs. 4000 and 9000, and Group D for below Rs. 4000.

the reservation status in groups A, B, C, and D is 2.78, 8.54, 5.04, and 6.75 %, respectively. The PwD Act, 1995,[6] provides for 3 % reservation in employment in the establishments of the Government of India and PSUs against identified posts which stand at 1900 after the revision in 2001.[7]

Private sector: "The appropriate Governments and the local authorities shall, within the limits of their economic capacity and development, provide incentives to employers both in public and private sectors to ensure that at least five per cent of their work force is composed of persons with disabilities" (Article 41 of the PwD Act, 1995, based on Article 41 of the Constitution of India[8]). The NPPD (2006) also recommends that proactive measures such as incentives, awards, and tax exemptions will be taken up to encourage the employment of disabled persons in the private sector.

Self-employment: Given that only a small percentage of the workforce is in the organized sector, self-employment of persons with disabilities is promoted (as per the NPPD, 2006). This is done through vocational education and management training. Further, the existing system of providing loans on softer terms from the NHFDC (National Handicapped Finance and Development Corporation, India) will be improved to make it easily accessible. The Indian government encourages self-employment by providing incentives, tax concessions, exemptions from duties, preferential treatment for procurement of goods and services by the government from the enterprises of disabled persons, etc. Priority in financial support is given to self-help groups formed by persons with disabilities.

3.2.1.2 Assistance Through Vocational Training

Rungta reported in 2004 that India had not ratified convention C159 of the ILO, entitled "Vocational Rehabilitation and Employment (Disabled Persons) Convention, 1983"; unfortunately, that remains to be the case, India is not among the 83 countries who have ratified the convention up till now.[9] However, NPPD (2006) provides for rehabilitative measures through vocational training in both education and employment. Assistance (up to 90 %) is provided through the Indian government to organizations providing training to PwDs. The Ministry of Labour through

---

[6]The Persons with Disabilities (Equal Opportunities, Protection of Rights and Full Participation) Act, 1995.

[7]This figure changed to 9975 by 2006–2007 as per a World Bank report (O'Keefe, 2009), which stated that the share of vacancies filled by PwDs in ministries and departments of the government was 0.37 out of 3.54 % identified posts for PwDs.

[8]Constitution of India, Article 41. Right to work, to education, and to public assistance in certain cases—The state shall, within the limits of its economic capacity and development, make effective provision for securing the right to work, to education, and to public assistance in cases of unemployment, old age, sickness, and disablement, and in other cases of undeserved want.

[9]From http://www.ilo.org/dyn/normlex/en/f?p=1000:11300:0::NO:11300:P11300_INSTRUMENT_ID:312304 (accessed on 26 May 2016).

DGE&T (Directorate General of Employment and Training) runs 17 vocational rehabilitation centres (VRC), free of cost with stipendiary provisions wherever needed. Apart from NPPD 2006, the government initiated a scheme—"Scheme for providing Employment to Persons with Disabilities in the Private Sector Incentives to the Employers"—in 2008 which covers any employee with disability earning more than Rs. 25,000 per month, including their contribution to provident fund.[10]

3.2.1.3 Employment Through Poverty Alleviation

Through various schemes of poverty alleviation,[11] the government undertakes to fulfil 3 % reservation for disabled persons in both rural and urban areas. However, except for SJSRY, which is run at urban level and has achieved assistance for self-employment to 5 % disabled persons, the others schemes (run in rural centres) have level of assistance varying from 0.02 to 0.96 %, which is much lower than the targeted 3 %.

3.2.1.4 Promises of the Private Sector

The International Labour Organization (ILO), Geneva, in 2010 published the CSR (Corporate Social Responsibility) profiles (ILO, 2010) of 25 companies which describes how companies address hiring and retention, products and services, and CSR from the perspective of disability. Out of the 25 companies, at least 13 of them have offices in India: Accor, Cisco, Dow, Ernst & Young, Honda Motor, IBM, Marks & Spencer, Microsoft, MphasiS, Nokia, Samsung Electro-Mechanics, Sony, and Wipro.

Here is an excerpt from the blurb of the company called MphasiS (situated in Bangalore, India):

> … We are committed to being an equal opportunity employer, and encourage employment of otherwise qualified persons with disabilities. We have recruited over 320 persons with disabilities in various capacities across BPO, Applications, ITO and Corporate Support towers. …[12]

Furthermore, the government constituted a committee of experts including representatives from the corporate sector which identified 1065 jobs[13] at various

---

[10]Accessed from: http://www.disabilityaffairs.gov.in/content/page/incentive-scheme1.php.

[11]Some of these schemes are as follows: Swarnajayanti Gram Swarozgar Yojana (SGSY), Indira Awaas Yojana (IAY), Jawahar Gramin Samriddhi Yojana (JGSY), and Swarn Jayanti Shahari Rozgar Yojana (SJSRY). The details of all such schemes can be found at http://www.indianyojana.com/.

[12]From: http://www.mphasis.com/csr_comm_initiative.html (accessed on 26 May 2016).

[13]From press release of the Ministry of Social Justice and Empowerment dated 13 August 2003, accessed from http://pib.nic.in/archive/releases98/lyr2003/raug2003/13082003/r130820031 3.html.

levels. These figures give a rosy picture where the government, public,[14] and private sectors seem to be too willing to welcome disabled persons at workplace. But is it really so?

3.2.1.5 The Census and Other Figures

According to the 2011 Census, the workforce participation rate of persons with disabilities is as low as 36.34 % (constituting 26.04 % of main workers and 10.30 % of marginal workers); that is, a total of 97, 44,386 disabled persons are employed out of a total of 26,810,557 disabled persons.[15] This figure does not compare too badly with, and in fact is higher than, the 29.94 % rate of participation in the workforce among the general population. However, it constitutes only 2.68 % (a rise from 1.87 % in 2001) of total workforce, which is a sad reflection since even by governmental estimates 2.21 % of the total population of India is disabled, a low workforce rate of participation reflects higher levels of unemployment among disabled persons.

A well-known survey conducted in 1999 by NCPEDP (National Centre for Promotion of Employment for Disabled People) (NCPEDP, 1999) exposes an even grimmer reality, namely that the rate of workforce participation of disabled persons is as follows: public sector: 0.54 %; private sector: 0.28 %; and multinationals: 0.05 %. Unfortunately, these data have not been updated since the NCPEDP survey.

This is one way of viewing the state of employment among disabled persons. However, there is another way, which involves examining the various levels of work that employed disabled persons are engaged in.

3.2.1.6 Levels of Work

As indicated earlier, the Government of India set up a committee of experts to identify private sector jobs at various levels. This committee identified 120 executive/management/supervisor level jobs and 945 skilled/semi-skilled/unskilled level jobs in the private sector; this indicates an eightfold variation between the two broad levels. This is similar to the study in Kaye (2009) which reported a tenfold variation from 1.8 % among advertising, promotion, and PR managers to 19.7 % among dishwashers in the USA. In a more recent study (Ali et al., 2011), this variation between the levels showed up even among the unemployed. They reported that while 16.7 % of the unemployed non-disabled population worked as a

[14]The difference between public and government sector is a subtle one; a public sector undertaking is a company where 51 % or more of share capital is held by government, whereas a government company is where 100 % share capital is held by the government.

[15]These and all other figures are calculated from total disabled population figures in Census of India 2011, accessed from http://www.censusindia.gov.in/2011census/population_enumeration.html.

Table 3.1 NCO 2004 classification of levels of work and their associated qualifications

Level I	Up to 10 years of formal education and/or informal skills
Level II	11–13 years of formal education
Level III	14–15 years of formal education
Level IV	More than 15 years of formal education

Source NCO (2004: 17)

Table 3.2 NCO 2004 classification of types of work

Legislators, senior officials, and managers	None
Professionals	Level IV
Associate professionals	Level III
Clerks	Level II
Service workers and shop and market sales workers	Level II
Skilled agricultural and fishery workers	Level II
Craft and related trade workers	Level II
Plant and machine operators and assemblers	Level II
Elementary occupations	Level I

Source NCO (2004: 18)

Table 3.3 Census of India 2001 figures for disabled workforce across levels

Groups	Types of work	Number of disabled persons	Percentage within disabled workforce
Group I	Managers and professionals	3,372,242	44.62
Group II	Associate professionals	183,247	2.42
Group III	Other	4,000,560	52.94

professional in their most recent job, the figure was 7.74 % across all disabilities for among the disabled population. However, in services, the respective figures are 21.5 and 34.9 %, showing a clear difference in level of the most recent job held by a (non-)disabled person.

Looking at governmental jobs, the levels of work are dictated by the National Classification of Occupation (NCO, 2004: 17), which identifies four levels (see Table 3.1). The NCO (2004: 18) further associates types of work with specific levels (Table 3.2).

If we take the first two as one group (Group I), namely the executive level, and third as the second group (Group II) and the rest as the other (Group III), we obtain some figures from Census of India 2001 (Table 3.3), which is a computation of different levels of work, according to NCO (2004), culled from bigger set of data for types of work in 2001. Interestingly, these data, in terms of levels of work, were not computed for the latest census (2011).

However, if we also look at the percentage of the total workforce on India, then a dismal picture emerges as only 0.83 % disabled persons out of the total working population of India are employed at Group I, 0.04 % at Group II, and 0.99 % at Group III. Thus, a clear case can be made that disabled workers at the top level still constitute a very low figure—only 0.83 % of the total working population. However, within the disabled working population, the percentage is high, namely 44.62 %, though the majority of disabled workers are employed at the lowest level, namely Group III.

3.2.1.7 Characterization of Workers

We see above that both the census figures and level of work perspectives provide a dismal picture of the rate of participation of disabled persons in the workforce and their levels. There is yet another aspect to it, namely the characterization of disabled workers as perceived by employers. Does that paint a dismal picture too?

Within the American tradition at least since Shafer et al. (1988), and most vocally in Kregel (1999), personal qualities such as productive, dedicated, responsible, reliability, inclusion in workplace culture, attendance, arriving to work, and returning from breaks on time have been stressed positively with regard to disabled workers. Although speed, quality, and independence are consistently rated as low, overall rating for work performance is quite high; that is, workers' performance in its entirety is considered satisfactory.

Even in the ILO (2010: 1) report, one business case for outlining the reason for hiring disabled persons is as follows: "People with disabilities make good, dependable employees. Many cases document comparable productivity, lower accident rates and higher job retention rates between employees with disabilities and a company's general workforce".

Further: "Hiring people with disabilities can contribute to the overall diversity, creativity and workplace morale and enhance a company's image among its staff, in the community and among customers".

However, against this rosy picture and good intentions, a close and careful reading of the existent literature reveals a world quite different, a world that in fact accounts for the massive fall (21.1 %) in employment among disabled persons in the USA in the period 1989–2000—the high period of the Americans with Disability Act (ADA), 1990; for valid reasons, therefore, this trend is identified as the anti-ADA backlash (Burkhauser et al., 2001). It was further revealed in a survey conducted in 2010 by Kessler Foundation and National Organization on Disability[16] that only 29 % of the companies had any disability policy or programme compared to 66 % in 1995. There are many reasons that were proffered for this so-called backlash, namely, that in the initial years of ADA, companies were merely complying, high recession in the country during the 1990s, employers' uncertainties over absenteeism, lesser productivity, accommodation, increase in

[16]Survey of Employment of American with Disabilities (2010).

health care cost incurred by a disabled employee, fear of legality, as well as the inability to find suitably qualified disabled employees.

Even in Shafer et al. (1988) and other works, it was noted that among the positive qualities of disabled workers were included the following as well: willingness to respond to employer supervision, accepting authority, loyalty to the company, and respect for authority. In other words, among the various other positive qualities, disabled workers are preferred because they are peaceful enough not to demand their rights or raise voice against mistreatment at workplace. However, Parent et al. (1996) report that disabled workers demand better jobs, increased earnings, changes in schedules and duties, promotion, career advancement, like any other group of workers.

In an interesting study, Kaye et al. (2011), using the method of structured projective questioning to remove social desirability bias, found over 80 % respondents agreeing to assign cost of accommodations, lack of awareness, and fear of legal liability as the top three reasons for employers not hiring and retaining disabled persons. A careful reading of this study also reveals a stunning fact (though not noted in the chapter) that whatever suggestions that are made in terms of practical or policy strategies for improving hiring and retention of disabled workers by employers and trainers (all non-disabled) are in fact, either external or systemic, absolving the employer of any accountability or responsibility in this regard. For example, in their Tables 4 and 5 (p. 532), practical strategies and policy strategies, respectively, are suggested, and responses sought. Among the findings, the ones that rank higher often contain suggestions such as external resources to get guidance on disability and accommodation requests, a government programme to pay for or subsidize reasonable accommodation for workers with disabilities, someone to come in and help solve disability- and accommodation-related issues without cost to the employer, an external mediation service, etc. In short, the suggestions have been designed to *fit in* the disabled person rather than any attempt to change the ethos of the workplace.

In summary, in spite of the rhetoric from both the state and private concerns, the reality in the workplace and the difference in the levels of work and characterization of workers indicate that there is no true diversity; in other words, as far as workplace is concerned, diversity is not welcome.

3.2.2 Disability and Educational Institutions

As per the census figures of 2001, the number of children across age groups and across disability attending school is not a major departure from the relevant figures with respect to the general population and is therefore comparable. For example, there is a steady increase in the number of children attending school from age 5 to age 12, a 507.7 % increase compared to a 330.22 % increase among the general population. Similarly as in the general case, there is a gradual fall from age 12 till age 17 which is 67.85 % as compared to 68.57 % in the general case. Finally, a

Table 3.4 Comparison of enrolment numbers at age 5 and age 19 across disabilities

Age	Disability	Persons
05	Mental	3473
19	Mental	3410
05	Hearing	2196
19	Hearing	2487
05	Speech	5876
19	Speech	5085
05	Visual	39,282
19	Visual	33,516
05	Locomotor	11,046
19	Locomotor	29,875
05	General	5,210,610
19	General	4,163,063

Source Culled from Census 2001, accessed from: censusindia.gov.in

sudden increase at age 18 (33.98 %) and a huge drop at age 19 (54.06 %) are noticed, again, as in the case of general children where the trend is a 25.18 % increase at age 18 followed by 52.80 % drop at age 19.

The somewhat erratic but nonetheless noticeable downward trend till age 17 is because the transition to upper primary and secondary is bad for all, especially wherever primary and upper primary classes are held in separate schools. Children with disabilities also have to face transition issues besides coping issues of the curriculum, etc. In this regard, note that the final figures across disability show hardly any increase between ages 5 and 19 (see Table 3.4).

For various reasons, there is a greater number of identification, followed by labelling, for locomotor disability than any other, and a combined average of enrolled children at age 19 is a false reflection of a more optimistic picture than it actually is. A truer picture emerges if we look at the percentage of disabled children not attending schools which ranges from a high 71.74 % for mental disability to a moderate 42.68 % for visual disability, which is still quite high as compared to the general class of children.

The percentage of total disabled and general population attending school at these ages (18/19) are 28.17/28.67 and 31.85/31.22 %, respectively, for disabled and general children. However, it must be pointed out that exactly like in the case of rate of participation in the workforce (see Sect. 3.2.1.5), on average, disabled children constitute a mere 1.63 % of general children going to school, which is way lower than the percentage of disabled population. Interestingly enough, Census 2011 completely bypassed the measure of enrolment of disabled children; thus, unlike in 2001, there is no table titled "Disabled population by type of disability, age and sex for India for Attending Educational Institute" in 2011; therefore, there is no census update for the enrolment figures for children with disability.[17]

3.2.2.1 Special Education/School

In an earlier work (Bhattacharya, 2010a), I have shown that the more modern the policies are with regard to education of disabled children, the rhetoric and metaphor of special schools attain more significance. That is, although not an integral part of the National Policy on Education (NPE) 1968, NPE 1986 onwards—for example, the Programme of Action (POA) 1992,[18] Person with Disabilities Act (PwD) 1995—special education/schools attain prominence, so much so that in POA 1992, the largest section is devoted to "Education in Special Schools".

I further show (in Bhattacharya, 2010b) that segregation as a political practice was already well established and therefore offered itself readily to act as an instrument for the promotion of special education during Enlightenment in the eighteenth century in Europe, especially in France where under the influence of Enlightenment, social concerns, dignity, and self-respect attained more importance than questions about God; the ideas of Enlightenment were "germane to the development of special education" (Winzer, 1993: 4). The connection between segregation and special education is nowhere more prominently spotlighted than in the case of education of African American children in the USA. This clearly stated in Allen (2010: 37):

> … America's historical suppression of people of African descent through slavery, limited citizenship, and government sanctioned segregation serves as a noteworthy prologue to the unique educational plight of African Americans today.

He further points out that laws in many "Southern states prohibited the teaching of Blacks [sic] to read and write through statutes created within their states" (p. 38). As a result of this pre-existing model of segregation, by the early twentieth century, special education classes were disproportionately comprised of African America children. Blanchett (2006: 25) notes that special education is the "new legalized form of structural segregation and racism".

I would claim that within the Indian context, this connection between segregation and special education is shown by five factors: (i) segregationist practices in women's education, 1948–1949 University Education Commission; (ii) consistent use of integration as the operative term; (iii) emphasis on special education (e.g. B. Ed., Special Education, of the Rehabilitation Council of India); (iv) home-based education, distance education; and (v) directly encouraging the role of NGOs in imparting special education as a sign of evading state responsibilities.

---

[17]However, there is some data available in the form of an update of the enrolment number of disabled children in the Annual Reports of the MHRD; see discussion in Sect. 3.2.2.2.

[18]POA 1992 refers to a revised version of POA 1986, the latter designed to implement successfully the National Policy on Education, 1986.

The University Education Commission of 1948–1949 (Ministry of Education, 1962), which included eminent learned men such as Sarvepalli Radhakishnan and Zakir Husain, the two former presidents of India, carefully prepared a document that laid out in detail, among other things, the future of women's education in India. Many insightful declarations, like the following, can be found in that report:

> There cannot be an educated people without educated women. If general education had to be limited to men or to women, that opportunity should be given to women, for then it would most surely be passed on to the next generation. (p. 343)

Alongside such sentiments, one can, however, also find statements like the following which (in)directly contribute to an emergent idea of "special" courses for women:

> The greatest profession of women is, and probably will continue to be, that of home maker. (p. 345)

> A well-ordered home helps to make well-ordered men. ... Probably there would be no quicker way to raise the general standard of economy and efficiency in Indian life than to make women interested and competent in the efficient, economical and convenient planning and management of their homes. (p. 346)

Special courses that are justified for women are home economics, nursing, teaching (primary and secondary schools), and the fine arts as the desirable vocations for women. This "redirection of interest" (p. 349) for women's education to less valued courses, I believe, would have considerably reduced their career opportunities and therefore economic independence. This in turn results in "segregation" if the latter is understood as involving "the separation of socially defined groups in space" (Massey et al., 2009: 74).

Furthermore, as pointed out in Bhattacharya (2010a: 19), as we move from NPE 1968 to POA 1992 and PwD 1995, the concept of "integration" and not "inclusion" takes over, along with the progressive emergence of the prominence of special schools in these policies and acts. It was also pointed (p. 19) that although the Comprehensive Action Plan of the Inclusion in Education of Children and Youth with Disability (IECYD), 2005, does address some of these concerns, it in turn gives rise to a new monster by the name of home-based and distance education for children/youth with disabilities, which directly encourages spatial segregation of PwDs by confining them to home. In addition, in the domain of designing assistive devices or special teaching material for training purposes, for that matter, for setting up teachers' training institutes, the PwD 1995 Act clearly considers non-governmental organizations as potential agents of change, thereby indirectly evading state responsibilities (Articles 28 and 29 of Chapter V).

The above discussion highlights the transformation from special education to special schools, a change from an educational philosophy with roots into European Enlightenment, to a segregated space. The representation *education* to *schools* in this context is highly significant as noted by Erevelles (2005). The change from *services* to *place* took place to maintain the "demands for conformity and rationality" (Erevelles, 2005: 72, quoted in Ferri, 2008: 418). Ferri (2008) expresses similar concerns when she comments that we label students rather than classroom practices (or teachers) as deficient, disordered, disabled.

One can thus realize that as in the case of workforce participation (concluded above at the end of Sect. 3.2.1.7), there is no true diversity in education of children with disabilities as the instrument of special education via special schools clearly marks out a separate space for those children.

3.2.2.2 Inclusion

Against this background of the segregationist view of special *education* (converted in practice to special *schools*), the idea of inclusion was posed as an antidote. Within the context of India, the only policy so far that actually mentions the word "inclusion" in the title of the policy is IECYD, or Inclusion in Education of Children and Youth with Disability, that was proposed by the Ministry of Human Resources and Development, Government of India, in 2005. This policy had a successful precursor, IEDC (Integrated Education for Disabled Children) scheme launched in 1974. However, by 1997, IEDC was being merged with other educational schemes such as SSA (Sarva Siksha Aviyan) and DPEP (District Primary Education Programme) [(Education of Children with Special Needs (ECSN), 2006: 6]. By 2002, this amalgamated scheme, aimed at providing educational opportunities for children with disabilities, to facilitate their achievements and retention, was extended to 41,875 schools, with more than 1,33,000 disabled children in 27 states and 4 Union territories (ECSN, 2006: 7). As per the 2005–2006 Annual Report of the MHRD on school education and literacy, the total number of disabled children enrolled was 15.85 lakh which represents almost 77 % of the nearly 20.14 lakh disabled children identified (Annual Report 2005–06: 75). The figures for 2013–2014 and 2014–2015, respectively, are 21.74 and 25.03 lakhs of children with special needs enrolled in schools, showing expected increase from 2005 to 2006 figures above.

However, IEDC was formally replaced by a new scheme under the name of Inclusive Education for Disabled at Secondary Stage (IEDSS) in 2009 to provide assistance for inclusive education of disabled children in classes IX–XII (Annual Report, 2013–14: 45), whereas primary education of disabled children falls under the purview of the SSA via its emphasis on inclusive education (ibid.: 187). Table 3.5 shows the enrolment figures from 2009 to 2015 (based on Annual Report 2013–14: 189 and from the MHRD, IEDSS site[19]):

Although the above table shows a steady and expected increase (barring 2011–2013) in enrolment figures for CWSN, the figures for children out of school and dropouts need to be also considered for assessing any programme of inclusive education. The National Sample Survey figures show that disabled children

[19]http://mhrd.gov.in/iedss (accessed May 2016).

Table 3.5 Children with special needs (CWSN) covered/approved to be covered under IEDSS 2009–2010 to 2014–2015

Year	CWSN covered/approved
2009–10	76,242
2010–11	146,292
2011–12	138,586
2012–13	81,207
2013–14	170,349[a]
2014–15	211,393

[a]There is a discrepancy in this figure between the MHRD Website figure (the one given here) and the one in the Annual Report (2013–14: 189), which is 123,356

constitute the highest percentage of 28.07 % among the out of school children, whereas the figure for all children out of school is 2.97 % (NSS,[20] 2014: 9). Unfortunately, the dropout rates (from classes IX–XII) are available only for 4 states as only 5 states returned any data out of which the figures for Nagaland are only available for 2011–2012. The figures for 2011–2012 for the other 4 states, namely Haryana, Odisha, Tamil Nadu, and Andaman and Nicobar Islands, all show a percentage increase from 2010 to 2011 in the range of 209 % for Haryana to 8.27 % for Tamil Nadu.[21]

Thus, both the out of school and the dropout figures of disabled children paint a much grimmer picture of the success of inclusive education policies of the government.

3.2.2.3 The True Nature of Inclusion

In spite of the argument in favour of inclusion in terms of the enrolment figures in Table 3.5, as pointed out towards the end of the previous section, the reality at the ground level is rather different. Often, it is some form of integration that the school practices which goes by the name of inclusion. Even the Centre for the Study of Inclusive Education (CSIE), well-known for its aggressive advocacy for inclusive education in the UK, accepts in its charter that some children with special educational needs can spend part of their time outside the ordinary classroom:

> Time spent out of the ordinary classroom for appropriate individual or group work on a part-time basis is not segregation. Neither is removal for therapy or because of disruption, provided it is time-limited, for a specified purpose.... Any time-out from the ordinary classroom should not affect a student's right to full membership of the mainstream (Thomas and Vaughn, 2004: 137, quoted in Norwich, 2008: 137).

Furthermore, as Norwich (2008) shows, based on an international study conducted across three countries, the most common resolution preferred by 132 policy

[20]National Sample Survey Estimation of Out-of-School Children in the Age 6–13 in India. Draft Report, 2014.

[21]These calculations are based on NCERT (2013).

makers and teachers for the placement dilemma for children with severe disabilities was a balance between included and separated provisions and a recognition of a reduced but persistent role of special schools.

Also, as noted in Bhattacharya (2010a), in terms of personal and social characteristics, experiences of deaf students in mainstream schools/classes have been found to be less positive than in deaf schools or separate classes. Similar results were obtained for self-esteem, measured in the Piers-Harris self-esteem scale.[22] In fact, one study (Murphy and Newlon, 1987) found post-secondary deaf students to be significantly lonelier than hearing students in mainstream classes. In general, for deaf students, the social environment of special schools and separate classes appear to be more positive than mainstream or general education classes.

These points argue for a mixed mode model where difference is preferably neutralized to achieve a certain unwritten, tacit equilibrium in the classroom. Inclusion here becomes what Hodkinson (2012: 7) terms, following Žižek (2009: 116), "part of a no-part"; in effect, it disfavours diversity and includes disabled persons merely as a spectacle since such inclusion is often restricted to the social sphere such as assemblies and mealtimes.

3.3 Conclusion: Diversity, not Inclusion, Is the Key

With respect to both participation in workforce and being included in regular schools, we have seen above that in spite of the rhetoric to the contrary, participation of disabled persons remains a mere Žižekian *part of a no-part*; that is, although they are included in the ambit of the organization or institution, they are not really included in activities that *they* would like to participate in. Thus, disabled persons are either not truly absorbed in an organization or are taken in through a school-within-school model.

In this connection, it is relevant to remember an important distinction that has been made (Fraser, 2000; Taylor, 1994) between *inclusion* as the notion that everybody is the same regardless of race, gender, disability, or sexual orientation and *recognition*, that demands a change in the basic norms by which a society is governed. Inclusion, in this view, leads to assimilation within the dominant culture at the cost of denial of other cultures[23]: "exclusion and assimilation are two sides of

[22]Pier-Harris Children's self-concept scale (Piers and Harris, 1969) is a widely used measure for children's self-esteem; it contains 80 statements about the self to which the child responds "yes" or "no". Out of these total scores are calculated which decide negative or positive values of self-esteem.

[23]However, in Bhattacharya (2014), I make the claim for the notion of "integrative difference" (ID) as the key to true inclusion, a position that accommodates, rather than contrasts, the present view. ID is shown to operate through a process of constant negotiation of the centre of knowledge in a curriculum whereby a disability centric knowledge system can be generated, empowering the disabled child in the classroom.

the same story" (Arneil, 2006: 21). Justice, therefore, requires the recognition of difference and the protection of cultural diversity. Thus, striving for identity may involve advocacy for inclusion through equality of treatment, or diversity and difference through preservation of difference; but it is only the latter that ensures preservation of rights of disabled persons.

The shift from service to advocacy, which clearly marks the beginning of the disability rights movement both in India and elsewhere, is a change that indicates recognition of diversity. This recognition, according to the proposals made in this chapter, is able to generate non-functional social capital (see Sect. 3.1.3.2) that can be "measured" and "quantified" for necessary interpretation through the lens of the disability experience. This instrumentalization of an interpretive concept like disability will afford a better understanding of the true nature of diversity that can address current imbalances at workplace and in institutions for disabled persons.

References

Ali, M., Schur, L., & Blanck, P. (2011). What types of jobs do people with disabilities want? *Journal of Occupational Rehabilitation, 21*, 199–210.

Allen, A. G. (2010). *A critical race theory analysis of the disproportionate representation of Blacks and males participating in Florida's special education programmes* (Doctoral dissertation). Boca Raton, FL: Florida Atlantic University.

Arneil, B. (2006). *Diverse communities: The problem with social capital*. Cambridge, UK: Cambridge University Press.

Bhattacharya, T. (2010a). Re-examining issues of inclusion in education. *Economic and Political Weekly, XLV*(16):18–25.

Bhattacharya, T. (2010b). *Education of students with disabilities: An evaluation of the Indian educational policies*. Paper presented at the international EDICT 2010 (enabling access to education through ICT) conference.

Bhattacharya, T. (2012). *Diversity at workplace and in education*. Paper presented at interrogating disability: Theory and practice conference held at the Institute of Development Studies Kolkata, September 27–29.

Bhattacharya, T. (2014). *Are we all alike: Questioning the pathologies of the normate*. Paper presented at the inequalities in India conference at the University of Delhi, 27–29 November.

Bhattacharya, T., & Hidam, G. S. (2011). Space-machine. In *Proceedings of Episteme 4, international conference to review research on science, technology and mathematics education*. Mumbai: Homi Bhaba Centre for Science.

Biklen, D. (2005). *Autism and the myth of the person alone*. New York: New York University Press.

Blanchett, W. (2006). Disproportional representation of African America students in special education: Acknowledging the role of White privilege and racism. *Educational Researcher, 35* (6), 24–28.

Bourdieu, P. (1986). The forms of capital. In J. G. Richardson (Ed.), *Handbook of theory and research for the sociology of education* (pp. 241–258). Slough: Greenwood Press.

Burkhauser, R. V., Daly, M. C., & Houtenville, A. J. (2001). How working age people with disabilities fared over the 1990s business cycle. In P. Budetti, R. V. Burkhauser, J. Gregory, & H. A. Hunt (Eds.), *Ensuring health and income security for an aging workforce* (pp. 291–346). Kalamazoo, MI: W.E. Upjohn Institute for Employment Research.

Coleman, J. S. (1990). *Foundations of social theory*. Cambridge, MA and London: Harvard University Press.

Coser, L. (1978). American trends. In T. Bottomore, & P. Nisbet (Eds.), *A history of biography studies*, *6*(1), 85–94.

Danermark, B., & Gellerstedt, C. (2010). Social justice: Redistribution and recognition—A non-reductionist perspective on disability. *Disability and Society, 19*(4), 339–353.

Davis, J. (1981). *Sociological construction of deviance: Perspectives and issues in the Field.* Dubuqu: William C. Brown.

EdCIL (India) Ltd., & SRI. (2014). *National sample survey estimation of out-of-school children in the age 6–13 in India, Draft Report.*

Erevelles, N. (2005). Rewriting critical pedagogy from the periphery. In S. Gabel (Ed.), *Disability studies in education: Readings in theory and method* (pp. 65–83). New York: Peter Lang.

Ferri, B. A. (2008). Doing a (dis)service: Reimagining special education from a disability studies perspective. In W. Ayers, T. Quinn, & D. Stovall (Eds.), *The handbook of social justice in education.* Lawrence Erlbaum.

Fraser, N. (2000). Rethinking recognition. *New Left Review, 3*, 107–120.

Ghai, A. (2015). *Rethinking disability in India.* New Delhi: Routledge.

Giddens, A. (1986). *The constitution of society*. Cambridge: Polity Press.

Gilman, S. L. (1985). *Difference and pathology: Stereotypes of sexuality, race, and madness*. New York: Cornell University Press.

Hauser, M. D., Chomsky, N., & Fitch, T. W. (2002). The faculty of language: What is it, who has it, and how did it evolve? *Science, 298*, 1569–1579.

Hodkinson, A. (2012). Illusionary inclusion—What went wrong with New Labour's landmark educational policy? *British Journal of Special Education, 39*(1), 4–11.

ILO. (2010). *Disability in the workplace: Company practices* (Working Paper No 3). Geneva: Bureau for Employers' Activities and Skills and Employability Department.

Kaye, H. S., Jans, L. H., & Jones, E. C. (2011). Why don't employers hire and retain workers with disabilities? *Journal of Occupational Rehabilitation, 21*, 526–536.

Kaye, S. H. (2009). Stuck at the bottom rung: Occupational characteristics of workers with disability. *Journal of Occupational Rehabilitation, 19*, 115–128.

Keller, E. F. (1985/1995). *Reflections on gender and science*. New Haven: Yale University Press.

Kregel, J. (1999). Why it pays to hire workers with developmental disabilities. *Focus on Autism and Other Developmental Disabilities, 14*(3), 130–139.

Krishna, A., & Uphoff, N. (1999). Mapping and measuring social capital: A conceptual and empirical study of collective action for conserving and developing watersheds in Rajasthan, India. *Social capital initiative* (Working Paper No. 13). Washington, D.C.: World Bank.

Kudlick, C. J. (2001). The outlook of the problem and the problem with the Outlook. In P. Longmore & L. Umansky (Eds.), *The new disability history: American perspectives* (pp. 187–213). New York: New York University Press.

Kymlicka, W. (1992). *Multicultural citizenship: A liberal theory of minority rights*. New York: Oxford University Press.

Lazer, D., Pentland, A., Adamic, L., Aral, S., Barabási, A.-L., Brewer, D., et al. (2009). Computational social science. *Science, 323*, 721–723.

Lévi-Strauss, C. (1966). *The savage mind.* London: Weidenfeld.

Linton, S. (1998). *Claiming disability: Knowledge and identity.* New York and London: New York University Press.

Lundberg, G. A. (1926). Case work and the statistical method. *Social Forces, 5*, 61–65.

Massey, D. S., Rothwell, J., & Domina, T. (2009). The changing bases of segregation in the United States. *The Annals of the American Academy of Political and Social Science, 626*, 74–90.

Matza, D. (1969). *Becoming deviant.* New Jersey: Prentice Hall.

McCagg, W. O., & Siegelbaum, L. (1989). Introduction. In *The disabled in the Soviet Union: Past and present, theory and practice*. Pittsburgh: University of Pittsburgh Press.

Ministry of Education. (1962). *Report of the University Education Commission* (December 1948–August 1949), Publication No. 606. New Delhi: Government of India.

Mitra, S., & Sambamoorthi, U. (2006). Employment of PWDs: Evidence from the National Sample Survey. *Economic and Political Weekly*, January 21; 41(3), 199–203.

Morris, D. B. (1991). *The culture of pain*. Berkeley: University of California Press.

Murphy, J., & Newlon, B. (1987). Loneliness and the mainstreamed hearing-impaired college student. *American Annals of the Deaf, 132*, 21–25.

NCERT. (2013). *Evaluation of the implementation of the scheme IEDSS in India*. New Delhi: NCERT.

NCPEDP. (1999). *Employment practices of the corporate sector*. Delhi: NCPEDP.

Norwich, B. (2008). What future for special schools and inclusion? Conceptual and professional perspectives. *British Journal of Special Education, 35*(3), 136–143.

O'Keefe, P. (2009). *People with disabilities in India: From commitments to outcomes*. Washington, DC: World Bank. http://documents.worldbank.org/curated/en/2009/07/11027298/people-disabilities-india-commitments-outcomes

Parent, W., Kregel, J., & Johnson, A. (1996). Consumer satisfaction: A survey of individuals with disabilities who receive supported employment services. *Focus on Autism and Other Developmental Disabilites, 11*, 207–221.

Piers, E. V., & Harris, D. B. (1969). *Manual for Piers-Harris children's self-concept scale (The way I feel about myself)*. Nashville, Tennessee: Counsellor Recordings & Tests.

Plummer, K. (2001). *Documents of life 2*. London, New Delhi: Sage Publications.

Putnam, R. D. (2000). *Bowling alone: The collapse and revival of American community*. New York: Touchstone.

Radford, J. P. (1994). Intellectual disability and the heritage of modernity. In M. H. Rioux, & M. Bach (Eds.), *Disability is not measles: New research paradigms in disability*. Institut Roeher: North York, Ontario.

Rudenstine, N. L. (2001). Student diversity and higher learning. In G. Orfield (Ed.), *Diversity challenged: Evidence of the impact of affirmative action* (pp. 31–48). Cambridge, UK: Harvard Education.

Rungta, S. K. (2004). *Training and employment of PWDs: India 2002*. International Labour Organization: Ability Asia Country Study Series.

Shafer, M., Kregel, J., Banks, P. D., & Hill, M. (1988). What does the boss think? An analysis of employer evaluations of workers with mental retardation. *Research in Developmental Disabilities, 9*, 377–391.

Snodgrass, J. (1976). Clifford R. Shaw and Henry D. McKay: Chicago criminologists. *British Journal of Criminology, 16*, 1–19.

Stouffer, S. A. (1930). Experimental comparison of statistical and case history methods in attitude research. Unpublished PhD dissertation, University of Chicago.

Supalla, T. (1986). The classifier system in American sign language. In Collette Craig (Ed.), *Noun classes and categorization*. Philadelphia: John Benjamins.

Taylor, C. (1994). The politics of recognition. In A. Gutman (Ed.), *Multiculturalism: Examining the politics of recognition* (pp. 25–73). Princeton, NJ: Princeton University Press.

Thomas, J. (1983). Toward a critical ethnography: A reexamination of the Chicago legacy. *Journal of Contemporary Ethnography, 11*(4), 477–490.

Thomas, G., & Vaughn, M. (2004). *Inclusive education: A reader*. Maidenhead: Open University Press.

Winzer, M. A. (1993). *The history of special education: From isolation to integration*. Washington, DC: Gallauded University Press.

Zborowski, M. (1960). *People in pain*. San Francisco: Jossey-Bass.

Žižek, S. (2009). *In defense of lost causes*. London: Verso.

Other Sources

Census of India. (2001). Registrar General of India (censusindia.gov.in).

Census of India. (2011). Registrar General of India (censusindia.gov.in).

Department of School Education and Literacy, Annual Reports 2005–06; 2012–13; 2013–14; 2014–15, Ministry of Human Resource Development (MHRD), Government of India.

Directorate General of Employment & Training. (2004). National classification of occupations, Ministry of Labour, Government of India.

Education of Children with Special Needs (Position Paper of National Focus Group). (2006). National Council of Educational Research and Training.

International Labour Organization (ILO). (1983). Vocational Rehabilitation and Employment (Disabled Persons) Convention (No. 159), http://www.ilo.org/dyn/normlex/en/f?p=NORMLEXPUB:12100:0::NO:12100:P12100_INSTRUMENT_ID:312304:NO

Ministry of Human Resource Development. (2005). Inclusion in Education of Children and Youth with Disability, Government of India.

National Policy for Persons with Disabilities. (2006). No. 3-1/1993-DD.III, Government of India, Ministry of Social Justice and Empowerment.

Persons with Disabilities (Equal Opportunities, Protection of Rights and Full Participation) Act. (1995). Ministry of Human Resources and Development, Government of India.

Survey of Employment of Americans with Disabilities. (2010, October). Conducted by Harris initiative for Kessler Foundation and National Organization on Disability. New York, NY: Harris Interactive. http://www.2010disabilitysurveys.org/octsurvey/pdfs/surveyresults.pdf

The Central Civil Services (Classification, Control, and Appeal) Rules. (1965).

Chapter 4
Right to Care, Home and Family: Ethics of Responsibility Towards Persons with Disability

Rukmini Sen

Abstract This chapter looks at the Rights of Persons with Disabilities Bill 2014 as a marked transformation from the Persons with Disabilities Act of 1995. Emphasizing the importance of family for everyday living of disabled persons and creating a separate category women with disabilities are two significant departures that the 2014 legislative moment underlines; this chapter discusses the importance of *inclusion* while pointing to the *constraints* as well. This chapter moves to engaging with the question, how enabling is a rights framework without contextualizing them within an ethicality of responsibility given that the former might just lead to an abstract rights-bearing (non) citizen without the latter?

Keywords Family · Home(s) · *Women* with disability · Care · Ethics

That all of us are temporarily able bodied[1] has now been said, medically proven and inevitably experienced in our everyday. If that is the case, then how do we deal with people in our families who are disabled? My first experiences of encountering disability (much before any law or my knowledge of the legal) happened in my neighbourhood—a man with visual impairment and a woman with speech impairment. The former used to take a stick, regularly study and work (later got married to a non-visually impaired woman), while the latter married and separated with a daughter, stayed in her brother's household and tried to get odd jobs. Much later, when I developed a course called disability and law in the middle of 2000s in a law school in Kolkata, most of the students who took the course had experienced someone in her/his family or household with disability and had questions and dilemmas around care/caregiving as well as inclusion/segregation. The statute that was available then to engage with was the Persons with Disabilities Act 1995, which had three daunting objectives—equal opportunities, protection of rights and

[1]Able bodied is used in contrast to disabled people or persons with disabilities.

R. Sen (✉)
Ambedkar University Delhi, New Delhi, Delhi, India
e-mail: senrukmini18@gmail.com

N. Ghosh (ed.), *Interrogating Disability in India*,
Dynamics of Asian Development, DOI 10.1007/978-81-322-3595-8_4

full participation. But, it seemed that the person with disability was abstracted from her/his primary location—the family. That care and empathy are essential first steps towards ensuring full participation (of course in the Act limited to public space) did not seem to occur to the lawmakers. It was as if family was invisibilized or that all disabled persons have a dignified living within the family seemed always already assumed. The 2014 Rights of Persons with Disabilities Bill is a major transition from 1995—home, family, and care all make a space within the legal. This paper together with interpreting the provisions around these in the Bill will make a theoretical engagement with rights and claims with ethics and responsibility. Can care inside the family be *enforced* through law? Or could there *only* be an ethic/ *responsibility* on care?

4.1 Family Enters the Disability Rights Paradigm in India

Ensuring labour for the person with disability dominated the rights framework for this community. If we go back to the Directive Principles of the Constitution the category, *disablement* included with sickness, old age and unemployment creates a responsibility on the state to provide work, education and public assistance. The idea of Directive Principles of State policies can be traced to the Declaration of the Rights of Man proclaimed by France and the Declaration of Independence by the American Colonies. The idea inherent is the concept of *duty* (wherein obligation is intrinsic) that the state has towards its citizens. And does it become a *moral* duty of the state to ensure welfare to its citizens? Interestingly that moral is about ensuring economic livelihood. Creating and facilitating the creation of a pool of workers and taking responsibility of their livelihood have been the philosophy of the welfare approach. By the early 1990s, the claim for rights started dominating the civil society discourses—where *abstract* individuals are rights bearing—but in a socially *ideal* context. In the Persons with Disabilities Act 1995, it was envisaged that education and employment will be made accessible—and therefore affirmative action in certain kinds of jobs on the one hand and, on the other hand, attempting towards inclusive education failing which special education for persons with disability were *guaranteed* in the Act. But an important question that came up was how do persons with disabilities reach these institutions of learning and work? The need for accessible roads and public transport was felt—although it was also a provision in the said law, yet it was dependent on the financial capacity of the government. Moreover, how does legislation ensure that families would be interested, willing and wanting to "bring out" their children/adults with disabilities overcoming the *shame* that exists in having such a person *as* family? Much has been written on the *coming out* of people in same-sex relationships (particularly gays); I consider non(or lack of)-visibility of persons in wheelchair, children with autism, and persons with speech impairment in public spaces have a lot to do with *stigma*, that of having an *ab*normal person in the family. A lot of sensitivity (not sensitization only) in the sense that is not restricted merely to legal awareness is required to overcome the stigma. One is not saying that efforts have not been made towards awareness, and in the last decade, issues relating to persons with disability have been popularized in mainstream commercial films and there has always been a care (or lack thereof) perspective in the portrayals—*Black* (visual impairment and Parkinson's), *Taare Zameen Par* (dyslexia), *Iqbal* (hearing impairment), *Barfi* (hearing–speech impairment and autism) and *Margarita with a Straw* (cerebral palsy). Families and/or caregivers have played significant roles in each of these films. Not getting into the critique of these films in the manner in which persons with disability have been represented in these films, what I want to highlight here is that there is a broader social, a personal in the social for any human being, and when we have created a category called persons with disability (rightly or not), they also have a network of people around them and that is extremely important for us to consider while guaranteeing any rights to them. This is because in many circumstances, the family or someone close to the person will provide the information, enable her/him to access the right and support her/him when the ensured right is violated.

After the ratification of United Nations Convention for the Rights of Persons with Disability (UNCRPD), family entered the disability rights framework in India (in the subsequent Bills), although earlier since 1999 *guardianship* dominated the legal regime where persons with cerebral palsy, autism and multiple disabilities legally could seek a guardian after attaining adulthood. Under the National Trust Act of 1999, facilities were created to provide support so that persons with disabilities could live with their own families. Moreover, providing early and comprehensive information, services and support to women with disabilities and their families to prevent concealment, abandonment, neglect and segregation of women with disabilities in relation to home and family life was a special provision for women. Since the Rights of Persons with Disabilities Bill 2011, there is a section on right to home and family which specifically talks about the children and the elderly having equal access to family, the right to marry a person of one's choice, adoption rights to persons with disabilities, guardianship/custody rights to persons with disabilities and non-separation of a child with disability from her/his parents. There is a separate section on right to home and family specifically for women with disabilities. Moreover, by ensuring reproductive rights for persons with disabilities, information about family planning will have to be ensured for persons with disability. There is a section on awareness raising within the Bill, which among others intend to target members of the family as well. Family caregiver is a person who is a member of the family of the person with disability providing voluntary care, support and assistance to her/him. In the 2014 Bill, special attention has been provided for those people living outside of family to be supported in situations of the need for their access to justice. The definition of family that we get in 2011 and 2012 Bills is a group of people related by blood, marriage or adoption to a person with disability, while the 2014 Bill does not define but assumes what a *family is*. The 2014 Bill has the guardianship clause alive for persons with mental illness with plenary (guardian takes all decisions, without even consultation, after incapacity proven) and limited guardianship (joint decision operating on mutual trust) provisions, thereby suggesting the *impossibility* of legal capacity for all kinds of disabilities as was proposed in the UNCRPD which was the guiding principle of the domestic Bills since 2011.[2]

Home is not defined in any of the Bills, although the section is right to home and family. Home is a powerful and rich word in the English language. As the cultural cliché "a house is not a home" suggests, "home" means far more than a physical structure. "Home" evokes thoughts of, among many other things, family, safety, privacy and community. The modern idea of the home developed hand-in-hand with the modern idea of privacy, and interests in safety, freedom and privacy is strongly reflected in the psychology of home. But there is another use of the word home in the context of disability. These homes are created and owe their existence to statutes and are governed partially by the law[3]. The law does not recognize the right to shelter or protection from the state when a woman seeks entry into an institution as a matter of choice, a choice usually emerging from desperation.[4] The possibilities of victim creation are major when one is within an institution called the home either due to deviance or mental illness. Liberty and privacy are lost, right to dignity, intimacy, creativity and mobility affected, and stigma is automatic.[5] Whatever the objectives of the institution protective, punitive or corrective, the consequence is lack of accountability on the part of the officials of the "home"; usually, there is absence of minimum standards of care and violation of right to life with dignity. When there is a situation of discharge, it can occur in three ways—discharge without rehabilitation meaning there is life back into poverty and marginalization, discharge with the hope to reintegrate with the family which usually ends in rejection by family members and another discharge where there is no follow-up on what happened to the people living in the "home".[6] So the Bills falter on two counts around this section on home and family—neither is there any meaningful contemporary engagement with the term family (redefining it to consider and include friends as kins to expand its meaning) nor is home understood in its institutional sense, which is an incompleteness considering that many disabled in reality persons spend many years of their lives in *home*s, without care and empathy.

I want to end this section by arguing that from the Act to the Bills, the *inclusion* of family has been a paradigmatic shift—although I am not stating that the inclusion necessarily is socially well contextualized and grounded—meaning that merely by including family into a legislation for persons with disability, it is a progressive step. However, what I want to highlight is that the absence may not be perceived

---

[2]For a detailed critique on legal capacity of this provision and rest of the Bill, please see http://kafila.org/2014/02/03/a-critqiue-of-the-draft-rights-of-persons-with-disabilities-bill-2014-amba-salelkar/.

[3]I am referring to mandated institutional care and protection under Mental Health Act, Juvenile Justice Act, Immoral Traffic Prevention Act, etc. Although surveillance is the real name for protection inside homes for the mentally ill, juvenile homes, homes for trafficked survivors, children's homes, vagrant homes.

[4]Ramanatha (1996).

[5]Ibid 201.

[6]Ibid 208.

merely as a lack but as *incomplete* assessment of lives and livings of persons with disability. This inclusion therefore is not *complete* but merely a recognition that when we think about people and not categories through our legislations; it is necessary to formally take into cognizance that they are connected/related with other people. Legislations based on the language and the perspective of rights considers an individual as the unit of/for intervention; while in everyday living all individuals live with/through relations. There seems to be a relational turn that the Bill proposes, only to falter. It is not true for only persons with disability who it is assumed are dependent on family and the temporarily able bodied people are independent, thereby not needing family for support or care. This is a different matter of debate altogether which does not form a part of this chapter. Of course the understanding of family is limited to kinship only, and there is no consideration that some adult friends who are disabled and those who are not could come and stay together in a household, or that "homes" for people with disabilities could become familial spaces and not the oppressive spaces that they usually are, or there may be other arrangements made which are not the conventional heterosexual monogamous family set-ups.

4.2 *Women* with Disabilities or *Disabled* Women: Marriage, Motherhood, Sexual Violence and Movement(S)

The UNCRPD had a separate section on women with disabilities and that is what was followed in the 2011 and 2012 national Bills, although not the 2014 one. The latter seems a shoddy shadow of 2011, although that detailed discussion is not within the purview of this chapter, and one important thing to note here is that in the 2011 Bill, there were three categories of people in the Bill—persons, women and children with disabilities. There were separate provisions in the 2011 Bill for women and girls with disabilities—right to education for women and girls with disabilities, right to work and employment for women and girls with disabilities and right to be protected against all forms of abuse, violence and exploitation although in the definition section of the said Bill violence included only physical and mental injury and not sexual violence. The 2014 Bill have no mention of sexual violence faced by women with disabilities—this seems strange because a number of discussions had been happening in the last few years (especially with the Criminal Law Amendment Act 2013) around sexual violence and the need to address specific issues experienced by women with disabilities, more so when the incidents happen inside "homes" which are supposed to protect and care. The disability Bills seem to be not in tune with the other legislative transformations occurring in India in the contemporary times. An important question to be addressed is whether issues of sexual violence should be a part of sexual assault provisions of Indian Penal Code, with special mention on women with disabilities or should those concerns come in a specific legislation for persons with disability. Are women as a category/community more important than disabled women, or the reverse? The *natural* space for voicing of the special needs on sexual violence of women with disabilities was the women's movement, and the rape law reforms with which the movement engaged itself for nearly four decades. The 2013 amendments did provide for assistance of interpreters and special educators to be taken at the time of recording of the complaint by the police and also during the trial, that the process of identification of the accused need to be videographed and that disabled women be exempted from recounting their testimony once again at the time of cross-examination in cases of sexual assault was affirmed through these changes.[7] Although these "achievements" happened, the 2011, 2012, and 2014 Bills did not in any way include these provisions at all. Was it because these Bills were heavily influenced by the UNCRPD and the analytical entry point there was disability and not sexual violence on women that the former still remained silent on one of the common experiences of women with disabilities? So although women got included in the Bills, there was not a feminist perspective yet to disability legislation. Although if only we had been a little more conscious of the reality in Indian contexts, we could not have forgotten the Pune mental asylum forced hysterectomy cases on mentally retarded women[8] or the popular perception that disabled women because of being sex-*deprived* made sexual *advances* on men. In 2001, in a case where a speech- and hearing-impaired girl was raped by two policemen inside a prison van in Kolkata, the Officer in Charge was of the candid opinion that the case need not be followed up because disabled girls were "sex starved" and it was the girl who had in fact attacked the policemen.[9]

One aspect to remember is women with disability entered the agenda of the women's movement much late, and only in the 2000s and interestingly, the disability movement also did not foreground women with disability from its outset that could be one reason why neither women, nor sexual violence or recognizing the importance of the family or caregiver was lacking from the initial legislative efforts through Persons with Disabilities Act 1995. It was more of an effort towards making a legal acknowledgement based on medical understanding of disability—so the doctors and the lawyers as professional experts dominated the disability discourse before and till 1995. There was not much connection between disability "movement" and other civil liberties movements in those days of arriving at the 1995 legislation, and international pressure played an important role (as well as state institutional aegis, the service-mode through which the issue of disability functioned for many years) which is in fact similar to the 2011 context. India was a party to the Proclamation on the Full Participation and Equality of People with Disabilities in the Asian and the Pacific Region, adopted at Beijing in December,

---

[7]Mandal and Sengupta http://infochangeindia.org/disabilities/analysis/not-a-safe-issue-disabled-women-and-sexual-violence.html.

[8]For details of the case and analysis read, Rajeswari Sunder Rajan, 2003.

[9]Ibid.

1992, and UNCRPD which came into effect in May 2008 had India ratifying the Convention as one of initial countries to do so. From being an excluded agenda in the women's movement issues on disabled women entered and shaped discourses since the middle of 2000s in India. In the 2008 Indian Association for Women's Studies Conference, Anita Ghai foregrounded the importance of the disability question within the women's movement in its plenary session. At the same conference, issues around disabled *bodies* perceived as asexual were also discussed. Since then in all the subsequent conferences, women with disability have been a recurrent theme in IAWS. Moreover, deliberations on sexual assault amendment-related laws in feminist circles since 2010 separately focused on women with disabilities and the results of which within the legal space are seen in the Justice Verma Committee recommendations of 2013 followed up with the amendments in Criminal Law Amendment Act 2013. However, what I want to raise in this paper is that women with disability became another new *identity* to be added to the list of identities based on caste, religion, sexual orientation or region. The risk about this creation was *disabled* women became a particular, *special* category within *women* as a universal category—this did not enable to appropriately challenge hierarchies between the universal and the particular, rather leading to the construction of centre(s) and periphery(s), as well as creating sub-hierarchies within the periphery, for example between physical and mental disabilities.

That women with disabilities depending upon the nature of their disability stand at multiple vulnerabilities is true, thus *enabling* provisions which will support her to submit her testimony in court need to be made. Also, the movement(s) need to internalize and be sensitive towards the *different* experiences of women with disabilities—around their sexuality and issues related to sexuality—sexual relations (within or outside marriage), sexual violence, menstruation, and reproduction. I am considering the last two issues within the larger ambit of sexual rights and the evidence of sexual wrongs that have been committed on women with mental retardation. Moreover, regular fear of sexual violence has been the reality of women within institutional care in West Bengal. In July 2012, it was reported that women inmates regularly raped and tortured by outsiders in Gurap, Hoogly rehabilitation home. Sexual abuse and murder of one Guriya led to the revelation of many other mentally ill and speech- and hearing-impaired persons being sexually assaulted in the home. In April 2012, there was reporting of sexual assault of woman in Pavlov mental hospital, while in February 2012, a deaf and mute woman was raped in Bankura medical college. This everyday reality of a "culture of fear" with which disabled women live (inside the home and also in the *home*),[10] in trepidation and vulnerability, is completely in violation of the rights framework that new legislations try to promote. It is important to note the shift in legal interpretations between 1994 Pune mental asylum hysterectomies case on mentally retarded women and the 2009 Haryana mentally retarded woman's continuance of pregnancy decision in the

[10]There is a right to home and family that the 2011 onwards Bills provide for, the home is understood as the household where members of the natal or matrimonial family resides.

best interest of the victim (Suchita Srivastava and Another v Chandigarh Administration). In the former, it was argued that they had no conception of motherhood; sterilization was a "solution" to the problem of menstruation and potential of becoming pregnant. The matter represented interconnectedness between custody and control, custody and closure of information, and custody and secrecy. Rajan in her 2003 essay brings out the complexity of the identity of mentally retarded woman in binaries of adult/child, woman/not really a woman, victim/citizen, and social responsibility/social threat through the Pune forced sterilization case. Considering mentally retarded women as minors and the state as a custodian, there is a need to recognize that the family is in a state of crisis—which is the cause of homelessness and institutionalization of women with disability. Binaries of safety and danger, freedom and confinement, sanity and insanity, and respectability and criminality are important issues to reckon with, and it is necessary for the movement(s) to talk about them. In the 2009 case, a woman had been raped inside a mental home and had become pregnant and the court expressed the presence of and respect for personal autonomy of mentally retarded woman (who expressed her willingness to bear the child). It insisted on the respect for woman's right to privacy, dignity and bodily integrity and stated that the woman in question will need care and assistance to raise her child, the costs of which will be borne by the government. What is interesting in this judgement is that although it is lawful to terminate the pregnancy when it is the result of rape in the Medical Termination of Pregnancy Act 1971, in this case the court decision went otherwise. Was the court making a distinction between a disabled woman and a temporarily able bodied woman because the latter will have probabilities of becoming pregnant through sexual relationship which is not forced? But for the former chances of becoming a mother is absolutely less-forced sex and the resultant pregnancy does not make it unwanted anymore—it gives her the *opportunity* to experience motherhood (according to the court) albeit through violence. Destroying chances of motherhood in Pune to considering the personhood of the woman to keep her child is a shift in the mentally ill women's judicial discourse. However, if the former action was violent, the latter decision cannot be simply looked upon as a *progressive* judgment, when considering the sexual violence angle in the matter. Renu Addhlakha (2005) while acknowledging that the Supreme Court ruling in the Haryana case is path-breaking as it unquivocally endorses respecting the autonomy of the mentally retarded persons in the area of reproductive choice; yet she raises a pertinent question: if this case had occurred in a family context, abortion would have been the automatic choice of the kin?

I want to end this section by foregrounding the need to look at people, their experiences and the institutions in which these experiences are lived in a continuum. The 2014 Bill does not provide right to make one's own choice in marriage. The family to which there has been a right guaranteed can take away the choice from the disabled woman, thereby suggesting the need for right to choose my partner (in marriage) as an important sub-section of right to family. By not bringing within the discussion home as an institution, the Bills since 2011 deny the reality of the violence through surveillance and institutionalizing sexual wrongs that happens in *homes*. There is therefore an intrinsic connection between home as in the familial home-sexual intimacy (in sexual wronging, as well)-marriage-reproduction and that remained dis-connected, unexplored in the Bills. I am in no way suggesting that the sexual violence happens in institutional settings only while consensual sexual intimacy with women with disability happen in familial (and familiar) contexts.

However, these discussions need to happen in movement(s) circuits in order for it to even enter the juridical realm. The characteristic feature that has dominated the disability *sector* has been providing for services, then to ensuring rights around education, employment, access to public roads or transportation. Service to rights trajectory took many decades—I am concerned how many years will it take for relationalities that play an important role in accessing rights and/or services be recognized? Since within disability sector, women were not the focused group, questions around sexual intimacy-marriage-reproduction all which of course impacts women differently than men never got the required importance.[11]

4.3 Responsibility/Ethicality to Care: Limitations of the Disability Rights Discourse

The limitation that I see in the rights discourse is that it is meant for individuals not taking into considerations the interdependency among individuals. That individuals live in and through relations, not always of blood, marriage and adoption but companionship nevertheless is something which the rights framework seems to consciously deny. Since having someone with disability at home means substantive *care* work, it might be important to raise this question: Is this care as *labour* or care as *relationship* or is this caring labour usually performed by women in the household or women hired as professionals performing an affective labour? Mothers of disabled children, wives of disabled husbands and daughters/ daughters-in-law of disabled parents' providing care *services*, not recognized as work, are common in many households. It is relevant to raise the question: Where are these mothers or daughters in the women's movement? How many times have the movement raised slogans in support of these women? Women who forgo their desires to care for the disabled relation, merely saying that this is patriarchal oppression coupled with state inefficiency, do not really provide a complete picture of a complex reality. Men in these situations either face the shame of being demasculinized if they are young disabled men, or try to arrange for the material resources needed for caring the disabled child or a parent—where are these men's voices in the disability movement or the women's movement? Speaking and

[11] I am in no way meaning to essentialize that these issues impact women (with disability) only and not men. However, incidents of sexual violence on women with disability have acquired statistical proportions, hiding the disabled daughter or marrying her off to anybody have been real issues to reckon with.

foregrounding education and employment accessibility for persons with disability have the lawyers, doctors, and even activists forgotten that there is love and lack of it, dependence and neglect, care and control, and protection and abandonment in any relationship, but when the latter affect in this binary is experienced by disabled men and women, their lives become extremely vulnerable.

The everyday humiliation that a disabled person faces requires more than rights to address it—a sense of moral inclusiveness, responsibility and the ethics of care rather than only guaranteeing rights. How does one instil responsibility of care-ing to the caregiver (paid, professional or unpaid learning by doing career) in a mental home or home? Thus, what I am arguing here is that right to home and family does not guarantee care, love or empathy. According to David Kennedy (2013), the hegemony of human rights discourse often wields more valuable emancipatory strategies less available, and it ends up strengthening the state, unwarranted faith in the "neutral" nature of human rights without cultural and political values. Legal regulation requires regulation and normalization of identities—fixing and universalizing of identities—in this case fixing disability identities, making these identities doctor-dependent to get the disability *certificate* in order to *claim* the rights. The importance of disability certificate in the national Bills is very different from UNCPRPD, and the fixity of identities makes it impossible to negotiate with these identities—as if someone with visual impairment does not have any other identity —s/he is known only for and because of this particular identity—her legal capacity/personhood all depends on this one *single* identity. This is where I see the disciplining as well as the punish of law—it does not just punish those who discriminate against persons with disability, but by disciplining disabled people into different blocks and brackets, it is the *force* of law. This force forgets that the visually impaired person is a mother of a child, employed as a teacher, is a regular commuter of the metro, and occasionally watches films in movie theatres with friends. It is too much to expect the juridical space to recognize all these identities, but is it not the responsibility of the movement to construct these myriad identities of this visually impaired person only to make lawmakers realize that by merely providing reservation for persons with visual impairment in certain government jobs, the *life* of this person is not holistically addressed.

Thus, I would imagine the limitation of law as a subversive site and law reform strategies are more limiting exercises than liberatory ones. Using existing provisions creatively and campaigning to repeal constraining provisions may be still worth exploring rather than writing new laws based on restricted/restrictive identities. But the question still remains: Whether litigation strategies will actually enable the differences to grow within the "fixed" category disabled? The challenge to the rights discourse can come by realizing the limitation of it—it is the task of the movement(s) to foreground the limits. I am not arguing a rights v care binary but definitely stating that for the well-being of persons with disability, a new language and politics of collectivization is necessary—merely taking UNCRPD provisions will multiply the problems of implementing them in a very different cultural and community context. Responsibility of caring (and not just providing livelihood) lies at various levels—with the members of the family and/or close relations, on the welfare state, on state-based institutions with the mandate of caring the abandoned or the very sick who cannot be cared in the home. It also lies with activists articulating and representing the multiple voices of the people from the community, with law makers who tend to reduce the multiplicity to a homogenous universality and with judges who would make creative interpretations of the fixated identities, thereby redefining identities and benefits/services that identities are supposed to receive.

I want to conclude by reiterating the importance of ethicality in legality rather than the legal being deprived of the ethical or the ethical being opposite to legal. For the community of temporarily able bodied people, this approach will only benefit them. Since nearly everyone from this community will someday enter the community of disabled, having a sensitive and empathetic approach to an already vulnerable (not victimized) population will give a sense of relief to those who encounter disabled persons on a regular basis as well as those who foresee themselves as *becoming* a part of the community.

References

Addhlakha, R. (2005). Disability selective abortions in India: Individual choice, disabling environments and the socio-moral codes, centre for women's development studies, occasional paper No. 55, New Delhi.

Menon, N. (2004). Recovering subversion: Feminist politics beyond the law University of Illinois Press.

Ramanathan, U. (1996). Women, law and institutionalization: A manifestation of state power. *Indian Journal of Gender Studies, 3*, 200.

Rajan, R. S. (2003). The scandal of the state: Women, law, and citizenship in postcolonial India. Permanent black.

Salelkar, A. (2014). A critique of the draft rights of the persons with disabilities bill, 2014, available online at https://kafila.org/2014/02/03/a-critqiue-of-the-draft-rights-of-persons-with-disabilities-bill-2014-amba-salelkar/, last accessed on 21st July 2016.

Sengupta, S., & Mandal, S. (2013). 'Not a safe issue: Disabled women and Sexual Violence' available online at http://infochangeindia.org/disabilities/analysis/not-a-safe-issue-disabled-women-and-sexual-violence.html, last accessed on 18th January 2016.

Chapter 5
Living Arrangement and Capability Deprivation of the Disabled in India

Achin Chakraborty and Subrata Mukherjee

Abstract The paper puts forward the argument that the living arrangement of a disabled individual, or his/her marital status in particular, can be taken as a proxy for some very important functionings that constitute his/her well-being, viz. emotions (being able to have attachments to others, able to love, etc.) and bodily integrity that includes "opportunity for sexual satisfaction" among others. In the process, we contrast our approach to the one that drags the notion of care into the relationship between disabled and non-disabled partners. Based on this conceptual foundation, which draws on the list of essential human functionings constituting freedom in the sense of human flourishing, as articulated by Martha Nussbaum, we examine the quantitative connections between the living arrangement, marital status, and other indicators that roughly correspond to various other relevant functionings. The main source of data is NSS 58th Round (2002), which is supplemented by such other sources as Census 2001.

Keywords Disability · Functioning · Marital status · Monthly per capita expenditure

5.1 Introduction

The observation that there is a high degree of correlation between disability and poverty/deprivation is rather commonplace now. A good number of quantitative studies based on survey data from developing as well as developed countries have all established connections between the two. Neither disability nor deprivation is one-dimensional. There are different types of disability, and within each type, the degree of disability may vary in a continuous manner. Disability is not a binary

---

A. Chakraborty (✉) · S. Mukherjee
Institute of Development Studies Kolkata, Kolkata, India
e-mail: achinchak@gmail.com

S. Mukherjee
e-mail: msubrata100@gmail.com

N. Ghosh (ed.), *Interrogating Disability in India*,
Dynamics of Asian Development, DOI 10.1007/978-81-322-3595-8_5

concept of all-or-nothing type. Therefore, the correlations between disability and deprivation can only be meaningfully discussed if both are identified with multiple dimensions that constitute them. It is now customary to conceptualise deprivation in terms of capability deprivation. Some studies, for example, have underscored the higher likelihood of the family with disabled member(s) to experience education deprivation and the resulting disadvantage the members of the family—both disabled and non-disabled—face in the labour market (Mont and Cuong, 2013). Studies have also highlighted the evidence that points to the existence of direct discrimination in the labour market as the disparity between disabled and non-disabled persons in labour market outcomes can hardly be explained by education and productivity of the persons concerned. In the past ten years or so, a good number of studies based on the Indian data on disabled persons and their households have come out, which have deepened our understanding of the nature of the connection between disability and various dimensions of deprivation in India (Mitra and Sambarmoorthi, 2008; O'Keefe, 2009). The importance of this understanding can hardly be overemphasized while designing public policies for capability expansion of the disabled. In this paper, we focus on a specific aspect of capability deprivation of the disabled which, as far as we know, has not been dealt with so far in the literature. Needless to say, any attempt to make specific inquiries of this kind cannot avoid the methodological challenges involved in quantification of both disability and capability deprivation. Thus, the paper starts with a conceptual and methodological prelude in Sect. 5.1. Some quantitative aspects of disability are presented in Sect. 5.2. Section 5.3 discusses living arrangement and marital status of persons with disability and their quantitative connection with certain other attributes of importance. In Sect. 5.4, we present the results of logistic regressions that explain the factors on which the likelihood of positive marital status seems to depend. We conclude in Sect. 5.5.

5.2 Conceptual and Methodological Prelude

The official discourse on disability in India continues to perceive disability as purely a medical condition, which is to be diagnosed for certification and assessment of eligibility for publicly provided support in the form of aid and appliances, concessions in education and employment, and so on. Forms of impairment are distinguished medically, and in most cases for the purpose of entitlement claims, according to such types as visual, communication (i.e. hearing or speech), locomotor, and mental. In the process, there is very little engagement with the wider social and cultural context. A person's ability to function properly depends to a considerable extent on his/her environment. Personal, social and environmental factors are all at play in "creating" disability. The World Health Organization's International Classification of Functioning, Disability and Health puts forward a functioning-based approach for assessing disability which integrates the so-called biomedical and social models of disability. However, the available sources of data may not conform to the methodological requirements of this approach.[1] Our approach is therefore limited to the extent it depends entirely on the available secondary data. The main source of data is NSS 58th Round (2002), which is supplemented by such other sources as Census 2001.

We broadly follow the capability framework here for its conceptual richness in underlining the freedom to do or be as the basis of assessing well-being of an individual. The capability approach assesses an individual's well-being in terms of her functionings and capabilities. While capability refers to what an individual can potentially do or be, which she has reason to value, functionings are what she manages to do or be. Being healthy, being well-sheltered, moving about freely, and being well-nourished are all examples of valued functionings. The list of valued functionings can indeed be very large ranging from such elementary functionings as being well-nourished to more complex ones such as having self-respect or taking part in the life of the community. Thus, the functioning-based assessment of an individual's well-being is clearly multidimensional and it focuses on the outcome rather than resources or "inputs". From the capability perspective, an individual is considered disabled if the impairment places restrictions on her functioning achievement, i.e. she cannot do or be what she values doing or being. Persons with disability suffer from lower income-generating capacity as well as lower capacity to convert income or resources into functionings. As Sen (1992) puts it,

> Sometimes the same handicaps, such as age or disability or illness, that reduce one's ability to earn an income, can also make it harder to convert income into capability. Often, a high proportion of the poor in the advanced countries have such handicaps, and the extent of poverty in such countries is substantially underestimated, since it overlooks the "coupling" of income-*earning* handicap and income-*using* handicap in generating capability. (p. 113)

Even if the lower income-generating capacity is compensated for targeted public policy, the "conversion handicap" remains a significant problem as the disabled person is not able to lead as good a life as an able-bodied can with exactly the same income. While some factors that determine conversion handicap can be seen as directly amenable to public policy, some are not so. Therefore, understanding the complexity of the conversion handicap is important in order to design meaningful public policy. We shall argue that the living arrangement and marital status of the disabled person are likely to influence the conversion handicap.

Thus, it is not difficult to see that there is a close correspondence between the capability approach and the social model of disability as the latter conceptualizes disability as arising from the interaction of a person's functional status with the physical, cultural, and policy environments.[2] Combining the capability approach with the social model of disability, it can be claimed that people with functional limitations due to impairment may not be considered as disabled if the environment

---

[1]The National Sample Survey (NSS), which is one of the two sources of data on disability in India, asks the respondent a set of questions of binary response type leaving no scope for capturing the degree of disability in any particular dimension.

[2]One of the few attempts to conceptually relate the two is Mitra (2006).

is so designed that an individual, whatever the nature of her impairment, is able to flourish and fully participate in society.

The paper puts forward the argument that the living arrangement of a disabled individual, or his/her marital status in particular, can be taken as a proxy for some very important functionings that constitute his/her well-being, viz. emotions (being able to have attachments to others, able to love, etc.) and bodily integrity that includes "opportunity for sexual satisfaction" among others (Nussbaum, 2000). In the process, we contrast our approach to the one that drags the notion of *care* into the relationship between disabled and non-disabled partners. Our approach is rather centred on the idea of realization of "opportunity freedom" through participation, where participation refers to the nature and extent of a person's involvement with life satisfaction. Based on this conceptual foundation, which draws on the list of essential human functionings constituting freedom in the sense of human flourishing, as articulated by Martha Nussbaum, we examine the quantitative connections between the living arrangement and other indicators that roughly correspond to various other relevant functionings. The prospect of having a positive marital status (i.e. married and living with a spouse) for a disabled person may depend on a number of factors, including economic status, level of education, occupation, and the type of impairment of the partners.

Questions can be raised about the value premise taken here which almost axiomatically accepts a positive connection between marital status and certain valued human functionings. Although we presume such a positive connection for the sake of analysis, it does not rule out the possibility of negative outcomes due to asymmetry of power within a marital relationship. The rhetoric of familial concern and protective paternalism can easily camouflage a callous lack of concern or indulgence in practices that go against the agency of the partner. In the Indian context, however, it has been observed that the quality of life of single women in general and widows in particular is much worse compared to women who live with their spouses (Chen, 1998). From the policy point of view, the government is supposed to respond to the market failure in providing insurance to the vulnerable. Where government fails to respond, family or community support is considered to be the only fall back option of the vulnerable. The expectation of reciprocity among the family members makes this organizational form important in alleviating capability deprivation of some form.

In discussions of marital relationships where one of the partners is disabled, the notion of "care" invariably gets entangled in the relationship which is typically constructed as a binary between caregivers and care-receivers. In this conventional representation, the sexual and emotional aspects of a relationship are often subsumed under the "need for care" in which the disabled partner is represented as only a care-receiver and the non-disabled partner as a caregiver (Smith, 2009). This kind of representation tends to ignore the positive functionings that are achieved by both the partners through marital relationship. The focus on the specific functionings mentioned earlier, by implication, rejects the tendency to assume that non-disabled partners experience only burden. Nonetheless, the scope of the paper remains limited as it does not address the question of gender justice within marital relationship.

5.3 Some Quantitative Aspects of Disability in India

Before we enter into the specific issue for inquiry in the present study, viz. the marital status and living arrangement of the disabled persons, we present a brief account of certain general quantitative aspects of disability in India. The National Sample Survey (NSS) 2002 estimated that 8.4 % households in rural areas and 6.1 % households in urban areas had at least one disabled person in the household, and the estimated number of persons with any disability in India, based on the NSS data again, turned out to be 18.5 million. According to Census 2001, the number was slightly larger—22 million. However, both the agencies seem to have underestimated the prevalence and the actual number, and according to some estimate, the number of disabled persons in India could be somewhere between 40 and 90 million (O'Keefe, 2009). Both NSS and census have been criticized on the ground that one is not sure what aspects of disability are in fact captured by them (Mitra and Sambamoorthi, 2006a, b; Jeffery and Singal, 2008). Even if they were clear on this, there would still be a possible underestimation for under-reporting at the household level.

Even though the overall estimate of NSS falls short of the actual prevalence, there is no reason why the estimated rural–urban or gender composition would be biased in either direction. In all the states of India, the proportion of households with disabled male members exceeds that with disabled female members. The prevalence rate is higher in rural than in urban areas and among men than among women. What is to be noted is that the gender difference in terms of certain basic functioning achievements is higher among the disabled than in the general population. For instance, while the illiteracy rate among the disabled females was 64 %, it was 43 % among the disabled males, according to NSS 58th Round (2002). Gender disparity is more pronounced among the children with disabilities than in the child population in general. Women with disabilities in India experience double disadvantage—the disadvantage due to disability is exacerbated by the pressure of traditional gender roles and expectations. In India, there are regional differences in the cultural aspects of people that determine the gender roles. Studies have found that the elderly women with disabilities in the northern part of India are more disadvantaged than their counterparts in the southern part of the country (Sengupta and Agree, 2002). Among different categories of disability, the conditions of the mentally disabled persons are the worst in terms of all the standard functionings.[3]

[3]We do not intend to present here any quantitative description of different aspects of relative deprivation of disabled persons. See O'Keefe (2009) for an elaborate picture of relative deprivation, and Mitra and Sambamoorthi (2006b) for employment situation.

5.4 Marital Status and Living Arrangement

The prospect of having a positive marital status (i.e. married and living with a spouse) for a disabled person may depend on a number of factors, including economic status, level of education, occupation, and the type of disability. Although there is evidence of education (general as well as vocational)-induced achievements in occupational status for the disabled persons in comparison with the non-disabled, there is little evidence on how higher educational status and associated occupational achievements make difference in their marital status.

Table 5.1 presents the distributions of disabled persons as well as the general population in India by marital status for males and females. As one would expect, in terms of marital status, the disabled persons on average differ substantially from the general population. The percentage of "ever married" among the disabled was 76.4 as against 84.3 % for the general population, which shows that the probability of entering into a marital relationship is significantly lower among the disabled compared to the general population. What is noticeable among the disabled persons is the significant difference between the two sexes. While the percentage of never married among the females (17.1) was substantially lower than among the males (28.1), a very high percentage of the "ever married" among the females was widowed or divorced/separated.

While 41.3 % of the disabled females aged 18 years or above were either widowed or divorced or separated, only 10.6 % in the case of disabled males belong to this category. If we compare the widowed among the disabled females with the widowed females in the general category, the difference seems to be rather sharp. One might wonder why so many disabled females were reported to be widows. In the absence of further evidence, we can only speculate about two possible explanations. First, the average age gap between the spouses might be wider among the disabled than in the general population, as such women are at a disadvantage in the marriage market. But more importantly, anecdotal evidence suggests that a good number of disabled women are abandoned by their husbands, and these women might report themselves as widows to avoid being despised and stigmatized by others. Therefore, we have good reason to suspect that the "widowed" category includes a good number of such women. In any case, such a high percentage of widowed women indicates that a significant proportion of the disabled women suffer from conversion handicap.

Table 5.1 Marital status of the disabled and general population (18 years and above)

	General population			Disabled population		
	Male	Female	Total	Male	Female	Total
Never married	22.7	8.5	15.7	28.1	17.1	23.6
Currently married	73.1	77.5	75.3	61.3	41.6	53.2
Widowed	3.7	13.0	8.2	9.0	38.1	21.0
Divorced/separated	0.5	1.0	0.7	1.6	3.2	2.2

Source Estimated from NSS 58th round unit-record data (schedules 1.0 and 26)

Further, the marital status varies significantly across different categories of disabled persons, which is revealed by Table 5.2. Almost 65 % of the mentally disabled are either never married or widowed/divorced/separated. Somewhat similar is the situation, although a little better, for persons having speech disability. Compared to these two categories, persons with disability in vision and hearing are not so deprived of conjugal life.

If one looks at the percentage of "ever married" among the disabled in different age groups, one does not find unusually large gender differences (Table 5.3). Among the disabled aged around 40, the percentages of ever married among males and females are almost the same (86.2 for males and 86.7 for females). What is to be noticed is that as they cross the age of 50 years, the male–female difference again increases. It is unlikely that, at an age above 50, more females get married than males. Therefore, this difference at higher ages might be indicative of higher mortality among the "never married" females compared to the "ever married".

The most striking difference between the disabled females and the females from the general population is observed in the age group 18–29 years. While the three-fourths of the females from the general population in that age group are currently married, only 36.5 % of the disabled females in the same age group are currently married. We already noted the high percentage of widowed among the disabled females. What is remarkable is that in all age groups, the percentage of widows among the disabled females is higher than that among the females in the general population. The gender difference in widowhood turns out to be much sharper among the disabled than in the general population. The percentage of widowed among females shots up much faster than that among males as they age (Table 5.3).

Does marital status vary across economic classes? Of course, there is no compelling reason to believe that it should, which is somewhat confirmed by the distribution of non-disabled persons of different marital status across MPCE (Monthly Per Capita Consumption Expenditure) classes.

Table 5.4 shows that while the proportions of widowed and divorced/separated in the disabled population are by and large uniform across all MPCE quintiles, they are not so in the case of "never married". As one moves from the bottom to the top quintile, one notices that while the proportion of never married increases, that of currently married slightly decreases, which means that the disabled in the relatively better off households are slightly less likely to get married. This particular pattern is observed in the general population as well. There is no obvious explanation for this.

As one would expect, the marital status of a disabled person is clearly associated with whether or not he/she is earning or able to work. In Table 5.5, the percentages of "ever married" in different occupational categories are shown for the disabled as well as the general population. "Poor" and "Rich" in the table refer to the bottom 30 % and top 10 % of the households, respectively, in terms of MPCE. Interestingly, while his status as an earner has stronger influence on the marital status of a man, in the case of a woman her marital status does not seem to be influenced significantly by her status as income earner. However, the disabled women who are not able to work due to disability are less likely to be ever married.

Table 5.2 Marital status of disabled persons with different types of disability and general populations (aged 18 years and above)

	Male				Female			
	Never married	Currently married	Widowed	Divorced/separated	Never married	Currently married	Widowed	Divorced/separated
Mental	56.2	35.0	3.1	5.7	40.1	34.4	15.6	9.8
Visual	16.2	64.6	17.8	1.5	6.5	31.6	60.7	1.2
Hearing	10.3	74.6	14.3	0.9	4.3	46.3	47.5	1.9
Speech	46.1	48.4	4.2	1.3	33.3	48.2	14.5	4.0
Locomotor	26.7	65.2	7.1	1.0	18.4	49.7	29.0	3.0
Multiple	36.8	51.3	10.1	1.7	26.2	27.3	42.4	4.0
All disabled	28.1	61.3	9.0	1.6	17.1	41.6	38.1	3.2
General population	22.7	73.3	3.7	0.5	8.5	77.5	13.0	1.0

Source Estimated from NSS 58th round unit-record data (schedule 26)

Table 5.3 Age group-wise distribution of marital status for males and females in disabled and general population (aged 18 years and above)

	Male				Female			
	Never married	Currently married	Widowed	Divorced/separated	Never married	Currently married	Widowed	Divorced/separated
Disabled population								
18–29 years	74.3	24.3	0.4	1.1	57.8	36.5	1.3	4.3
30–39 years	26.5	69.2	1.9	2.4	24.1	62.0	5.9	8.0
40–49 years	13.8	79.3	4.1	2.8	13.3	66.8	15.5	4.3
50–59 years	8.4	81.1	8.9	1.7	4.8	57.8	34.9	2.5
60 years and above	3.5	72.6	23.0	0.9	1.0	25.9	72.1	1.0
Total	28.1	61.3	9.0	1.6	17.1	41.6	38.1	3.2
General population								
18–29 years	58.5	40.9	0.3	0.3	22.3	75.7	0.9	1.1
30–39 years	5.8	92.6	1.1	0.6	1.5	93.8	3.4	1.3
40–49 years	1.8	95.8	2.1	0.4	0.9	87.2	11.0	1.0
50–59 years	1.5	92.4	5.7	0.4	0.8	74.8	23.4	1.1
60 years and above	1.1	79.3	19.0	0.6	1.7	39.4	58.4	0.5
Total	22.7	73.3	3.7	0.4	8.5	77.5	13.0	1.0

Source Estimated from NSS 58th round unit-record data (schedules 1.0 and 26)

Table 5.4 Distribution of marital status of disabled and general population for each MPCE quintiles (aged 18 years and above)

MPCE quintile	Disabled population				General population			
	Never married	Currently married	Widowed	Divorced/separated	Never married	Currently married	Widowed	Divorced/separated
Poorest	20.5	55.2	21.8	2.5	9.6	80.2	9.3	0.9
2nd quintile	22.5	54.7	20.6	2.4	12.7	78.1	8.4	0.8
Middle	23.6	53.3	21.1	2.1	15.2	75.8	8.1	0.9
4th quintile	26.4	50.2	21.2	2.2	16.8	74.0	8.6	0.6
Richest	28.3	50.1	19.9	1.8	21.6	70.8	7.1	0.6
All	23.6	53.2	21.0	2.2	15.7	75.3	8.2	0.7

Source Estimated from NSS 58th round unit-record data (schedules 1.0 and 26)

Table 5.5 Percentage of "ever married" in different occupational categories (aged 18 years and above)

	Poor		Rich		All	
	Male	Female	Male	Female	Male	Female
Disabled population						
Earning—self-employed or regular wage earners	88.6	82.2	78.8	80.6	83.9	76.7
Earning—labourer	83.1	87.1	48.0	76.9	78.6	86.3
Engaged/capable in working but not earning	53. 2	83.5	27.8	82.3	46.2	84.2
Not working due to disability	72.1	83.5	67.5	72.6	68.9	80.9
Others	70.7	88.8	67.6	76.4	68.2	84.7
Total	75.5	84.6	68.4	77.9	71.9	82.9
General population						
Earning—self-employed or regular wage earners	93.8	95.4	84.5	80.8	88.9	87.5
Earning—labourer	85.2	96.5	73.7	89.3	79.8	94.6
Engaged/capable in working but not earning	64.5	95.2	41.7	94.0	53.0	94.1
Not working due to disability	64.3	84.5	68.8	77.6	65.8	82.7
Others	69.0	88.0	40.5	39.7	49.4	65.8
Total	84.1	95.0	71.3	84.8	77.4	91.5

Source Estimated from NSS 58th round unit-record data (schedules 1.0 and 26)

Table 5.6 Living arrangement of disabled persons (aged 18 years and above)

	Poor (bottom 30 % MPCE)		Rich (top 10 % MPCE)		All	
	Male	Female	Male	Female	Male	Female
Alone	1.4	3.7	8.3	6.3	2.8	5.7
With spouse	62.5	39.1	52.5	37.8	58.6	38.7
Without spouse	36.0	57.2	39.3	55.9	38.6	55.6
With parents	20.9	15.8	22.5	18.6	23.4	16.6
With children	7.8	31.3	8.4	25.3	7.5	29.5
With others	7.3	10.1	8.4	11.9	7.7	9.6

Source Estimated from NSS 58th round unit-record data (schedule 26)

This particular aspect points towards the dark side of the so-called family support. Women's ability to work is what is most valued in a prospective marital contract.

As far as the living arrangement of the disabled is concerned, there is a large male–female difference. While a high percentage of disabled men have the advantage of living with their spouses (58.6), the disabled women are not so lucky —only 38.7 % of them live with their spouses. A greater proportion of females than males live all alone (Table 5.6).

In this section, we have tried to explore the possibility of association between the marital status of a disabled person and certain other features which may throw some light on the question of how the marriage market works in the case of disabled persons. Even if we ignore the asymmetric power relation that may prevail between the partners and assume reciprocity as the basis of a marital contract, it is clear that the ability to work makes a big difference in achieving the desired functionings through marital relationship. The tentative observations presented in this section will be further examined through logistic regressions.

5.5 Results of Logistic Regressions

To examine empirically how different individual-level characteristics of a disabled person including his/her economic status and place of residence are statistically associated with his/her marital status, we have estimated a logistic regression. The dependent variable that we have considered is the marital status of the disabled person, and like other estimates, we have restricted our sample to include only those aged 18 years and above. The independent variables that we have considered are sex, age group, working-earning status, education, type of disability, extent of disability, per capita monthly consumption expenditure of the household in which the disabled person lives, and place of residence of the disabled person.

Table 5.7 presents select summary statistics of the dependent and independent variables which have been used in the logistic regressions. Although a slightly more than three-fourths of the disabled persons (aged 18 years and above) have the *ever married* status, the percentage is higher for the females (83 %) than the males (72 %). This is an indication that as far as the *ever married* status is concerned, the disabled females do not show disadvantageous position in comparison with the disabled males. The sample of disabled persons (aged 18 years and above) which is used for our analysis has almost 40 % females indicating a highly skewed disabled population sex in favour of the female. This feature significantly deviates from the sex ratio of the general population. The distribution of disabled males and females by age groups clearly shows that the group of disabled females has remarkably higher share of elderly (60 years and above) population. So the disproportionately higher share of females we observe in our sample of disabled persons is mainly due to higher share of disabled elderly females. The distribution of disabled males and females across *working-earning* status too reveals a striking difference. While the percentage of males and females who are *not able to work due to disability* shows comparable figures, the share of earning (high or low) disabled females is far lower than that of the disabled males (11 % for the females against 40 % for the males). A very high percentage of disabled females are able to do some work but they are not engaged in any earning activity. It is therefore evident that even though both disabled males and females have almost comparable percentage of their population *not able to work due to disability*, they differ markedly in terms of employability. The present data do not allow us to enquire whether disabled women's lower

Table 5.7 Select summary statistics of dependent and independent variables

Dependent/independent variables	Male	Female	Total
Ever married disabled person (%)	71.90	82.88	76.45
Female (%)	–	–	41.44
Distribution of age group (%)			
18–29 years	26.51	19.67	23.67
30–39 years	16.05	12.93	14.76
40–49 years	14.92	11.77	13.61
50–59 years	12.93	13.15	13.02
60 years and above	29.59	42.48	34.94
Distribution of working-earning status (%)			
Earn-high	26.43	4.49	17.35
Earn-low	13.10	5.32	9.87
Work-not earn	9.32	38.67	21.48
Not able to work	35.75	34.82	35.36
Others	15.40	16.70	15.94
Distribution of educational status (%)			
Illiterate	46.24	75.77	54.48
Primary	38.56	18.39	30.20
Second and high second	11.52	4.40	8.57
Above high second	3.68	1.44	2.75
Distribution of type of disability (%)			
Hearing	10.37	13.19	11.34
Mental	9.31	8.00	8.77
Visual	12.37	20.55	15.76
Speech	3.24	2.55	2.95
Locomotor	54.67	43.98	50.24
Multiple	10.04	11.73	10.94
Distribution of extent of Disability			
Can take self-care without aid/appliance	63.16	53.18	54.34
Cannot take self-care without aid/appliance	10.65	14.61	12.29
Can take self-care with only aid/appliance	10.90	16.44	17.88
Aid/appliance not tried/available	15.29	15.77	15.49
Average MCE (Rs)	534.26	533.36	533.89
Urban (%)	22.74	22.98	22.84

Source Estimated from the unit-record NSS data (58th round)

employability is due to choice or discrimination in the labour market. The evidence in this regard is rather mixed, which is discussed in a subsequent section. The distribution of disabled males and females across education categories shows a dismal picture as 85 % of the disabled males and 93 % of the disabled females are either primary educated or have received no education. Such a low level of education of the majority of the disabled females probably explains their low employability. The distribution of disabled persons by types of disability does not show a similar pattern for the male and female disabled persons. While the relative shares of hearing, mental, speech, and multiple disabilities are almost comparable between the males and the females, significant male–female difference is found in the burden of visual disability and locomotor disability. While females share a higher burden of visual disability, males share a higher burden of locomotor disability. As far as the extent of disability is concerned, almost comparable percentage of disabled males and females can take care of themselves either without any help or aid or with help or aid. The per capita consumption expenditure and concentration in urban locations do not show any significant male–female difference.

In the logistic regression, sex is included to see whether marital status favours one gender over the other. Age group is included in the regression mainly as a confounding variable since the likelihood of having the *ever married* marital status must be monotonically increasing with age. We have excluded individuals below 18 years since the legal minimum age of marriage is 18 years, and ideally, we should not expect to see an individual aged below 18 years having "married" status. Since ability to work and earning capacity are two important traits that are likely to be considered most important in the marriage market, especially for the disabled persons, we have included an independent variable *working-earning* status which combines both working capability and earning capacity of the disabled person. The variable "working-earning" status is classified into four categories, namely *earn-high* (which is used as a reference category in the logistic regression), *work-not earn*, *not able to wor*k (due to disability),[4] and *others*. Apart from its own importance as an important individual trait in the marriage market in general, education can be additionally important for a disabled person as having higher education expands his/her job opportunities and increases likelihood to earn his/her own income. A disabled person's acceptability or lack of it in the marriage market is expected to be dependent on his/her degree of disability since the ability to live a conjugal life depends on the nature and severity of disability. Therefore, in order to capture the effect of the type and severity of disability on the marital status, we have included both the *type of disability* and *extent of disability* as independent variables. The monthly per capita consumption expenditure of the household where the disabled person lives is included to capture his/her current economic status, since consumption expenditure is considered a good proxy for permanent income. We have made log transformation of the consumption expenditure to remove the positive skewness in its distribution. The place of residence (sector) is included to

[4]The category earn-high includes those working in the household enterprise (self-employed) own account worker, working in household enterprise (self-employed) employer, working as regular salaried/wage employee, rentiers, pensioners, remittance recipients, etc. The category earn-low includes casual wage labourers in public and other types of work, beggars, and prostitutes. The category "working but not earning" includes those who are working as helpers (or unpaid family workers) in household enterprise, attending educational institutions, attending domestic duties only, attending domestic duties and also engaged in free collection of goods (vegetables, roots, firewood, cattle feed, etc.), sewing, tailoring, weaving, etc., for household use.

Table 5.8 Results of the logistic regression

Independent variable	Odds Ratio	$P > z$
Sex (Ref = Male)		
Female	1.99	0.000
Age group (Ref = 18–29 years)		
30–39 years	6.74	0.000
40–49 years	15.85	0.000
50–59 years	39.59	0.000
60 years & above	174.74	0.000
Working-earning (Ref = earn-high)		
Earn-low	0.96	0.535
Work-not earn	0.57	0.000
Not able to work	0.23	0.000
Others	0.19	0.000
Education (Ref = Illiterate)		
Primary	1.16	0.000
Second and high second	0.92	0.190
Above high second	0.88	0.114
Type of disability (Ref = hearing)		
Mental	0.31	0.000
Visual	0.59	0.000
Speech	0.34	0.000
Locomotor	0.70	0.000
Multiple	0.31	0.000
Extent of disability (Ref = can take self-care without aid/appliance)		
Cannot take self-care without aid/appliance	0.86	0.023
Can take self-care with only aid/appliance	0.97	0.545
Aid/appliance not tried/available	1.06	0.339
LnMPCE	0.83	0.000
Sector (Ref = Rural)		
Urban	0.73	0.000

Dependent variable: marital status of the disabled person is 1, if ever married; 0, if never married
Note Sample size = 56145, Wald $\chi^2_{19} = 7374.76$, pseudo $R^2 = 0.42$
Source Estimated from the unit-record NSS data (58th round)

examine whether living in the rural or urban areas makes any significant difference in the marital status of a disabled person. The results of the logistic regression are presented in Table 5.8. The odds in favour of "marital status of the disabled person is ever married" are higher (OR = 1.99) if the disabled person is a female than a male. Since the age group variable is included as a confounding variable, we do not attempt to provide any explanation for this. In comparison with *earn-high* disabled persons, odds are lower for the disabled who earn-low (OR = 0.96 but not significant), who work but do not earn (OR = 0.57), those who are *not able to work* due to disability (OR = 0.23), and lowest for *others* (OR = 0.19). This clearly indicates that earning, irrespective of its level, makes a difference in the marital status of a disabled person. In comparison with the illiterate disabled persons, odds are higher for disabled persons with primary education (OR = 0.96). Although *secondary and high secondary* (OR = 0.92) and *above high secondary* (OR = 0.88) show lower odds ratios in comparison with illiterate disabled persons, neither of them is statistically significant. This is an indication that a disabled person's literacy status makes a difference in his/her marital status, but no significant difference is observed across disabled persons with different levels of education. Since it is generally observed that hearing disability restricts one's ability to live a normal life to a much lesser degree in comparison with other forms of disability, we have considered "hearing disability" as a reference category and tried to see what difference other types of disability make to marital status of a disabled person. The results show that in comparison with *hearing disability*, odds are lower for *locomotor disability* (OR = 0.70) followed by *visual disability* (OR = 0.59) and *speech disability* (OR = 0.34) and lowest for *mental disability* (OR = 0.31) and *multiple disability* (OR = 0.31). However, it should be noted that data used for the analysis are what were then observed at the time of the survey and there is no way to know whether the disability and other characteristics (such as education, occupation etc.) observed at the time of survey were the same as that at the time of marriage. As far as the *extent of disability* is concerned, in comparison with a disabled who *can take self-care without aid/appliance*, odds are lower for a disabled who *cannot take self-care without aid/appliance* (OR = 0.86). The odds are not significant for the categories *can take self-care with only aid/appliance and aid/appliance never tried or unavailable*. A less than unity value of the odds ratio (0.83) for log of monthly per capita consumption expenditure indicates that having higher economic status reduces the odds favouring *ever married* marital status. In this context, it is worth mentioning that Mitra and Sambarmoorthi (2008) found non-labour income having a negative and significant effect on the probability of employment for persons with disabilities but not for the non-disabled. Odds favouring marital status *ever married* is lower for the disabled persons living in the *urban* areas compared to the *rural* areas (OR = 0.73).

Regression results presented in Table 5.8 clearly show an association between sex and marital status of a disabled person, and such an association does indicate a favourable situation for the females as the odds favouring a disabled person having *ever married* marital status are higher for the females in comparison with the males. It was interesting to observe that there are individual-level characteristics other than *sex* which show strong association with marital status of a disabled person. It may be interesting to examine whether other individual characteristics have similar influences on marital status for the male and female disabled persons. For example, the effect of education or occupation or economic status on the marriage prospect of a disabled person may be different between a male disabled person and a female disabled person. It has been noted by scholars that the disabled females are often forced to accept the material reality of their impairments and deal with the requirements of their impairments while perfecting their performance as women (Ghosh, 2010).

The results of the logistic regression where this connection is investigated are presented in Table 5.9. We have used the same set of dependent and independent variables except sex. The odds ratios are found to be higher for the male disabled persons in comparison with the female disabled persons for a given age group. This should not be interpreted as male disabled person's higher likelihood to be married with age compared to a female disabled person. In the Indian context, the average

Table 5.9 Results of the logistic regression

Independent variables	Odds ratio Male[a]	Odds ratio Female[b]
Age group (Ref = 18–29 years)		
30–39 years	8.49***	4.50***
40–49 years	20.22***	9.86***
50–59 years	41.80***	35.65***
60 years and above	150.39***	267.97***
Working-earning (Ref = earn-high)		
Earn-low	0.98	1.63**
Work-not earn	0.30***	1.82***
Not able to work	0.25***	0.41***
Others	0.21***	0.33***
Education (Ref = Illiterate)		
Primary	1.51***	0.73***
Second and high second	1.26***	0.51***
Above high second	1.28**	0.49***
Type of disability (Ref = hearing)		
Mental	0.29***	0.37***
Visual	0.65***	0.52***
Speech	0.39***	0.25***
Locomotor	0.78***	0.57***
Multiple	0.38***	0.22***
Extent of disability (Ref = can take self-care without aid/appliance)		
Cannot take self-care without aid/appliance	0.81***	0.97
Can take self-care with only aid/appliance	0.96	0.98
Aid/appliance not tried/available	1.15*	0.90
LnMPCE	0.89***	0.77***
Sector (Ref = Rural)		
Urban	0.70***	0.78***

Dependent variable: marital status of the disabled person is 1, if ever married; 0, if never married
Note [a]Sample size = 33206, Wald χ^2_{19} = 5216.80, pseudo R^2 = 0.4241
[b]Sample size = 22939, Wald χ^2_{19}= 2270.64, pseudo R^2 = 0.4225
*Significant at 10 % level
**Significant at 5 % level
***Significant at 1 % level
Source Estimated from the unit-record NSS data (58th round)

age at marriage is always found to be lower for females than for males. Therefore, moving from a lower age group to a higher age group shows greater changes in marital status in favour of "ever married" for the males than for the females. In comparison with the *earn-high* group, for the male disabled persons the odds are lower for *work-not earn* (OR = 0.30), *not able to work* (OR = 0.25), and *others* (OR = 0.21) groups but not significantly higher or lower for the *earn-low* group. For the females, the odds are higher for the *earn-low* (OR = 1.63) and *work-not earn* (OR = 1.82) groups but lower for *not able to work* (OR = 0.41) and *others* (OR = 0.33) groups. It is evident that capacity to work irrespective of the earning status favours *females' ever married* marital status or marriage prospect more than that of males, but for the male disabled persons, both capacity to work and earning level matter. It is worth noticing the contrasting effects of education on ever married status for the male and female disabled persons. Being literate increases a male's prospect of favouring *ever married* marital status, but odds are higher for disabled male with *primary* education (OR = 1.51) than disabled males with *secondary and high secondary* (OR = 1.26) and *above high secondary* education (OR = 1.28). Being literate and having more education monotonically reduce ever married status for the female disabled persons as in comparison with the *illiterate* reference group; odds favouring *ever married* marital status are 0.73, 0.51, and 0.49 for the *primary, secondary and high secondary,* and *above high secondary* educational groups, respectively. The real reason behind this pattern is not obvious. While higher education can increase a disabled person's prospect of getting a job and capacity to earn his/her own livelihood, having higher education can make him/her more conscious and careful about his/her physical limitation to live a normal married life and at the same time entails more empowerment and gives confidence to live a life without seeking support from others. Moreover, a disabled person's preference and sense of vulnerability also changes with higher education. A decision and an opportunity to get married must be an outcome of all these complex factors. In comparison with *hearing disability* (which is considered least restrictive for a person's life in comparison with other forms of disability), odds are lower for all other forms of disability for both the males and females. Except *mental disability*, odds are lower for females than males indicating that a female's marriage prospect gets more affected than a male's for any given type of disability. The effect of the extent of disability on the marital status seems to follow distinct patterns for the male and female disabled persons. For example, in comparison with a male disabled person who *can take self-care without aid/appliance*, odds are lower for a male disabled person who *cannot take self-care without aid/appliance*, but for other categories of the *extent of disability*, no statistically significant association is observed. In case of female disabled persons, none of the extent of disability categories is significant. Having better economic status reduces the odds favouring *ever married* marital status for both male and female disabled persons, but it reduces more for the female disabled than for the male disabled persons. Similarly in comparison with *rural* areas, living in the *urban* areas lowers the odds for both male and female disabled persons, but it lowers more for the males.

It is obvious that disability imposes constraints on employability of a person. In their study in the context of Tamil Nadu, (Mitra and Sambarmoorthi, 2008) find that 52.3 % of males with disabilities work compared to 79.1 % of males without disabilities. A decomposition analysis of this difference suggests that responsible factors are related to differences in demographic, human capital, health, and other observed characteristics between males with and without disabilities. The results of their analysis suggest that this employment difference perhaps arises from different returns to productive characteristics (e.g. education) across disability status or because of discrimination by prejudiced employers.

There are a number of studies which have tried to understand the well-being effects of marriage or spousal relationship on disabled females. For example, the association between marriage, gender, and physical impairments is explored by Sengupta and Agree (2002) who compared the gender and disability among older adults in north and south India and found that female disadvantage is stronger in the absence of a spouse. The females in southern India are more likely to report impairments than the males when they are currently unmarried. They argue that women benefit more from marriage or spouse since marital protection for women in India is not only associated with better economic conditions when the spouse is alive but also with a higher status within the household and kin network. Though it is observed as expected that households with members with disabilities fare significantly worse as compared with households without people with disabilities, Menon et al. (2014) further observes that in comparison with families with male adults with disabilities, those with female adults with disabilities appear to experience no statistically discernible penalty. This goes contrary to the widely prevalent belief that households with disabled female are especially disadvantaged in comparison with households with disabled male. This finding is in line with that of Thomas (2005), who argues that when males and females have comparable levels of disability, females have higher likelihood of work participation.

It is worth mentioning that Mitra and Sambarmoorthi (2008) found negative attitudes among persons with disabilities themselves and heads of households as the factors that discourage persons with disabilities from entering the labour market. As far as Becker's theory of discrimination is concerned (Becker, 1971), the limited labour supply by the persons with disabilities probably explains the absence of a wage gap.

5.6 Conclusion

That a disabled person who faces great disadvantage in the marriage market can be easily understood, but the nature of such disadvantage and how it varies across different types of disabilities and in the presence of other characteristics of the individual and the household to which she belongs are not clearly understood. This paper has made an attempt to fill this gap. We find that the nature and extent of disadvantage follow distinct patterns among men and women. Disabled women are a lot more likely than men not to live with their spouses, and an overwhelming proportion of them are widowed or separated. This seems to be the most vulnerable group among all the disabled persons. We also find that capacity to work irrespective of the earning status favours the marriage prospect of females more than that of males, but for the male disabled persons, both capacity to work and earning level matter. More interestingly, higher levels of education reduce the prospect of the married status for both males and females and it reduces more for the females. Only micro-qualitative kind of inquiry can throw some light on the real reason behind such systematic patterns. While higher education can increase a disabled person's prospect to get a job and capacity to earn his/her own livelihood, it gives her more freedom to choose between a married life that is likely to be affected by the lack of mutual respect and living an unmarried life. Findings of this kind help us think about the appropriate design of public policies.

References

Becker, G. (1971). *Economics of discrimination*. Chicago: University of Chicago Press.

Chen, M. A. (Ed.). (1998). *Widows in India*. New Delhi: Sage.

Ghosh, N. (2010). Embodied experiences: being female and disabled. *Economic and Political Weekly, 45*(17), 58–63.

Jeffery, R., & Singal, M. (2008). Measuring disability in India. *Economic and Political Weekly, 43*(12–13), 22–24.

Menon, N., Parish, S. L., & Rose, R. A. (2014). The "state" of persons with disabilities in India. *Journal of Human Development and Capabilities, 15*(4), 391–412.

Mitra, S. (2006). The capability approach and disability. *Journal of Disability Policy Studies, 16*(4), 236–247.

Mitra, S., & Sambamoorthi, U. (2006a). Disability estimates in India: What the census and NSS tell us. *Economic & Political Weekly, 41*(38), 4022–4026.

Mitra, S., & Sambamoorthi, U. (2006b). Employment of persons with disabilities: Evidence from the national sample survey. *Economic and Political Weekly, 41*(3), 199–203.

Mitra, S., & Sambarmoorthi, U. (2008). Disability and rural labour market in India: Evidence for males in Tamil Nadu. *World Development, 36*(5), 934–952.

Mont, D., & Cuong, N. (2013). Does parental disability matter to child education? Evidence from Vietnam. *World Development, 48*, 88–107.

Nussbaum, M. (2000). *Women and human development: The capabilities approach*. Cambridge, MA: Cambridge University Press.

O'Keefe, P. (2009). *People with disabilities in India: From commitments to outcomes*. Washington, DC: World Bank. http://documents.worldbank.org/curated/en/2009/07/11027298/people-disabilities-india-commitments-outcomes

Sen, A. (1992). *Inequality re-examined*. Cambridge MA: Harvard University Press.

Sengupta, M., & Agree, F. M. (2002). Gender and disability among older adults in north and south India: differences associated with coresidence and marriage. *Journal of Cross-Cultural Gerontology, 17*, 313–336.

Smith, S. A. (2009). *Love, sex, and disability: The ethics and politics of care in intimate relationship*. Ph.D. thesis, Ohio State University.

Thomas, P. (2005). *Mainstreaming disability in development: India country report*, DFID Policy Project Report on Disability Knowledge and Research Programme.

Chapter 6
The Right to Be Different: Autism and Advocacy in Urban India

Shubhangi Vaidya

Abstract This chapter attempts to engage with the heterogeneity of the disability experience by foregrounding the lived experiences and subjectivities of persons with intellectual and developmental disabilities and their caregivers. Specifically, it takes up for examination the diagnostic category of autism and its location at the intersections of biology and culture. The chapter attempts to map cultural and contextual understandings of disability and the impact of globalization and information flows on shaping these understandings. It argues for an appreciation of different ways of being in the world and the webs of mutual dependence and care in which we are all implicated. In this context, it examines the role of family driven NGOs and presents a case study of Action for Autism, an NGO in Delhi. The "right to be different" is a fundamental aspect of the plurality and diversity of the world in which we live.

Keywords Autism · Care · Family · Intellectual and developmental disabilities · Difference · NGO · Action for Autism · Advocacy

6.1 Introduction

Disability scholarship and activism over the past few decades have brought about a sea change in the reconceptualization of disability, from a narrative of loss, deviance and deficit to one of inclusion, rights and entitlements on par with the non-disabled. However, on the ground, many of these ideas remain unfructified and large sections of the disabled population continue to lead sub-human existences on

The discussions in this chapter are included in the author's book "Autism and the Family in Urban India: Looking Back, Looking Forward" (S.Vaidya, Springer, 2017).

S. Vaidya (✉)
School of Interdisciplinary and Trans-Disciplinary Studies (SOITS) IGNOU, New Delhi, India
e-mail: svaidya2404@gmail.com

N. Ghosh (ed.), *Interrogating Disability in India*,
Dynamics of Asian Development, DOI 10.1007/978-81-322-3595-8_6

the margins of society. Even within the disability sector itself, persons with intellectual and developmental disabilities find themselves at the margins of the margins. Due to the very nature of their impairments, collective action, contestation of stereotypes and self-advocacy become difficult for them and they continue to be "spoken about" rather than speaking for themselves. Families and caregivers, their chief interlocutors, are frequently regarded with distrust and suspicion within the Disability Rights Movement; this came into sharp focus during the often acrimonious debates that ensued over the Rights of Persons with Disabilities Bill (2014) when it was sought to be taken up in Parliament by the United Progressive Alliance (UPA) government in what was to be its last parliamentary session. Yet, it is parental activism and advocacy that has been instrumental in creating and disseminating awareness and putting in place services (albeit vastly inadequate) for persons with mental and intellectual disabilities; and there is an urgent need for the DRM and disability studies to engage productively with these stakeholders.

Disability discourses emerging from a Western, rights-based model that privilege the autonomy of the self-reflective actor, do not adequately capture the sheer variety of the disability experience nor differently embodied ways of being in the world. While persons with physical disabilities may share similar aspirations and desires with non-disabled persons and feel a sense of injustice and discrimination at being excluded from the 'normal' activities of society, persons with profound intellectual disabilities may experience the world in very different ways which may not at once be accessible or make sense to the non-disabled (Klotz, 2003). It has been observed that persons with physical disabilities feel slighted if they are considered under the same category as those with intellectual disabilities and go to great lengths to prove that their intellect is unimpaired. It is worth reminding ourselves that the Disability Rights Movement emanated from the mobilization of persons who had become physically disabled and therefore felt themselves suddenly diminished and rendered 'dependents' upon society. At the same time, there is a need to engage with the heterogeneity of the experience of disability by engaging with the life-worlds of those whose voices remain unheard, as well as their families and caregivers. A rights-based approach is incomplete without caring practices that emerge out of intimate engagement with the life-worlds of those who are 'different', and whose minds and bodies may not work in the ways society deems as 'normative'. This chapter draws attention to the issues of persons with intellectual and developmental disabilities, their caregivers and interlocutors and argues for a more inclusive and nuanced understanding of the disability experience and disability rights.

In the case of persons with mental disability, there is also a need for a more nuanced understanding of difference and inclusion. The discussions around the Right to Education Act (2009), for example, resulted in it being extended to children with physical as well as mental disabilities. This is in consonance with the view that inclusion will foster empowerment and challenge prejudice and discrimination. A provision for home-based education and other non-formal kinds of education for children with severe disabilities met with criticism from some NGOs and activists who viewed it as a retrogressive step that would result in exclusion. However, lumping together children with differential learning styles and challenges without making appropriate provisions by way of trained staff and pedagogical clarity is to do a grave injustice to those who are to be 'included' and who might have spent their time far more productively in a 'special' setting tailored to their needs or at home in a setting that they are familiar with (see Vaidya, 2014, for a reflexive account of my quest for an appropriate educational placement for my child with autism). It is sometimes argued that until children with disability are compulsorily placed in 'inclusive' settings the attitudes and capacities of teachers, and by extension, the wider communities are not likely to change. In the meantime, children with disability must suffer rejection and hostility and poor service delivery until such time as the system actually deigns to accept them! It is also implicitly assumed that 'going to a normal school' is a desired goal for all children with disability and that special school will deepen the stigma of disability. This approach denies the possibility of different subjectivities and life-worlds that do not need the affirmation of the 'normal' world or engage with it in 'normal' ways.

This chapter draws attention to sociohistorical and cultural contexts that define ability and disability across time and place. It opens up the complex and situated nature of disability and difference through a discussion of the diagnostic category of autism spectrum disorder (ASD). There is a vast and growing body of multidisciplinary literature on autism in the West, including cross-cultural studies documenting the experiences of persons with autism and their families (see e.g. Daley, 2002, 2004; Grinker, 2007). In India, autism is a marginal category, virtually unknown outside the medical and psychiatric community and almost totally absent within disability studies scholarship. Many individuals with mild autistic symptoms go through life without a diagnosis or appropriate support and may often struggle hard to live up to familial and societal expectations of 'acceptable' behaviour. Those with more severe symptoms and challenging behaviours may be stigmatized as mad or insane and a 'burden' to be borne by family and community. The lived realities of persons with disabilities and conditions such as these and the families who are intimately engaged with them must inform disability scholarship and activism in order for it to become truly inclusive.

6.2 Mental/Intellectual Disabilities in a Cross-cultural Perspective

As medical anthropologists remind us, the categorization of certain kinds of physical and mental states such as "disabilities", "disorders" or "conditions" is determined as much by cultural factors as merely organic ones. Within classical anthropology, Benedict's (1934) paper *Anthropology and the Abnormal* (which looked at epilepsy in a cross-cultural perspective) problematized the notions of normality and abnormality, arguing that they are culturally and morally defined and based upon culturally variable definitions of appropriate behaviour and social roles. Mehrotra and Vaidya (2008) in their examination of constructs of intellectual disability, personhood and gender identity draw upon historical and cross-cultural sources to understand how societies and cultures understand cognitive difference and mental disabilities. In Western civilization, where the values of individuality, material success, productivity and literacy are culturally prized, persons with intellectual impairments have historically been viewed as deficient or even sub-human. During the Middle Ages, such people were simultaneously seen as possessed by the devil or as "holy innocents" protected by the Church; their intellectual deficits were believed to make them closer to God and Nature than "normal" people corrupted by culture (Jenkins, 1998). The Enlightenment in eighteenth-century Europe saw the identification and incarceration of persons who were seen as a burden on society, namely criminals, the unemployed and the insane in the name of social control (Foucault, 1967). Modernity brought with it the notion of the "normal" and human behaviour came to classified against deterministic criteria of what was considered the statistical norm (Davis, 1995). The measurement and testing of intelligence is an apt example. The eugenics movement, a social philosophy that believed in the transmission of culturally desirable and "superior" traits (such as intelligence, skin colour.) through "selective breeding" also played a role in confining the mentally disabled to institutions so that they would not be able to reproduce "defective" offspring. Eugenics was operationalized by the Nazis during the Second World War, and the human rights abuses and atrocities committed against persons with disability and other marginalized populations are well known.

In the post-war period, the practice of sending disabled children to special institutions became prevalent, in tune with dominant psychodynamic discourses of the time which viewed disability as a pathology and its impact upon the rest of the family in largely dysfunctional terms (see Ferguson, 2001). The move from institutionalization of the mentally disabled to community-based rehabilitation and intervention was the fallout of the "normalization principle" that emerged in the Nordic countries and the concept of "social role valorization" articulated by scholars like Wolfensberger (1972) in the USA. They emphasized the need for intellectually disabled persons to be given a chance to be part of their communities and follow their cultural norms. However, the pervasive "othering" of persons with special needs in social institutions and practices like education is deeply ingrained. Murray (2006) writes that these children are seen more as cardboard cut-outs rather than real individuals and their presence a threat to the well-being of the non-disabled ones.

Anthropological studies of intellectual disabilities were pioneered by scholars like Edgerton (1967), whose best known work *The Cloak of Competence: Stigma in the lives of the Mentally Retarded* (1967) attempted to understand the experiences of deinstitutionalized people with mild intellectual disabilities in the USA and how they coped with life on "the outs", i.e. outside the institution. His ethnography highlighted their attempts to resist the label of mental retardation by utilizing a "cloak of competence" that would mitigate the stigma of their diagnostic labels. However, as Klotz (ibid) points out, Edgerton did not attempt to analyse the core issue of why cognition and intelligence are considered so fundamental to Western notions of personhood and human identity.

Deploying a social constructivist perspective, Bogdan and Taylor (1982) challenged the validity of the category of mental retardation, arguing that it was not an objective condition but dependent upon social and cultural concepts in a given society. In a similar vein, Langness and Levine (1986) also regard the category as social and cultural, as much as a medical or psychological one. Interpretivist studies of mental retardation link the category to the growth of the educational infrastructure in the West, which categorizes, labels and then discards children who are deemed unfit or incompetent (Goodley, 2011). However, Klotz (2003: 12) cautions that interpretations that only take sociocultural structures and constructions into account disregard the fact that "intellectual disability is an ontological reality that makes a real difference to one's experience of being in the world. Researchers who adopt a constructivist perspective ignore the real implications of difference as *both* productive of the sociocultural world *and* the product of it". Similar debates have taken place in the context of autism and the reality of the category, which we shall discuss later. Attempting to understand the experiential reality and subjectivity of persons with profound disabilities, researchers like Goode (1980) and Gleason (1989) tried to place themselves in their shoes, closely observing and initiating contact and communication with them on their own terms and in their own ways. Klotz (2003: 23) observes that disability theorists rarely engage with these diversities and that their theories, concepts and methodologies prove inadequate to understand these worlds. Long-term ethnographic engagement offers rich possibilities for forging relationships with the lived experiences of the intellectually disabled and making their life-worlds accessible and knowable.

The edited volumes by Ingstad and Whyte (1995) and Jenkins (1998) brought together cross-cultural studies examining disability management within non-Western societies and the impact of culturally shaped notions of humanness and personhood on the lives of persons with a range of impairments. The latter collection of papers specifically focused on intellectual disability and culture. Whyte's (1998) study of the Nyole people in rural Uganda and Nuttall's (1998) work on the Inuit community in Greenland highlight how competence is not based on the ability to read or write or performance in intelligence tests, as in the West, but in terms of social functioning and participation in the local culture and systems of subsistence. Similarly, Devlieger (1998) argues that among the *Shona* and *Songye* peoples of south-eastern Africa, personhood is defined as the ability to interact with others within broader social contexts. Physical or mental deficiencies are viewed as the result of "wronged relationships" with nature, relatives, ancestors and God, and witchcraft is employed to restore "relational embeddedness". These studies demonstrate how persons with disability are absorbed and accommodated within the networks of family, kin and neighbourhood, creating spaces and opportunities for them to function as per their capacities; interdependence, relatedness and affiliation are valued above individual abilities. This is in sharp contrast to the Western biomedical understandings and interventions that seek to fix or cure the deficient or damaged individual body or mind.

In the Indian context, authors like Miles (1995, 2000), Dalal (2002), Ghai (2003, 2015) have written extensively about local understandings of disability, drawing upon history, mythology and cultural practices. The Hindu and Buddhist worldview on disability can be explained through the *karma* theory, wherein illness or disability in this life is viewed as a consequence of past misdeeds, the outcomes of cosmic factors to be accepted in a spirit of resignation. Belief in supernatural causation, the impact of the "evil eye" (*nazar lagna*), the proliferation of faith healers, *tantriks, babas, swamis* and traditional folk remedies coexist with modern biomedicine, particularly in the context of mental illnesses and similar afflictions (Ghai, 2015). With regard to intellectual disability, Mehrotra (2004) in her ethnographic work in rural Haryana mentions that the categories used to describe such persons are *bhola* or *bawla* (naïve, innocent). They are assigned household chores, and their reduced mental capacities are viewed as disabilities if coupled with any kind of physical impairment. Thus, the mere fact of being mentally "defective" is not stigmatizing in itself in the context of agrarian/pastoral societies. Mehrotra and Vaidya (2008) note that as societies transit from tradition to modernity, notions of competence also shift. The processes of industrialization and urbanization, biomedical and psychiatric interventions, improved access to education, etc., all play a role in the categorization of mental/intellectual "deficits" as conditions that need external intervention. The growing recognition and salience of categories such as learning disabilities and autism spectrum disorder in urban India may be seen in this context.

6.3 Between Biology and Culture: The Case of Autism Spectrum Disorder

Autism Spectrum Disorder provides an interesting site for sociological and anthropological research, opening up the complex and situated nature of the category of disability and the experience of disablement/difference. Autism as a diagnostic category emerged from relative obscurity in the 1950s to an alleged epidemic in the twenty-first century. In the USA alone, it is reported there has been a ten-fold increase in autism prevalence over the last four decades. According to the Centres for Disease Control and Prevention, one out of every sixty-eight children in the USA is identified as being on the autism spectrum. The increase in number of persons diagnosed has been explained by some scholars and practitioners as the consequence of far better screening and diagnostic practices and more liberal criteria for diagnosis (Grinker, 2007). Ongoing debates about causation attribute it to a host of factors from environmental toxins to childhood vaccines; and a range of 'cures' and therapies have been in vogue over the years, ranging from gluten- and casein-free diets to chelation, hyperbaric oxygen treatments and lately stem cell therapy. None of these therapies have as yet been scientifically validated, and the view largely subscribed to in the scientific community is that autism is a neuro-developmental condition with a strong genetic component. The pioneering clinical work of Kanner (1943) in the USA and Asperger (1944) in Vienna established it as a distinct diagnostic category of childhood psychiatric disorders. Derived from the Greek word "autos" meaning "self, same, spontaneous, directed from within", autism was associated with intense self-absorption and inability or unwillingness to relate with others. Kanner's descriptions of his young patients capture their intense self-focus and self-absorption, their apparent immunity to the presence or absence of significant others in their environment. Asperger's patients, while more verbal and apparently highly intelligent, also displayed social disconnectedness and extreme naiveté. The idea of autism as a 'spectrum' condition captures individuals with a range of abilities and levels of functioning, from the severely impaired, non-verbal ones, to those with milder symptoms who none the less find it extremely difficult to negotiate the complex demands of social intercourse and understand the perspectives of others.

The psychoanalytical view saw it as withdrawal of the child into his/her own inner world as a consequence of the coldness and inability of the primary caregiver (usually the mother) to engage in 'normal' human interaction with the child. The stigmatizing term "refrigerator mother" (unfortunately coined by Kanner) and the resultant mother-blame were to cause incalculable psychological damage to a whole generation of mothers of children with conditions like autism. This view has been debunked and discredited, but the notion that bad parenting results in children developing mental illnesses and disorders is a pervasive construct that refuses to go away.

So was autism an unknown quantity before Kanner and Asperger named and described it? Straus (2010) remarks that even though it may today appear, as a "secure, natural category", it is a historically and culturally contingent one (536). Grinker (2007) points out that autism is new because it is only in the past century that Western psychiatry has described mental disorders more precisely and made distinctions between categories. It is old because people exhibiting its features have always been around and often subsumed under other categories such as madness, feeble-mindedness and schizophrenia. There are cultures where the symptoms of autism are not regarded as pathological, but rather as a sign of divine grace or conversely, possession by evil spirits.

Autism, plainly explained, is a condition that impacts the language, social and imaginative capacities of an individual. Persons with autism may experience difficulties in the everyday aspects of social interaction such as reading social cues, facial expressions and body language and understanding the mental states, feelings and thoughts of other persons in their environment. Baron-Cohen (1997) uses the term "mind-blindness" in this context. Many persons on the autism spectrum also report sensory perceptions or modalities that are qualitatively different; they may experience intense sensitivity to light sound, touch, colour or taste. This has profound effects on their way of being in the world and embodied subjectivities. Autism thus occupies a singular place on the continuum from the medical to social model; it is held to be a biological disorder but manifests in social behaviour and normative social functioning; its nature can only be defined with reference to culture. It presents sociologists with a range of issues, human identity, difference, perception and subjectivity within a social and cultural context (Silverman, 2008). The cultural fascination with autism in Anglo-American countries is also linked with the idea of autistic savants, individuals displaying islands of extreme brilliance or genius in a sea of profound disability, the iconoclastic individual or the creative genius with scant regard for social codes and niceties, who defies time and tide and lives life on his or her own terms. However, the reality is that the majority of persons with autism are not savants; many of them experience difficulties in coping with the demands of a world that cannot understand their ways of being and perceives them as aberrant or abnormal.

Over the years, autism as a construct and category has travelled to parts of the world where it was earlier unknown or unnamed; with globalization and the Internet revolution, information about symptoms, diagnostic procedures, therapies, treatments and 'cures' circulates freely and intensely among ever increasing numbers. The Internet has also facilitated sharing of experiences between families and individuals with autism across time zones and geographical space. The virtual world of autism discourse and transnational flows is a potentially exciting site for research.

In the absence of epidemiological studies or Census data, autism figures in India must necessarily be tentative; researchers peg the figure at anything between 2 million (Daley, 2004) and 10 million depending upon prevalence rates in other countries. The identification and perception of autism as a marginal, rare disorder that is diagnosed only in a certain class of the population and therefore a middle-class problem does a grave injustice to the vast numbers of children and adults whose difficulties are never identified or named but who experience stigma and ridicule nonetheless for their distinctive behaviour which fits the cultural definition of 'madness' (*paagalpan* in Hindi). While the acquisition of a biomedical diagnosis may be seen as reifying the category and labelling the individual it also opens doors for acceptance and accommodation. While those with a biomedical label have possibilities for rehabilitation and remediation, those stigmatized as mad or abnormal remain relegated to the social margins and may suffer terribly for no fault of their own.

6.4 Families of Persons with High Support Needs

In any discussion on disability in the Indian context, the role of the family in providing care, sustenance and support assumes centrality. The family is the key site within which the disability is managed and very frequently has to act as the voice of the disabled individual and the bridge between him/her and the wider community. With the growth of urbanization, migration and the advent of the neoliberal economy the traditional networks of care and support of the aged, ill and disabled are crumbling. It is quite clear that the contemporary family in India is under stress and hard pressed to care for the lifelong needs of children with disabilities especially in view of the sheer paucity of services, infrastructure and social attitudes towards disabled persons.

The issues of persons with severe and profound disabilities with high support needs who will require assistance and aid in performing even the most basic tasks of self-care throughout their lives, and the families who are disabled by the unending care work demand attention. In a situation where families have to struggle to survive, provide life-long care and are beset by worries about who will look after their child when they are gone, the DRM has to reflect critically upon the issue of disability, dependence and the provision of care. In her thoughtful analysis of the politics of caregiving and its gendered nature in urban India, Chakravarti (2008) presents case studies of young adults with cerebral palsy in Delhi and their care-givers, highlighting the individual and social suffering they experience. She highlights the existential difficulties of ageing parents looking after the high support needs of their disabled adult children, the double burden of working for a living and providing care, the unreliability of non-familial help or support and the lack of any institutional mechanisms for long-term care of persons with severe disabilities. The only ray of hope of these families is the support they receive from the NGO and special school that caters to people with cerebral palsy; when their wards have to leave to make way for new clients, they feel abandoned and helpless with no place to go. Despite receiving a good deal of emotional and practical support, Chakravarti's respondents expressed disappointment that the special school and NGO have not been able to plan for the needs of adults with disability and address their educational, vocational, psychological and social needs. Exhausted by a lifetime of care and worried about the future of their children, parents lamented that the organizations that had supported them for years were not doing enough for their children now.

In my ethnographic fieldwork conducted with families of autistic children in Delhi during the course of a doctorate, I attempted to understand how families mobilized personal, social and cultural resources to negotiate with their child's condition and cope with the daily demands of parenting a child with a complex and challenging condition. My personal location as a parent of a child with autism, a social scientist interested in participatory and reflexive research methods and an advocate for the rights of persons with disability and their families informed the research endeavour. Narratives of the families chronicled the processes of symptom recognition and diagnosis, acceptance and coping, and the daily routines and quotidian activities through which the personhood of the child was constructed and represented to the world. The onus for identifying the child's problem rests squarely on the family; as a result, only those families who had the resources and social capital to consult the right specialists and sometimes travel long distances to do so could hope to secure an appropriate diagnosis and facilities for treatment and rehabilitation. The differential and gendered experiences of fathers and mothers and the re-calibration of roles and responsibilities as a consequence of the child's autism came out in sharp detail, with mothers being relegated to the domestic space and becoming the full time care givers, teachers and playmates, and fathers treading an uneasy balance between providing for the family and participating in the care giving for their child. The anonymity of urban existence, the stigma and social isolation and the paucity of familial and kin networks resulted in the nuclear familial unit withdrawing into a shell and seeking affiliation and support from other similarly placed families (Vaidya, 2011, 2015).

6.5 Parental Activism and Social Change: Case Study of an NGO

In their essay “Enabling Disability: Rewriting kinship, reimagining citizenship”, anthropologists and mothers of developmentally disabled children, Ginsburg and Rapp (2010) write about the efforts of families of children with disability to expand the scope of kinship ties beyond the biological family to the realm of public culture, expanding “the social fund of knowledge about disability” (p. 239) and making it available to society at large. By transforming and extending their personal experiences and expertise gained within the kin group to the larger social realm, they sow the seeds for social change.

Disability NGOs appear to straddle the domestic as well as the sociopolitical space as many of them are founded and led by parents and caregivers of persons with disabilities. Bereft of traditional support structures and struggling with the demands of urban existence, families under difficult circumstances are compelled to seek alternative models of support and engage with people and groups outside the ambit of traditional networks. The growth of the autism advocacy movement in India is a pre-eminently urban phenomenon, led by educated, middle- and upper-middle-class English-speaking parents who could mobilize social and cultural capital to find out what was “wrong” with their children and ways to deal with it. The activism and advocacy of parent-driven organizations put autism on India’s disability map; over the past two decades, it has become a recognized category (it was included as one of the disabilities in the National Trust Act, 1999, and is included in the new Rights of Persons with Disability Bill, 2014, which has yet to be passed in the Parliament).

Action for Autism, a parent-driven organization in Delhi, has been a pioneer in the area of autism in south Asia for the past two decades (Grinker, 2007; Mehrotra and Vaidya, 2008; Vaidya, 2015). Its genesis from the efforts of a handful of motivated parents to a multipronged and dynamic organization at the vanguard of autism rehabilitation and disability activism is a fascinating story of commitment and courage. The organization, which began its life as a small school established by a mother to teach her child who was rejected by mainstream and special schools alike, is now a multitasking hive of activity, engaged in teaching and training, research, advocacy and providing sheltered employment options to adults. Plans to establish a residential centre to address the long-term needs of autistic adults are underway.

The philosophy of the organization reflects in its vision statement, which envisages “a society that views the interdependence of people of every ability as valuable and enriching and seeks to provide equal opportunities for all”. Its mission is to “facilitate a barrier free environment to empower families of persons with autism and to act as a catalyst for change that will enable persons with autism to live as fully participating members of the community” (www.autism-india.org).

Parental empowerment is a key goal of the organization and is actualized through annual workshops which are well attended by parents and professionals from across the country. These workshops aim at providing an understanding of autism not merely as a set of symptoms but rather by foregrounding the humanity of the person of autism and drawing attention towards how the non-autistic can better understand and respond to the child's needs. The organization conducts an intensive 'Parent-Child Training Programme' (PCTP), a twelve-week-long residential programme where participants receive hands-on training in early intervention strategies with their children and also on their own perceptions and attitudes regarding their child's autism. A recent evaluation of the programme revealed the positive impact of the programme on parental attitudes and the key role of parental empowerment and acceptance as agents of change (Daley and Weisner, 2015).

Its model school for children with autism, Open Door School is also backed by a well-articulated philosophy of education based upon what Merry Barua, AFA's founder–director, terms an "unconditional acceptance of difference". The emphasis is on helping children learn communication and language, appropriate social behaviour and work skills. Sessions such as community education programs, community visits and celebration of festivals are structured to help children participate in a variety of social experiences. There is a strict zero-tolerance policy towards the use of aversive methods and punishment. AFA's educational programmes are not merely confined to academic or vocational training; rather, they focus upon integrating the child into the community. This is in consonance with its vision of a society built upon interdependence and participation.

Its vocational centre, *Aadhar* about which I have written in detail elsewhere (Mehrotra and Vaidya, 2008) is a sheltered work place where adults with autism work in a structured environment where they are engaged in making bags, costume jewellery, household decorative items, etc. The organization has also initiated a programme for training young adults in work skills and soft skills that will enable them to seek employment in semi-sheltered as well as open settings.

AFA's vision of a society based on "interdependence of people of every ability" implies an inherent belief in the equality of all humans, irrespective of ability or disability and emphasizes the "valuable and enriching" aspects of such interdependence. What is also implied is that the less equal members of society also can contribute to this interdependence in a valuable and enriching way, rather than always being at the receiving end. The vision of "providing equal opportunities for all", although an oft-used phrase, assumes greater salience when we bear in mind that personhood of the mentally disabled is often undermined or questioned; they are seen as not quite human, and hence, the question of providing them with "equal opportunities" is rarely taken up seriously. It aims to do away with barriers that restrict or prevent the full participation of disabled people in the life of the community, be it physical barriers like disabled-unfriendly architecture or public spaces, and, even more significantly, discriminatory practices that deny them access to appropriate education, recreation, etc. It will be interesting to see how a new-generation cadre of functionaries and leaders will match up to the missionary zeal and selfless dedication of the founders and what new forms and structures these organizations will evolve over time. Disability scholarship can engage productively with these organizations and initiatives.

6.6 Concluding Remarks

The heartfelt question asked by families is: "What will happen when we are gone"? This question is as relevant in the case of autism as it is for any other disability given the near total absence of a social security net that will address the long-term needs of vulnerable populations. While reservation in education and employment hold out promise for persons with physical disabilities, for those with difficulties like autism the issue is far less straightforward. The language of rights and the emphasis on autonomy, agency and independence that has underpinned the disability rights discourse finds itself on shaky ground in this context. Rights alone cannot guarantee a humane society until they are backed by caring practices (Reinders, 1999). Sarrett (2012), drawing upon Kittay's (1999) formulation of universal and shared relations of dependence and Turner's (2006) depiction of the frailty and vulnerability of the human body, suggests that these provide the conceptual apparatus for constructing a model of human rights for persons with autism and similar disabilities. Such a model would be based upon an acknowledgement of mutual dependence as the common human condition, the creation of ethical caring communities where individual worth is not measured in utilitarian terms and the right to live and die with dignity is guaranteed to all irrespective of the way their minds and bodies work.

How can these entitlements be fructified in the Indian context? One of the possibilities is the setting up of supported living centres that will cater to the lifelong needs of persons with disability and foster an environment wherein they can participate in the community. Rather than being closed communities like the institutions and asylums, give-and-take with local communities and sharing of facilities and services such as schools, playgrounds, health services should be fostered. Running a facility of this nature would entail job opportunities in the fields of education, rehabilitation, health care and provision of services which would also benefit the wider community. Thus, an entire ecosystem based upon a model of community responsibility and the need for support and care could emerge. Group homes for persons with disabilities are common abroad; however, an indigenous model that draws upon our traditions of community care is the need of the hour. Changing notions of family responsibility and care in a globalizing world have implications for the welfare of vulnerable categories of people. From a disability studies perspective, this can truly become a 'social model' wherein rights, responsibilities and caring practices fuse together to affirm a shared humanity and the 'right to be different'.

References

Asperger, H. (1991/1944). Autistic psychopathy in childhood. In U. Frith (Ed. & trans.), *Autism and asperger syndrome*. Cambridge: Cambridge University Press.

Baron-Cohen, S. (1997). *Mindblindness: An essay on autism and theory of mind*. Massachussetts: M.I.T. Press.

Benedict, R. (1934). Anthropology and the abnormal. *Journal of General Psychiatry, 10*, 59–80.

Bogdan, R., & Taylor, S. (1982). *Inside out: The social meaning of mental retardation*. Toronto: University of Toronto Press.

Chakravarti, U. (2008). Burden of caring: Families of the disabled in urban India. *Indian Journal of Gender Studies, 15*(3), 341–363.

Dalal, A. K. (2002). Disability rehabilitation in a traditional Indian society. In M. Thomas & M. T. Thomas (Eds.), *Selected readings in community based rehabilitation* (Vol. 2)., Disability and rehabilitation in south Asia Bangalore: National Printing Press.

Daley, T. C. (2002). The need for cross-cultural research on pervasive developmental disorder. *Transcultural Psychiatry, 39*(4), 532–551.

Daley, T. C. (2004). From symptom recognition to diagnosis: Children with autism in urban India. *Social Science and Medicine, 58*, 1323–1335.

Daley, T., & Weisner, T. (2015). Evaluation of the parent child training programme. *Autism Network, 10*(3), 2–6.

Davis, J. L. (1995). *Enforcing normalcy: Disability*. Deafness and the Body. London: Verso Press.

Devlieger, P. J. (1998). Incompetence in America in comparative perspective. In R. Jenkins (Ed.), *Questions of competence: Culture, classification and intellectual disability*. Cambridge: Cambridge University Press.

Edgerton, R. B. (1967). *The cloak of competence: Stigma in the lives of the mentally retarded*. Berkeley: University of California Press.

Ferguson, P. M. (2001). Mapping the family: Disability studies and the exploration of parental response to disability. In G. L. Albrecht, K. D. Seelman, & M. Bury (Eds.), *Handbook of disability studies*. New Delhi: Sage.

Foucault, M. (1967). *Madness and civilization: A history of insanity in the age of reason*. Cambridge: Cambridge University Press.

Ghai, A. (2003). *(Dis)embodied form: Issues of disabled women*. New Delhi: Shakti Books.

Ghai, A. (2015). *Rethinking disability in India*. New Delhi: Routledge.

Ginsburg, F., & Rapp, R. (2010). Enabling disability: Rewriting kinship, reimagining citizenship. In L. J. Davis (Ed.), *The disability studies reader* (3rd ed.), NY: Routledge.

Gleason, J. J. (1989). *Special education in context: An ethnographic study of persons with developmental disabilities*. Cambridge: Cambridge University Press.

Goode, D. (1980). The world of the congenitally deaf-blind: Towards the grounds for achieving human understanding. In J. Jacobs (Ed.), *Mental retardation: A phenomenological approach*. Charles C. Thomas: Springfield, Illinois.

Goodley, D. (2011). *Disability studies: An interdisciplinary reader*. New Delhi: Sage.

Grinker, R. R. (2007). *Unstrange minds: Remapping the world of autism*. New York: Basic Books.

Ingstad, B., & Whyte, S. R. (Eds.). (1995). *Disability and culture*. Berkeley: University of California Press.

Jenkins, R. (Ed.). (1998). *Questions of competence: Culture, classification and intellectual disability*. Cambridge, UK: Cambridge University Press.

Kanner, L. (1943). Autistic disturbances of affective contact. *Nervous Child, 2*, 217–250.

Kittay, E. F. (1999). *Love's labor: Essays on women, equality, and dependency*. New York: Routledge.

Klotz, J. (2003). *The culture concept*: *Anthropology, disability studies and intellectual disability*. Paper Presented to Disability studies and Research Institute (DsaRI) Symposium, "*Disability at the cutting edge*: *A colloquium to examine the impact on theory, research and professional practice*". University of Technology, Sydney. September 12, 2003.

Langness, L. L., & Levine, H. G. (1986). *Culture and retardation: Life histories of mildly mentally retarded persons in American society*. Dordrecht, The Netherlands: D. Reidel.
Mehrotra, N. (2004). Understanding cultural conceptions of disability in rural India: A case from Haryana. *Journal of Indian Anthropological Society, 39*, 33–45.
Mehrotra, N., & Vaidya, S. (2008). Exploring constructs of intellectual disability and personhood in Haryana and Delhi. *Indian Journal of Gender Studies, 15*(3), 317–340.
Miles, M. (1995). Disability in an eastern religious context: Historical perspectives. *Disability and Society, 10*(1), 49–70.
Miles, M. (2000). Disability in south Asia: Millenium to millenium. *Asia Pacific Rehabilitation Journal, 11*, 1–10.
Murray, P. (2006). Being in school? Exclusion and the denial of psychological reality. In D. Goodley & R. Lawthom (Eds.), *Disability & psychology: critical introductions & reflections*. Basingstoke: Palgrave Macmillan.
Nuttal, M. (1998). States and categories: Indigenous models of personhood in northwest Greenland. In R. Jenkins (Ed.), *Questions of competence: Culture, classification and intellectual disability*. Cambridge, UK: Cambridge University Press.
Reinders, H. S. (1999). *The limits of rights discourse*. Paper Presented to the Roundtable of the Special Interest Research Group on Ethics, International Association for the Scientific Study of Intellectual Disabilities. Doorn, The Netherlands, April, 1999.
Sarrett, J. (2012). Autistic human rights: A proposal. *Disability Studies Quarterly*, 32.
Silverman, C. (2008). Fieldwork on another planet: Social science perspectives on the autism spectrum disorders. *BioSocieties, 3*(3), 325–341.
Straus, J. N. (2010). Autism as culture. In L. J. Davis (Ed.), *The disability studies reader* (3rd ed.). New York and London: Routledge.
The Rights of Persons with Disabilities Bill (2014). Retrieved from http://www.prsindia.org/uploads/media/Person%20with%20Disabilities/The%20Right%20of%20Persons%20with%20Disabilities%20Bill.pdf
The Right of Children to Free and Compulsory Education Act (2009). Retrieved from http://eoc.du.ac.in/RTE%20-%20notified.pdf
Turner, B. S. (2006). *Vulnerability and human rights*. University Park, PN: The Pennsylvania State University Press.
Vaidya, S. (2011). Mothering as ideology and practice: The experiences of mothers of children with autism spectrum disorder. In M. Walks & N. MacPherson (Eds.), *An anthropology of mothering*. Bradford, ON: Demeter Press.
Vaidya, S. (2014). Lessons in disability: Acceptance and inclusion. *Fortell* (29):15–18 (Special Issue).
Vaidya, S. (2015). Developmental disability and the family: Autism spectrum disorder in urban India. In A. Hans (Ed.), *Disability, gender and the trajectories of power*. New Delhi: Sage Publications.
Whyte, S. R. (1998). Slow cookers and madmen: Competence of heart and head in rural Uganda. In R. Jenkins (Ed.), *Questions of competence: Culture, classification and intellectual disability*. Cambridge, UK: Cambridge University Press.
Wolfensberger, W. (1972). *The principle of normalisation in human services*. Toronto: National Institute on Mental Retardation.

Chapter 7
Power and Leveraging in a Disability Context

Madhura Nagchoudhuri and Srilatha Juvva

Abstract This chapter explores the dynamic of use of power by subordinate groups particularly persons with disability, through leveraging their vulnerable status, and argues for a healthy use of power and agency. People with disability have often been viewed as "dependent", a burden or victims of a "personal tragedy" and have remained marginalized and invisible in the society. Consequently, the notion of a person with an impairment having "agency" or having power in any shape or form including the most basic form of having power over oneself is difficult to imagine. This notion has led to persons with disability systematically being conditioned to become "helpless" and dependent. However, this paper argues through the use of illustrations and anecdotal evidence that developing an understanding of disability as "socially constructed" is essential to realize personal power for persons with disability. Persons with disability no matter how disenfranchised they are have the potential ability to exercise the "power within" to become empowered themselves and also work towards empowering others both disabled and non-disabled. This may be done by partnering with others in positive ways to co-create power rather than using power in negative ways by leveraging their disability.

Keywords Power · Agency · Leverage · Disability · Abilities · Partnering

M. Nagchoudhuri (✉)
Centre for Equity and Justice for Children and Families, School of Social Work,
Tata Institute of Social Sciences, Mumbai, India
e-mail: madhuranag@tiss.edu

S. Juvva
Centre for Disability Studies and Action, School of Social Work,
Tata Institute of Social Sciences, Mumbai 400088, India
e-mail: juvvas@tiss.edu

N. Ghosh (ed.), *Interrogating Disability in India*,
Dynamics of Asian Development, DOI 10.1007/978-81-322-3595-8_7

7.1 Introduction

Traditionally, persons with disability have been viewed as "dependent" and "a burden"—people are incapable of being independent or self-sufficient physically, financially or emotionally. The state of being impaired has been viewed as a "personal tragedy" where the person's condition cannot be changed or fixed. Consequently, the notion of a person with an impairment having "agency" or having power in any shape or form including the most basic form of having power over him/herself is difficult to imagine. This notion has led to persons with disability systematically being conditioned to viewing themselves as (and also becoming) "helpless" and dependent. Years of reinforcing the viewpoint that the individual is "deviant" or "faulty" and hence powerless has been deeply ingrained in the cultural archetype of any society. This kind of a view of disability has been propagated and crystallized through the depictions of persons with disability in mainstream media, including television and cinema, in ways that stereotype and label such persons, assigning them roles of "dependent victims". Such beliefs are so ingrained in both persons with disability and those without disability that all people subscribe to this at an unconscious level to the extent that it has become an accepted way of living and interacting. These kinds of views are often propagated by the families of the disabled themselves as well as others in the immediate environment of the person. According to Bhambhani (1999), this is particularly true for families having women with disability where parents tend to either neglect or overprotect and "infantilize" their disabled daughters, discouraging them from taking independent decisions. This feeds into learnt helplessness and internalized ableist attitudes resulting in a mindset that makes the person expect and feel satisfied with sympathy and pity rather than being able to see themselves as "agents" capable of giving expression to their "inner voice" (Bhambani, 1999).

In the past, individual models were used by professionals and society at large to understand disability where the underlying assumption was that persons with disabilities have something inherently wrong with them for which the blame and responsibility rested solely on that individual (Reid-Cunningham and Fleming, 2009). According to the medical model, disability was "a functional impairment" deviating from an "assumed norm of human form and functioning" (Reid-Cunningham and Fleming, 2009: 12). This view perceived disability as a fixed condition resulting in relationships of dependency between persons with disability and their non-disabled counterparts (Smith, 2008). These beliefs also had other repercussions in terms of the formation and understanding of the notion of identity among persons with disability. The identity of an individual essentially refers to the social categories that he/she belongs to as well as to the sources of his/her self-respect and dignity (Fearon, 1999). There are two key aspects to the notion of identity which include "social" and "personal" identity. An individual's social identity primarily indicates the social category or categories that the individual belongs to where a social category refers to a set of persons marked by a label and distinguished by rules deciding membership and supposed characteristic features or attributes. An individual's "personal" identity on the other hand refers to some distinguishing characteristic (or characteristics) that the individual takes special pride in or views as socially important but more-or-less unchangeable (Fearon, 1999). In case of persons with disability, the person's social identity is often connected to their disability where they are categorized and labelled by society based on the nature of their disability and functional limitation as "blind" or "deaf" which is over and above their gender, class or caste identities which are other aspects of social identity. This is as opposed to the person's "personal" identity connected with the individual viewing himself/herself in terms of their personality or talents as being part of their identity which may be linked to their occupation, hobbies or their role within the family such as being a "good mother" or a "good daughter", etc.

7.2 Philosophical Underpinnings

We believe that all human beings are equal, irrespective of differences and diversity. We stand for human values that are geared to preserving, upholding and restoring dignity, respect, confidence and full potential of human beings. In doing so, there is a natural inclination to harmonize and plug divisive gaps that serve to create inequality and marginalize certain groups of people. Such an orientation focuses more on the individual's agency and power that boosts growth and development. This gives us the freedom and space for acceptance and inclusion that is at the root of being human.

However, we confront an alternate reality. Due to the notions propagated through the medical and individual model, the disabled individual's identity has been viewed as a stigmatized or a "spoiled identity" (Goffman, 1963) where the disability is a "deeply discrediting" attribute resulting in the person with disability becoming reduced from a "whole and usual person to a tainted, discounted one" (Goffman, 1963: 3). According to Fine and Asch (1988), the notion of disability as a stigmatized identity is based on certain assumptions including the belief that disability is located solely in biology such that persons with disability are victims of biological injustice in need of help and social support. Moreover, it is assumed that being disabled is central to the disabled person's self-concept and self-definition and all the problems of such individuals are resulting from their impairment. This is dominantly understood as the medical model—wherein the individual and the impairment are considered responsible for the limited functioning of the individual. While the predominant problems that arise from the impairment are manifested in the form of activity participation and functioning of the individual, the concomitant social and psychological ramifications of the impairment are often overrated. The feelings of incompetence, lack of self-esteem, distorted identity and poor self-concept, lack of acceptance of self, lack of acceptance by others, exclusion and stigma are some of the problems that result from impairment. This does not necessarily focus on the society's inability to understand its role in contributing to the functioning and activity participation of the individual with impairment in the form of posing barriers in his/her life. These barriers may not loom so large for persons without impairment, but it restricts the capacity of the individual with disability to function. This is the contestation of the social model of understanding disability.

However, the stigmatization of any social category is entirely dependent on social, economic and political power. In the case of persons with disability, they are less likely to have access to social, political or economic power since they are more vulnerable to being impoverished, having lower levels of education, having incomes below poverty level with fewer savings and other assets in comparison with non-disabled populations in both developed and developing countries (Elwan, 1999). In general, they are less likely to participate in all manner of societal processes be they social, economic or political. Such situations increase the chances of persons with disability having very little social, economic or political power making them most vulnerable to stigmatization.

Productivity has been a defining factor in understanding disability and labelling persons as having a disability. The conceptualization of productivity has been largely related to power. If a person has the capacity to be productive as conceived by the hegemonic able-bodied majority who believe in enhancing economic contributions, he/she is said to have power and influence. Even among persons with disability themselves, there has been a pecking order in terms of the way they have been perceived with regard to the relative powerlessness since the social construction of "disability" is such that their capacity to be productive or the absence of such a capacity serves as a structural factor that greatly influences the understanding of disability. Thus, a person who becomes disabled in old age is not as marginalized or stigmatized since they have in the past been productive and contributed to society as opposed to a child with disability who has been disabled from the very beginning and is therefore seen as someone lacking the potential to contribute in future leading to greater powerlessness and marginalization (Chakravarti, 2008).

This chapter is an attempt to understand leveraging of power in the context of a dominant individual model that stigmatizes, excludes and devalues the respect and dignity of individuals with disability, thus rendering them powerless. Based on anecdotal and experiential narratives, the authors put forth their propositions to help understand the perpetuation of the power dynamic that limits disabled individuals. The arguments proposed in this discourse reflect an etic perspective and not necessarily the first rights holder's perspective. Therefore, these contestations are merely points of view that are stated from an outsider's perspective.

7.3 Power and Disability

In the context of exclusionary practice, the identity of disabled persons being viewed as stigmatized indicates a lack of power in the hands of persons with disability. Power may be understood as the potential ability of one group or person to influence another within a given system (Martin, 1971). It is not an attribute of a person or a group, but rather it is a "relationship" between individuals or groups which pervades all social relationships (Vago, 1989). It is concerned with personal and social relationships where one person or group consistently prevents others (seen as powerless) from achieving their needs and aspirations. Power is strongly linked with the concept of oppression since it divides persons into the categories of "oppressor" and "oppressed". Oppression is characterized by personal and social relationships based on the assumption of inequalities of power with society being divided into those who are powerful and those who are powerless (Dalyrymple and Burke, 1995). Persons or groups who are powerless are characterized by not having any authority, status or a sense of self (Young, 2000). Though power exists both within a person and without, often individuals are rendered powerless by their environment and a larger social system which reinforces and assumes the powerlessness of certain groups of people as is the case with persons with disability.

Persons with disability have, in the past for several generations, had to deal with being in a subordinate position or having to remain invisible most of the time. In order for an individual or group to become empowered, realizing this "power within" is essential. However, more often than not the lack of power is internalized by individuals and therefore perpetuated through their behaviour resulting from internalized oppression. The process of internalized oppression is one through which dominant or powerful groups, in this case persons who are non-disabled, convince subordinate group members (persons with disability) that the current social hierarchies are acceptable and/or cannot be changed (Weber, 2001; Hardiman and Jackson, 1997). Internalized oppression results in subordinate groups not challenging the social order and thereby accepting a definition of self that is hurtful and limiting resulting in behaviour that devalues the group as a whole and themselves as members of that group (Hardiman and Jackson, 1997).

In the context of persons with disability, ableism and internalized ableism are related concepts that have a deeper relevance. Ableism is associated with the production of ableness and the perfectible body resulting in any other kind of body having any type of impairment being viewed as negative and undesirable which should, if possible, be ameliorated, cured or eliminated (Campbell, 2008). It tends to induce internalized ableism or disabled self-hatred, which is manifested through the two-pronged strategy of the person with disability distancing himself/herself from other disabled persons and the emulation by disabled people of ableist norms (Campbell, 2008). So, for example, when persons with disability devalue or doubt their own competence or the competence of other persons with disability as compared to non-disabled persons, internalized ableism/internalized oppression is demonstrated. Vijay[1] is an example of a young man who is very severely hearing-impaired, with severe hearing loss in both ears such that he uses hearing aids for both ears. He was diagnosed early, and intervention was done when he was very little such that he became proficient at using whatever residual hearing he had with the help of hearing aids. He was integrated into the mainstream from a young

[1]All names mentioned in the manuscript have been disguised to protect confidentiality.

age with his family providing him with a lot of encouragement and support to become as "normal" as possible. Today, he has a postgraduate degree and a career and has integrated well with the hearing world. He does not like to acknowledge his impairment and is unwilling to engage with others who are hearing-impaired or disabled in other ways most of the time. Though he is able to speak more than one language, he is unwilling to learn "sign language" since he does not wish to be seen as a hearing-impaired person nor is he keen to interact with the hearing-impaired particularly those who are not part of the "oral deaf" community. He is unwilling to consider "deafness" as a part of his identity. It is quite apparent from Vijay's case that he has internalized ableist norms, in that he is concerned about bodily perfection as well as with distancing himself from the deaf community and the larger disabled community. In doing so, he negates an aspect of himself that also gives him an identity. By cutting off this identity, he negates having impairment and this can come in the way of his accepting this part of himself. When there is a lack of total acceptance of the impairment and a struggle towards ableism, the tug of war between two conflicting identities can be energy-consuming and makes a person feel like being in a liminal state of being and existing.

7.4 Agency and Leveraging Personal Power

The gradual development of the understanding that disability is "socially constructed" has been an important step in the direction of realizing personal power for persons with disability. The way a person interprets his/her impairment influences the way he/she deals with it subsequently. This is also related to issues of identity, acceptance and using an individual's agency in a manner that promotes and optimizes growth of the self. When a person recognizes and uses opportunities to grow, he/she in turn creates space and opportunities for others to realize their potential too. For example, Chitra has a sensory impairment and is totally blind. She recognizes her limitation, has learnt to manoeuvre her way through mobility training, has learnt to accept her limitation and has constructed her reality. Her reality includes recognizing her strengths, skills and talents as well as her limitations in a manner that has encouraged her to become strong enough to overcome societal restrictions/barriers, deal with quizzical behaviours of her non-disabled peers, and make others comfortable with her impairment.

Some of the strategies which Chitra has used to make others comfortable with her impairment are to use the words "see", "look" and "I turn a blind eye to others who tease me". She uses politically incorrect language that portrays her disability in a casual manner; she senses that people who she meets for the first time are uncomfortable referring to or asking about her impairment, while at the same time, they are in awe of her ease in functioning. She initiates casual conversations about her impairment and explains it to them in such a simple and lucid manner that it immediately makes them comfortable with her and her impairment; on seeing the comfort that her family and close friends share with her, they see potential to emulate them and have a "referent" power that gives them an edge over others who are seemingly ignorant and perplexed. These behaviours have forced her family and others to interact with her as they would with any other non-disabled person, and these experiences have enabled her to consolidate her self-image and self-concept which puts her on par with non-disabled peers.

When Chitra normalizes life for herself and others, she is able to exert an influence on not only others, but it gives her an opportunity to be in charge of her situations and interactions with people. Armed with this self-acceptance and positive self-concept, she is able to help not only herself but others to realize their potential and contribute meaningfully in their lives and their work. On interacting with Chitra, her non-disabled and disabled peers have been able to not only accept impairments, but also learnt to optimize their own capacities and resources so that they accomplish what they wish to. Further, the non-disabled peers have learnt to support other people with disability with ease and comfort, drawing inspiration from her. She has been able to use her personal power to co-create meaning for herself and others, thus establishing her position as well as facilitating others to establish theirs. This is indicative of using personal power to enable her to stake her claim in society. In such a leveraging of power, the individual is able to use his or her agency to their own advantage as well as that of the society at large. This has been at the core of the disability rights movement in various parts of the world, where the power from within has been catalyzed to activate the power from outside and thus advocate for rights and inclusion. When the person uses the power from within, not only he/she has the potential to transform self and the environment/context, but also he/she has the power to attain inclusion and commit to action.

7.5 Leveraging Impairment

Although it is true that the environment has restricted persons with disability to access and use their power, both within and without, there are other ramifications to such a situation. These include traces of other patterns of use, or lack of use of power that interplays with this environmental limitation that influences functioning and agency. For example, Rudy, a person with locomotor impairment who uses crutches, faced difficulties in accessing both his house and his previous workplace that did not have any suitable accommodation. He therefore had to change jobs and found work in a moderately accessible multinational company. While the physical environment at work had some limitations, he attributed home-related limitations also to the current workplace. Therefore, he refused to take on responsibilities that were a part of his job, including being punctual at work, on the ground of having an inaccessible work environment. He was able to recognize the reasons for his late coming and pointed these out to friends outside work, on a couple of occasions. He described that while his workplace was reasonably convenient to work in, he had difficulty moving around his house and getting ready on time to leave for work.

This was despite the fact that the company provided him with a transport facility. However, when his boss raised the issue of lack of performance and accountability, he was unwilling to distinguish between the two environments and continued to attribute home-related limitations to his workplace. Moreover, he was not open to feedback and learning from these lapses.

Persons with disability have, in the past, had to deal with being in subordinate positions or being rendered invisible and forced to remain so (Buckingham, 2011; Young, 2000). Due to this constant subordination, persons with disability have been forced to and have also learnt to use their image of a "powerless" and "helpless" person as a tool to gain power and to have influence. This is done by using their impairment to draw attention to themselves or to gain sympathy and influence people around them. Such behaviour may be viewed as a cover to camouflage the unwillingness of the person to take on tasks that pertain to the next higher level of functioning that one is aiming for, as this involves a risk of success or failure. For example, in the case of Rudy, he was unwilling to take on responsibilities such as writing reports or travelling to the field in the company car, when he did not wish to. Instead, he continuously pointed out to colleagues how he was being exploited by the company, was not given tasks commensurate with his qualifications and was not oriented appropriately about his work and roles by seniors and colleagues when he joined work a year ago. This had led to poor and inadequate performance of roles and tasks on his part, resulting in difficulties for himself and the company. As Rudy continued with this behaviour, he became more and more isolated from his colleagues at the workplace, as they could not deal with his constant complaining and negative energy and could not rely on him to complete and contribute to work-related tasks. Consequently, he also lost an opportunity to build on his competencies and strengths.

Risks for success are often attempted when an individual is quite confident of learning lessons and thus benefitting through the risk taking. The willingness to make such an attempt stems from a personal power of "knowing" what one is going to risk or what one is unsure of. In instances where there is leveraging of the impairment to gain power, the person with disability often "gives up all too quickly" citing his/her disability as the reason for not being able to accomplish the task. This kind of a dynamic may be observed among various types of vulnerable groups including children who also use their understanding of being "young" and "vulnerable" and incapable of understanding complex notions to manipulate adults around them to get a toy they want or other little concessions. Such tactics give the person with disability agency for that moment, as was with Rudy. However, in the larger context, such behaviour, especially when repeated frequently, tends to limit his/her access to realizing capabilities and opportunities for growth in the long term. Such behaviour runs contrary to the notion that persons with disability have abilities that are underutilized and neglected. Moreover, it emphasizes the person's impairment, recognized in the past as a "deficit" and loss, as if it needs to be compensated for. Therefore, the person with impairment tends to prefer concessions and "adjustments" by others, to deal with the situation that he/she is in.

Another scenario is when a person with disability does not accept his or her impairment and this limits his or her performance in all spheres of life. For example, Ankita is a person with a hearing impairment. From early on, she received messages that to be disabled is to be “less” than others, since in society disability may be tolerated but is mostly considered as inherently negative (Campbell, 2008). She has had to find her way in a hearing world and has faced quite a few difficulties while growing up. She had to hone her competencies to be accepted in the hearing world. She struggled hard for this acceptance; she pushed her boundaries, making tremendous progress and accomplishments. In the process, she internalized the ableist perspective and did her best to overlook her impairment by refusing to acknowledge or accept her impairment. She was able to achieve and succeed in her chosen profession and most other spheres of life, but due to overlooking her impairment, she faced a lack of inclusion with others. In some ways, it resulted in almost cutting off one aspect of the self. Subsequently, when she actually encountered limitations due to her impairment, she was faced with an onslaught of emotions associated with lack of acceptance. The lack of acceptance as a learnt behaviour prevented her from coping healthily with the impairment. She is unable to cope with the impairment and easily resorts to what she knows best, that is, use the very impairment to gain attention from others, or leverage it to offset the risk of failure or lack of accomplishment. Such behaviour is viewed as manipulation by others, as she underutilizes her potential and competency and thus hinders healthy interpersonal relationships, which reinforces and perpetuates the “deficit” model. The root of this acceptance of disability, claiming and owning one’s personal power (and thus offering others a chance to claim theirs) remains unaddressed and hence compounds the issue. This influences Ankita’s agency to perform and succeed in a similar manner as Chitra does. Ankita’s propensity to ignore her agency makes her devoid of power both from within and from outside, thus imposing restrictions in her life and maintaining the “disadvantaged” status.

When there is insight about acceptance or non-acceptance of the impairment, the individual will work towards overcoming this barrier. Insight is often gained through life experiences and through feedback from significant others, not necessarily the family. Often, significant others hesitate to give this feedback for the fear of hurting the person with disability or demoralizing him/her. However, this leads to negative consequences for the person, both in the short term and in the long term, as this action unwittingly restricts opportunities for growth and acceptance of the impairment. When this situation is commonly prevalent, as it is for any human being, for a person with disability it has far-reaching consequences that deprive him/her of agency and personal power. During such times, the person legitimizes the power of the impairment. In Ankita’s case too, this was quite apparent since like many other women with disability, Ankita too was brought up in an environment with a lot of expectations as well as overprotection, first from her family and later on in the professional sphere. She had a mentor who tended to treat her in the same way and as a part of this same behaviour tended to underestimate and underplay her capacities. This resulted in Ankita spending a very large part of her life in an overprotected environment within her family as well as in the professional sphere.

As a part of the overprotection in the professional sphere, she was often not given responsibilities or leadership opportunities, resulting in her confidence being undermined. However, with changes in environments and situations, attitudes and behaviours can also change, as happened in the case of Ankita. At one point, she got an opportunity to work in a new office and new environment, among unfamiliar people, in an unfamiliar place, without her mentor. Here, she had no choice but to be independent with regard to decision making and she was also exposed to peers who had disabilities but were independent with regard to making their life choices. When she interacted with them, she was able to identify and relate to them as persons with disability, and this enabled her to enquire into her own disability and related behaviour. Thus, she gained a new perspective and the ability to realize the "power within". In the process of accepting her impairment, she was able to convert a problem into an opportunity or possibility, thus expanding her options of choices and actions. This enabled her to push herself beyond the known territory, explore unknown pastures and experience the freedom of growth and potential, thus giving her power over herself and her situation.

Realizing the "power within" also assists individuals to exercise power outside and use their agency to benefit the larger community of disabled people or others, who may be vulnerable or in a disempowered position by virtue of their gender, age, experience, caste, class, etc. This was seen in the case of Chitra, who worked in the disability sector with sensitivity and inspiration, such that she changed the trajectory of others who were also disabled. She enrolled disabled people and women who were violated and abused, who had given up on their lives and who helped them to be transformed into people with meaningful accomplishments through her actions and by being who she was.

Self-advocacy is one such mode through which power has been exercised by persons with disability to advocate for themselves and for others like them through the development of "common spaces", which in turn promotes self-determination wherein people with disability feel empowered to take their own decisions as a group and as individuals (Scotch, 2009). Self-advocacy entails that persons with disability develop an understanding of their rights and responsibilities and assess their abilities and interests as well as their strengths and weaknesses. It also requires that persons with disability become aware of the options and opportunities that are available to them and connect themselves with others in order to accomplish their goals (Douglas, 2004). It therefore allows for positive partnering between persons with disability so that they may individually and collectively exercise the "power within" and utilize each other's agency and "voice" to grow. This is what happened in the case of Chitra as well as Ankita, who after a change in their environments were able to thereafter advocate for themselves, express their own needs openly to others around them wherever they faced genuine limitations, and were able to take independent decisions as well as risks and leadership roles and carry them with ease.

7.6 Partnering for Power and Leverage

At times people who have experienced vulnerability tend to garner support and expect collusion from those who have or are presumed to have been in similar situations or contexts. For example, Rudy had a co-worker with hearing impairment. The co-worker did not face similar limitations in the work environment as Rudy did. However, Rudy looked up to him for support with regard to his stated difficulties related to access in the workplace. Though the co-worker was unsure about Rudy's contestation (as stated earlier), he felt obliged to support a person due to his disabled identity, rather than looking objectively at the issue at hand (inaccessible workplace that Rudy alleged). The co-worker had mixed feelings about wanting to support Rudy since he felt that Rudy might be taking advantage of the situation. There are situations when one feels camaraderie with fellows in a similar state and thus lobbies for garnering and sharing of sentiments that are commonly experienced as a person with disability. This leads to coming together as allies, for reasons which are not growth-promoting but on the contrary that are growth-limiting and spirit-defeating. Such camaraderie is unhealthy as it pits one against the other. This further splits the divide between the disabled and the non-disabled, as it happened in the case of colleagues and co-workers at Rudy's office, wherein there was a divisive opinion about what accommodation was actually required. Rudy quit his job within a year of joining. On Rudy's departure, his co-worker felt let down as he (Rudy) did not complete what he had initiated as fair policies for persons with disability. He continued to experience discomfort and perceived further exclusion in the office. While such negative experiences are located within the objective reality of exclusion and marginalization, interpreting and transcending them allow a person with disability to take responsibility for inclusion, like Chitra did. Attempts may be made by the individual to get others as allies, to partner with them based on powerlessness of having impairments. In so doing, he/she gains power in the situation by claiming commonality of identity and experiences, because only such people would be able to understand difficulties or challenges that people with impairments face. While making this proposition, the authors are painfully aware of the structural factors of stigmatization that are commonly seen in society towards any marginalized group, especially persons with disability.

The impairment may be leveraged as a threat against others to get them to comply or tolerate their "undesirable" behaviour, one of which is perceived powerlessness. Compatriots then rally around this concept to view the person as a "victim", who is perforce provoked to retaliate against rude behaviour of their non-disabled counterparts and hence such an undesirable behaviour. For example, Hiral, a person with learning disability, uses her impairment to avoid responsibilities given to her at the students' union in college. Hence, gradually the union members allocate work only when she indicates interest. During the annual college festival, she complains to the principal of the college that she is excluded and not given tasks because of her impairment. She garners support from the enabling cell of her college. This behaviour is the result of provocation rather than a desire to manipulate or gain attention, which is totally unrelated to the impairment.

On analysing this further, it may be noticed that the "undesirable" behaviour stems largely from discomfort with oneself (in this case, it resulted from the fact that she did not use her entitlement for concessions, therefore scored poor grades and experienced ridicule in her family) and particularly the non-acceptance of the impairment and internalized ableism, which drives the individual to project in order to protect. Hiral has good interpersonal skills otherwise, but her lack of acceptance of her impairment provoked her to blame others for her consistent non-performance in the students' union activities. She complained to the principal that the members of the students' union ridiculed her about her impairment. Therefore, she projected her own perceptions about her impairment onto others, thus protecting herself from consequences of what she faced in her family with regard to grades, thereby establishing her role as a "victim".

Recognizing one's limitations permits one to operate and function within the framework of one's strengths and capabilities. When an individual is unmindful of his/her limitations and does not accomplish what he/she has set out to do, there is a tendency to blame external factors for the non-performance—hence using the impairment to justify non-performance, as it is far more formidable to face risks. This is also a source of relinquishing personal power and misusing the impairment to condone non-performance. It is done partly because the individual has not learnt to accept or cope with the impairment and relative comparisons only offset the impairment. By comparing her grades with others, Hiral has overlooked the fact that she had not used her entitlements rightfully so as to score better. This would have been done, had she accepted her impairment. In doing so, she further perpetuates the "helplessness" myth. This serves to create an impression that he/she is being marginalized by being given undue and excessive work/burden, which is not commensurate with the impairment and hence the non-performance—as was also seen in Rudy's case. It may be considered as another instance of leveraging disability to claim helplessness and powerlessness in order to condone non-performance.

Some other instances of the linkages between partnering and power were obtained from experiences of an NGO worker and former caregiver. Aniket has worked with persons having various types of impairments. He indicated that in his experience on some occasions, he had found that the person with disability he was working with exaggerated the extent of his/her impairment to seek attention and also to obtain help. Though such behaviour had helped this individual to gain access to resources and assistance where required in the past, he had tended to seek assistance for things that he could or should be able to accomplish on his own or with minimal assistance. This devalues his power from within. The constant seeking of help from various individuals to accomplish any and all tasks had become a survival mechanism which had a range of negative consequences. One such consequence of constantly seeking assistance from others led to the formation of mostly need-based relationships. Since all tasks were accomplished with assistance from others, this person with disability did not gain competence to accomplish tasks independently. The need-based relationships also had negative repercussions in that it tended to isolate this person with disability as only a few long-term social networks were being formed. These factors together reduced the disabled individual's ability to realize the power "within".

There are multiple ways to leverage impairment as is seen above. One such modus operandi is to seek the attention of people in power and authority, to draw attention to the impairment, so that it serves as a reason to apply pressure on peers to succumb. Therefore, this perpetuates the misuse of personal power. When one does so, he/she does not utilize his or her inherent power. The person with disability constantly seeks support and succour from the outside and fails to tap his or her inner resources that are readily available, but often underutilized. Often society's construction of impairment as that which needs to be "taken care of" or "allowed for" or "excused" also tends to perpetuate the "helplessness" myth and the relinquishment of personal power. This was seen in Rudy's case, where he wanted his workplace to provide him with all the facilities besides the accommodations that were provided as per his requirements, but he chose to continue to complain and not perform.

While hierarchies exist between disabled and non-disabled groups, these structures are also seen among the diverse types of persons with disability as well. The more severe the disability, the more powerlessness is perceived by that group of persons. This is particularly true in case of groups of persons who cannot fully articulate their thoughts in a manner understood by others, such as those with cerebral palsy or autism or those who have difficulty in comprehension of complex concepts as may be the case with those with intellectual impairments. In such cases, they may require others to speak for them. For example, Ankita shared her experiences about behaviours of people at a meeting of diverse types of persons with disability to discuss a common agenda related to framing a plan of action for themselves. She remarked that one group of people with one type of disability were boisterous and vociferous and did not allow others a chance to participate in the meeting. The groups of people with other two types of disability felt they were being marginalized due to their difficulties in articulating their thoughts, such as persons who were not oral and were aural deaf. The dominant paradigm continues to reign in the case of cross-disability groups. The seemingly more forceful and domineering groups tend to overshadow their disenfranchised counterparts.

While leveraging disability tends to give an individual a momentary sense of power and control, in the long run, it does not promote the abilities of the person to cope with his or her impairment. This leads to unhealthy and perhaps dysfunctional ways of living and relating that tend to limit the person. On the contrary, if the individual is able to, and is taught to accept the impairment and yet push boundaries, raising the bar for himself/herself, thus raising others' expectations and respect, he/she accomplishes and leads a fulfilling life.

7.7 Co-creating Power

In order to promote effective use of power and agency, the authors recommend the leveraging of skills, abilities and talents while accepting one's impairment. The projection of one's strengths not only enhances oneself, but also provides for opportunities of empowerment of the person with disability. There have been success stories where "enabling niches" (Rapp and Goscha, 2006) have served as empowering experiences for success and accomplishments. The environmental context, which includes the family, school and workplace contexts, should serve as enabling niches that enhance and promote personal power. A healthy fit between the person with the impairment, his/her abilities and the environment will ensure that the boundaries are stretched in order to accomplish. For example, Shakuntala is a person suffering from severe mental illness and mild intellectual impairment and is currently in the phase of recovery. She was symptom-free when we met her. She had a graduate education and was extremely creative in arts and crafts. She crochets, paints, sketches and embroiders, besides writing limericks and poetry in her mother tongue. Initially, she was on a high dose of antipsychotics, which came in the way of pursuing her creative passion in arts and crafts. When she was able to recognize the consequences or effects of her dosage, she negotiated with her treating physician to decrease the dosage. In turn, she promised to keep her symptoms at bay through self-management. One of the strategies she used for this was to control her voices by engaging them in her painting or craftwork. As a result, she was able to deflect the disturbances of her symptoms into meaningful activity. While the treating doctor agreed to decrease her dosage reluctantly, her family stood by her and provided her with not only the required resources, but also the necessary supervision and support to see her through her tough phases. On bad days, she was able to recognize it and she informed her family and friends about it. When they were forewarned, they contributed to her recovery by not disturbing her and letting her "be". During such times, Shakuntala felt that she was able to use whatever power and potential she had in a positive manner. She enabled herself, along with her support systems, to preserve her power, realize her strengths and draw succour from them to promote personal power. She felt that she had "control" over symptoms. This way, both Shakuntala and her family, friends and the treating doctor aided her recovery through the process of co-creating opportunities for her to realize her potential. She went on to conduct exhibitions and sell her products at competitive prices that added to her self-esteem and self-concept.

Efforts to encourage personal power enhance the agency of the individual to succeed and accomplish. Together, these help in empowering the individual at various levels including at a personal level which implies the individual's sense of power and control over their life and destiny as well as their self-efficacy. At an interpersonal level, empowerment is reflected in the ability of the disabled individual to influence others, and at a larger political level, empowerment entails bringing about social change and social action to further the efforts of the disability rights movement in terms of transferring power across groups (Dempsey and Foreman, 1997). Through her efforts, Chitra was able to get her peers and friends to participate in all activities, campaigns, fund-raising shows and other such events, for the organization she worked with. Further, she was instrumental in initiating self-help groups for persons with disability keeping in mind gender concerns of women and men with disability. This enabled her to create awareness among stakeholder groups in a traditional and patriarchal society towards gender-specific needs, respect for equality and dignity of both men and women with disability. In another instance, Chitra had initiated a campaign for ensuring access to all public spaces and all kinds of public transport, by initiating policy-level changes in the local administration. These efforts resulted in making visible what was hitherto not noticed by or was invisible to the general public and local governance systems.

In order to empower agency, one needs to look at leveraging abilities rather than impairments and encourage better fit between persons–abilities–context to maximize agency and highlight strengths. This is what Chitra and Shakuntala have accomplished by optimizing their strengths, educating or teaching other non-disabled peers in order to lead their lives in a productive and respectful manner. This inspired others to join hands and partner with them for the cause of disability. This will be beneficial to individuals with impairment both in the long and the short run in addition to further facilitating changes in the balance of power between persons with disability and the non-disabled.

7.8 Conclusion

Primarily, there is a need to create positive and long-term relationships which facilitate empowerment of the persons with disability, in the long run rather than focussing on short-term survival mechanisms. Instead, the emphasis should be on strengthening the "power within", so that individuals have opportunities to realize the power within. This will facilitate relationships based on trust rather than survival. Partnerships should be positive and empowering with sustainable results rather than quick-fix solutions. This facilitates the prospects of leveraging strengths and capacities to influence agency, rather than leveraging the impairment, which is a weak substitute. When a person with disability leverages enabling niches to co-create meaning and power, the individual not only operates from the depths of wisdom, but also uses leverage points appropriately to facilitate inclusion of self and others, in the true sense of its meaning. Focusing on abilities allows for a paradigm shift in the disability sector, thus encouraging the utilization of agency existing in each individual (disabled or non-disabled) towards growth and transformation.

References

Bhambhani, M. (1999). The burden of women with disabilities. *Actionaid Disability News, 10*(1&2), 22–24.

Buckingham, J. (2011). Writing histories of disability in India: Strategies of inclusion. *Disability & Society, 26*(4), 419–431.

Campbell, F. K. (2008). Exploring internalized ableism using critical race theory. *Disability & Society, 23*(2), 151–162.

Chakravarti, U. (2008). Burden of caring: Families of the disabled in urban India. *Indian Journal of Gender Studies, 15*(2), 341–363.

Dalyrymple, J., & Burke, B. (1995). *Anti-oppressive practice: Social care and the law*. Buckingham and Philadelphia: Open University Press.

Dempsey, I., & Foreman, P. (1997). Toward a clarification of empowerment as an outcome of disability service provision. *International Journal of Disability, Development and Education, 44*(4), 287–303.

Douglas, D. (2004). Self-advocacy: Encouraging students to become partners in differentiation. *Roeper Review, 26*(4), 223–228.

Elwan, A. (1999). *Poverty and disability*. A Background Paper for the World Development Report, Banque Mondiale, Washington.

Fearon, J. D. (1999). What is identity (as we now use the word)? Retrieved from http://www.stanford.edu/~jfearon/papers/iden1v2.pdf on September 17, 2012.

Fine, M., & Asch, A. (1988). Disability beyond stigma: Social interaction, discrimination, and activism. *Journal of Social Issues, 44*, 3–22.

Goffman, E. (1963). *Stigma: Notes on the management of spoiled identity*. Englewood Cliffs, NJ: Prentice Hall.

Hardiman, R., & Jackson, B. W. (1997). Conceptual foundations for social justice courses. In M. Adams, L. A. Bell, & P. Griffin (Eds.), *Teaching for diversity and social justice*. New York: Routledge.

Martin, R. (1971). The concept of power: A critical defence. *The British Journal of Sociology, 22*(3), 240–256.

Rapp, C. A., & Goscha, R. J. (2006). *The strengths model: Case management with people with psychiatric disabilities* (2nd ed.). Oxford: Oxford University Press.

Reid-Cunningham, A. R., & Fleming, V. C. (2009). Theories of disability: Findings from an analysis of textbooks on human behavior and the social environment. *Journal of Human Behavior in the Social Environment, 19*(1), 10–25. Retrieved September 5, 2011, from Taylor and Francis online database.

Scotch, R. K. (2009). "Nothing About Us Without Us": Disability rights in America. *OAH Magazine of History, 23*(3), 17–22.

Smith, S. R. (2008). Social justice and disability: Competing interpretations of the medical and social models. In *Arguing about disability*. Routledge.

Vago, S. (1989). *Social change*. Englewood Cliffs, NJ: Prentice Hall.

Weber, L. (2001). *Understanding race, class, gender and sexuality: A conceptual framework*. New York: McGraw-Hill Higher Education.

Young, I. M. (2000). Five faces of oppression. In M. Adams, W. J. Blumenfeld, R. Castaneda, H. W. Hackman, M. L. Peters, & X. Zuniga (Eds.), *Readings for diversity and social justice: An anthology on racism, antisemitism, sexism, heterosexism, ableism and classism* (pp. 31–35). New York: Routledge.

Chapter 8
Negotiating Femininity: Lived Experiences of Women with Locomotor Disabilities in Bengal

Nandini Ghosh

Abstract This paper explores the lived experiences of women with locomotor impairments in the cultural context of Bengal in India and elaborates the ways in which women with disabilities construct their selves, negotiate their identities and live their lives in adherence with, redefining or subverting the accepted ideas of femininity and ability. An embodiment that is shaped by an impaired female body coupled with the sociocultural valuation of a disabled person as well as of the different social roles a woman plays greatly influences the way in which disabled femininity is constructed, nurtured and contested. This paper illuminates and illustrates the ways in which disabled women strive towards normative femininity, despite facing negation and denial of the sexuality in the form of suppression within the household to stigmatizing encounters in the public sphere. Disabled women also redefine, the ideal of a *bhalo meye* in the different domains of their daily lives, whether in the private realms of their homes and personal processes or in the public sphere.

Keywords Gender · Disabled women · Lived experiences · Body · Femininity

8.1 Introduction

Both feminist scholars and disability theorists have stressed the importance of the body, female or disabled, in the construction of identity. The process of embodiment is fundamental to the construction of identity, whereby individuals come to be socially constructed through the meanings connected to particular bodily characteristics and the practices in which these bodies are involved. The possession of a body with specific features within society becomes critical for everyday recognition and identification of persons as well as for interpreting individuals' interactions with their bodies and through their bodies with the world around them

N. Ghosh (✉)
Institute of Development Studies Kolkata, Kolkata, West Bengal, India
e-mail: nandinighosh@gmail.com

N. Ghosh (ed.), *Interrogating Disability in India*,
Dynamics of Asian Development, DOI 10.1007/978-81-322-3595-8_8

(Davis, 1997). Differences between bodies become important for understanding embodiment as the possession of particular bodies, inscribed by markers like gender or impairment, results in socialization into and internalization of cultural constructions and ideologies governing it, which profoundly influence construction and performance of the self through the medium of gendered or disabled bodies. The gendered/impaired body is constructed through social practices and cultural interpretations inscribed on physically different bodies located within and thus defined, understood and shaped by social and historical contexts.

This paper explores the lived experiences of women with locomotor impairments in the cultural context of Bengal in India and elaborates the ways in which women with disabilities construct their selves, negotiate their identities and live their lives in adherence with, redefining or subverting the accepted ideas of femininity and ability. This qualitative ethnographic study has been conducted in West Bengal, where a form of benign patriarchy operates, with the status of women as mother being the most predominant in gendered constructions. In Bengal, with its stress on motherhood as the only goal for women, the domestic arena is recognized as the most suitable for girls. Socialization processes and socializing institutions that turn women into gendered subjects interact and draw upon historical, religious, political and economic structures and ideologies to shape the lives of women in the socio-cultural context of Bengal.

8.2 Constructing the Disabled Woman in Bengal

According to Bagchi (1995), Indian womanhood is based on a multi-layered accretion of myths that serves patriarchy in both its global and local manifestations. In India, over the last three centuries, there has been a complex process of construction of gender through cultural symbols, social ideologies and invoking of the so-called indigenous belief systems. The Indian Nationalist movement redefined Indian womanhood in order to argue for the superiority of Indian culture over that of the West and to establish its claim for sovereignty (Bagchi, 1990; Tharu and Lalitha, 1991; Chatterjee, 1993). In order to project the superiority of the Indian identity over the colonial masters, nationalist leaders separated the domain of culture into 2 spheres, the material and the spiritual, which corresponded to an ideologically more powerful dichotomy between the inner and outer. The inner/outer distinction separated social space into the *ghar* and *bahir*, the home and the world. The *bahir* was seen as the domain of the male, of practical considerations and dominated by the profane activities of the material world, while the home was posited as the representation of one's true identity, one's spiritual self, and women became the representation of this inner/spiritual domain. This ideological distinction between the public/private, the *bahir/ghar* and the material/spiritual led to the identification of social roles by gender and spheres of operation of men and women in Bengali society (Chatterjee, 1993). The strict segregation of private feminine spaces from the public, male areas led to the formulation of two completely different worlds of physical experience and quality of life, governed by varying norms and expectations which affected the relationships between the sexes and created distinct spheres of functions and influence. From this period of early nationalism and high imperialism first emerged the figure of the chaste upper-caste, upper- and middle-class Hindu woman, who in her role initially as wife, and later as mother, became the supreme emblem of a consolidated Hindu nationalist selfhood (Mazumdar, 1994; Mookerjea-Leonard, 2005).

For women in Bengal, all relationships centre around the men in their families—their fathers, brothers and later their husbands and sons. The emphasis on a woman's behaviour is in relationship to men, wife/husband, mother/son, daughter/father and sister/brother (Wadley, 1999). The phase of wife and mother were the two most important phases in the life of any woman (Chakraborty, 1998; Bannerji, 2002). Motherhood was seen as the ultimate identity for Bengali women and was an excellent ploy to keep the women out of privileges like education and glorifying womanhood only through her reproductive powers. Women's lives can be divided into 3 phases: one before her marriage spent at her *baper bari* as daughter, and the other after, at her *sasur bari* as wife and mother. In Bengal, there are 2 models for women to follow, one for young unmarried girls and the other for married women who are expected to model their lives on those of their mother or mother-in-law. There are neither aspirations nor models associated with spinsterhood in this society. Bengali girls are trained by female relatives and kinswomen from a very early age to fulfil her future role as a good wife and mother by the family and society at large (Roy, 1972; Bagchi, 1993; Chakraborty, 1998).

Feminine bodily norms are influenced and determined by the way in which an entire society constructs femininity and women. Practices based on cultural ideologies reflect not only the value attached to male members of the family, but also the ways in which female bodies are seen as needing containment, especially at puberty (Dube, 1985). The growing girl is sought to be socialized into restraining her sexuality by enforcing rules of feminine comportment and ideas of decency and modesty (Das, 1989). From a young age, girls learn proper attitudes and modes of behaviour, and the differing social expectations from female bodies and internalize an ideal of the body and physical appearance they needed to attract a good proposal of marriage. In arranged marriages, the examination of the prospective bride includes her physical appearance such as skin colour, hair and facial features and girls are tested on their manners of speech, gait, learning as well as other skills to judge her abilities, physical beauty and to ascertain that she did not have any deformity or disability (Roy, 1972; Engels, 1996).

Feminist theorists have highlighted the fact the bodies that women experience are always mediated by constructions, associations and images which most patriarchal sociocultural formations accept and endorse (Bordo, 1993, 1996). Certain images of gendered/able bodies are put forward as the norm, which are internalized and reinforced by state agencies and social institutions, such as education and medicine, and portray and legitimize certain bodily forms and shapes as more desirable in different sociocultural contexts. Dube (1985) and Bagchi (1995) have argued that gender differences are culturally produced, inscribed and interpreted though social practices. The female body is therefore produced through the cultural practices that shape and manipulate not only the physical body but also the women's lived experiences of their bodies. The acquiring of a socially acceptable body by "normal" women becomes important to the presentation of self, in order to conform to the norms of femininity. As ideal embodied femininity is linked with social acceptability, to have a feminine body—a body socially constructed through the appropriate practices—is most crucial to a woman's sense of herself as a female sexually desiring and desirable subject (Bartky, 1992).

As women have been traditionally identified with their bodies, they are taught from early childhood to be conscious of body shape, size, hair and facial features, which are determined by culturally prescribed appearance norms. Such norms portray defective bodies as inadequate and reinforce the traditional conceptualization of the disabled body as deficient and in need of reconstruction or "improvement" (Begum, 1992; Garland-Thomson, 1994, 2002). The disciplinary practices of physical normalcy, which are learnt early and unconsciously, create a standard of physical normality, as the disciplines of femininity create the ideal woman (Wendell, 1996). Hillyer (1993 cited in Tighe, 2001) feels that all women, including women with disabilities, are evaluated by a body code that requires strict adherence to culturally constructed feminine disciplinary practices. From girlhood, women and disabled women especially, learn to feel uncomfortable with their bodies (Campling, 1983; Rimassa, 1997). Feminine body ideals and standardization of female bodies tend towards the normate—the corporeal incarnation of culture's collective, unmarked, normative characteristics (Garland-Thomson, 2002). Disabled women are just as likely to internalize and be influenced by dominant norms and values about attractiveness and physical appearance as other women, and perceive themselves to be lacking the popular standard of beauty.

8.3 Embodied Experiences: Bengali Women

Disabled girls are socialized into and follow, from a young age, social attitudes, expectations and modes of behaviour considered appropriate for women. As they grow up, girls learn and internalize the ideal of a *bhalo meye* (good girl) in all senses of the term, which is closely related with the notions of the acceptable female body, with associated expectation regarding physical beauty, functional capacities and productive and reproductive roles, which govern the daily lives of all women in Bengal. Bengali gender culture upholds an ideal of the body, physical appearance and functionality that is considered to be desirable in all women, especially if they are to fulfil the role of wife and mother. The concept of *bhalo meye* is used by disabled girls in a dual sense, referring to women with unimpaired "normal" bodies, as well as to women who conform to and actualize the ideal notions that the gender culture attributes to women. Young girls internalize an image of the ideal body and the particular kind of physical beauty, notions of appropriate and acceptable feminine comportment as well as functional capacities that is desirable among women.

This ideal, however, varies from prescribing acceptable range of height, weight, skin tone, arrangement of features and behaviour patterns that determine one's dress, appearance, hair style, etc., which are learnt from the verbal and visual messages projected by other women and the media. Disabled girls, also socialized into such body ideals, however, find it difficult to accommodate the imperatives of their impaired bodies to some of these notions and prescribed behaviour patterns which become increasingly important to all girls as they grow up.

8.3.1 Fashioning a Feminine Identity

The notion of a "*bhalo meye*" or a physically attractive woman dominates the minds of disabled women as someone who is physically unimpaired, and hence a "complete" woman. Socialization into sociocultural ideologies governing lives of women results in internalizing notions of feminine beauty, attractiveness and appropriate feminine behaviour. Patriarchal/ability systems that construct the female norm also specify the visual nature of desirability in women, which for disabled girls, depend not only on the arrangement of their physical features but also on the kind and degree of disability. For disabled girls, socialized into an identity that exhorts them to be like girls, yet relaxes feminine norms based on their impairments, being recognized as women becomes of vital importance. Keeping this in mind, most women set out to fashion a feminine appearance and a feminine self, by adopting typically feminine modes of behaviour and appearance as well as adapting notions of femininity to suit the requirements of their particular impairments. Women come to realize that although they are expected to conform to other "feminine" norms, they are excluded from gendered notions of sexuality. This affects the ways in which disabled girls experience, adapt and deal with culturally valued notions of femininity, desirability and attractiveness. While severely disabled girls accepted that social ideologies exclude them from notions of attractiveness, girls with mild and moderate disabilities found it more difficult to accept and negotiate because of the semblance of "normality" that they had in their lives.

8.3.2 A Feminine Gait

In the course of "appearing" to be a woman, the first concern of women with locomotor disabilities and their families is to fashion a feminine gait. This is more important for girls with mild-to-moderate impairments than for girls with severe disabilities, mainly because participation in daily life activities and reducing the visible impact of the impairment are easier to achieve. Girls undergo surgery, physiotherapy and fitting with mobility aids so that they could walk better, straighter and like other "normal" people. However, the use of post-rehabilitative mobility aids, ranging from wheelchairs and tri-wheelers for the severely disabled to callipers and crutches, depends on a range of situational factors that either help or hinder the continued use of the mobility aid.

One of the primary reasons for rejection of the mobility aid by the women with severe disabilities is because the mobility aids were not suited to the rough and uneven beaten tracks in the villages and because they used to go out of the home only occasionally, either for school or very rarely to relatives outside the village. Mobility aids were experienced as painful and restrictive and girls, who could not use their callipers at home for daily life activities like bathing and toileting or even household work, discontinued its use. At home or in familiar spaces, where acceptance is assured and presentation of the feminine self is not so imperative, girls prefer not to use their mobility aids as it hampers their performance of household work or attending to their daily needs. Asha, who is severely disabled, recalls that within the home and with family it did not matter how she moved around, as everyone knew of her disability. Within the home, Sulekha moves on her hands and feet as she can do things faster and move around with more ease than with her calliper. Women with mild disability like Manju, however, stressed that she always felt more comfortable in her callipers as she realized that she could walk straight wearing it. Without the calliper she has to walk with a hand to her knee, but that used to emphasize her impairment and call attention to her in public spaces. The mobility aid helped Manju to present an image of herself as more "normal" and like all other women. "Without my callipers I would have had to use crutches all my life or walk with a terribly lopsided gait".

Mobility aids are attuned to not only the needs of their disability but also to the notions of femininity internalized through the processes of socialization. Sandhya felt that the metallic aid attached to leather boots diminished her as a woman. Mita recalls that she used to hate the fact "the calliper was very visible especially because I used to wear skirts at that age. Somewhere it clashed with my idea of a feminine self". Sulekha uses her callipers only outside the home as she feels more dignified if she is walking in the public spaces, as she is able to project herself as a "normal" woman better in callipers than while crawling. With newer technology coming in, Sulekha requested the technicians to adapt her mobility aid to feminine codes of dress and notions of beauty so that it now allows her to give full expression to her feminine tastes, rather than the older heavy boots accentuating her impairment. "I am happy that I can wear my calliper inside my *salwar* (loose pants worn with the *kameez*) when I go out such that the calliper is not visible to all. I bought new fashionable *chappals* (sandals) to go with the new callipers. Now I can wear platform heels also if I want with my calliper".

The social valuation of perfect bodies not only accentuates visible differences but coupled with teasing comments and taunts gives rise to feelings of inferiority and devaluation. Girls, who are unable to walk, feel a sense of shame because of the way in which they move, either by crawling or by dragging their hips, which makes them the object of ridicule and pity in public. The performance of a feminine self becomes central as they grow up, especially in public spaces where they encounter the "gaze" more than in familiar surroundings. Girls seek to minimize the visual impact of their physical impairment by adopting gaits that seem "normal" in order to gain greater acceptance. Although Sandhya moves by crawling within the home, she uses a tri-wheeler when she goes out. "People realise I am disabled but they never can make out the extent of my disability when I drive my tri-wheeler down the road. To them, I am a woman, dressed well and that is the image I like to project. It is only when I start crawling that the admiring looks turn to one of pity". Jahanara has taught herself to walk slowly and wear *saree*s, which conceal her disability effectively.

8.3.3 Presenting a Feminine Self

The chief emphasis of the training of girls for womanhood is on modesty, which is linked with femininity (Cormack, 1953). The concept of lajja or shame governs and underlies all references to civilized or proper behaviour appropriate to girls and women, which deals with the realms of morals and manners (Bannerji, 1994). Disabled girls are subjected to the same processes of socialization as their sisters and other women and have learnt, accepted and internalized notions of modesty, shame, morality and prescribed norms of behaviour for girls as they step into puberty. Like all other girls in the family and neighbourhood, they, too, are subject to rules of seclusion and avoidance, more so as they pass from childhood to adolescence. Women with mild-to-moderate disabilities are more likely to adhere to acceptable feminine modes of dressing, as it is one way of asserting their femininity. However, the degree of disability determines the choice of clothes to a great extent and girls, who had been wearing skirts and blouses, continue to do so, citing convenience of movement in such clothes. Asha prefers to wear skirt-blouses or a nightgown, as they are easy to manage while crawling. "Ma cuts them short for me, so that I am well covered and yet when I crawl, the dress doesn't get very dirty nor is there too much cloth to encumber my movements". Notions of modesty are tailored to the needs of their impaired bodies and different gaits, and girls who crawl prefer blouses and skirts, which can be hitched up and notched carefully at the thighs so that modesty is preserved and yet movement is easy. The adoption of adolescent modes of dressing is suggestive of an arrested womanhood and a modified code of decency that grants use of such clothes for convenience. Such modes of dressing are then justified citing ease, expediency and a dogged resignation regarding their condition. Sandhya prefers to wear skirts and blouses rather than nightgowns and salwar kameezes, which tear easily because of the way in which she moves and restrict her movements. "Going to the toilets, I hitch up my clothes to knee level. Sometimes it is embarrassing in front of other people but what to do? As a girl, I have my modesty and I try to preserve it as best as I can".

Notions of feminine beauty impel many of the disabled women to adhere to feminine dress and make-up codes, especially because they too "want to be identified as a woman. I like to wear womanly clothes and I want to be known as a woman rather than anything else". Chobi likes wearing bindis and earrings. "Sometimes when I feel very dressy, I wear necklaces also. I wear long gowns at home in summer and salwar kameezes in winter. I like wearing such feminine attire like frocks and gowns". Other markers of a feminine self like having long hair, wearing jewellery and using make-up are accepted and employed to "look like a woman" and thus be accepted as one. "Now that I have grown my hair and am wearing long earrings and bindis, suddenly everyone has realized that I am a girl. My friends tell me that now I am looking like a girl and give me advice on make-up. I like the fact that my colleagues are identifying me as a girl".

However, notions of femininity are revised depending on the nature of their impairments. Agatha rarely wears *sarees* as she finds it difficult to manage it with her callipers and crutches. "Someone has to help me to wear a saree as I cannot do it myself, standing with my crutches. So I have given up on *sarees* now. During college days, I wore *sarees* for the farewell and welcome parties, as everyone else was also wearing and I wanted to be like them". Asha, who wears skirts would like to wear *sarees* but accepts that they would get dirty while crawling. "It is very difficult to crawl around in a sari, especially outside the house as so much of cloth hampers one's movements". Mita, who wears *sarees* regularly at work and whenever she goes out, feels comfortable in a saree as it makes her feel "feminine". "I love to wear *sarees*, which I wear always outside the house. For me, it is a very feminine way of dressing". For her, wearing the saree every day became the symbol of reaffirmation of herself as a woman, and as it covered her calliper, very few people could discern that she was disabled.

Girls with severe disabilities usually downplay their femininity by dressing conservatively, so as not to call any more attention on themselves that they already are subjected to, because of their impairments. Asha scorns at dressing in fine clothes and putting on make-up and states that she never liked doing so from her childhood. "It is not because I am like this—disabled. I don't like showing off to the world. I like dressing simply with just earrings and maybe a *bindi*. Sometimes when I put on many things and look in the mirror I feel that I am too dressed up. Dressing up is not for me". Sandhya reiterated the same sentiment when she asserted that she does not like "*saj goj*" (dressing up). "Girls like us have no right to dress up". These feelings are further strengthened through the encounters in the public domain. Manju recalls that when she was in college, if she dressed up and went out, boys would invariably taunt her, "'She can't walk properly yet see how she dresses up.' So I also started feeling that I shouldn't dress up or put on makeup to make myself pretty. I refused to wear *sarees*, although other girls would be wearing them". Disabled women, considered to be unfeminine and unattractive, are relegated to the sidelines of femininity and hence made to feel that they need not attempt to beautify themselves. Krishna, who travels regularly by bus, often has to hear derogatory comments about being "overdressed". "One day, in a crowded bus, when I got a seat, I bent down to release the knee-lock of my calliper. I like to wear long dangling earrings and these were dangling as I struggled with the task. One man said to the other, 'Look at her, disabled and she is so dressed up!'"

8.3.4 Dealing with Menstrual Processes

For disabled girls, too, puberty is a process of becoming women, with its associated fears and promises. Yet the social conditioning experienced by most of the disabled girls from late childhood was of negation of puberty, as opined by mothers, other women in the extended family and friends. Agatha's mother told her, "a normal girl would have got it by the age of thirteen but you are a different kind of child". This creates a feeling of being deficient in one of the most basic identification of themselves as women. This is further compounded by the fact that most of the girls with locomotor disabilities start menstruating much later than their sisters and other girls. Girls are worried about the late onset, as it seems to them another dimension of their difference with other women, and a questioning of their femininity. Asha, the eldest of six sisters started her menses after all her sisters and found it to be extremely embarrassing. "Everyone used to ask me if my menses had started and it was shameful. All my sisters were getting it every month while mine were not starting at all. Sometimes I used to worry that I would never become a woman".

While delay in menarche leads to frustrations and anxiety about one's femininity, the onset of menstruation is also characterized by fear and worry about negotiation of impairments with the periodic needs of their cycle. Saraswati recalls that when her periods started, she had no idea about it. "When I saw my pants soaked in blood one day, I was very frightened. No one had told me that it would happen like that". Jahanara's first menses started when she was at school and the teachers gave her cloth and taught her how to use it. "I went home and told my sisters and cousins, but not my mother, as I was feeling ashamed". Sisters, female cousins and other women directed them in ways of taking care during the menstrual periods. Disabled girls, especially those living in the rural areas, usually use cloth for sanitary pads, which are convenient as they are not only cheaper, but also thicker than the regular ones, which allows them to balance the requirements of their menses with the needs of their impairment. Mita says that she feels comfortable using thick cloth pads because of her weak legs and unstable hips. "Even though I used to tie a string around my hips to hold it in place, the pad would continuously shift when I walked. I could not manage it properly". Manju recalls that she used to have more problems during her periods at home as she did not wear the calliper at home. "Keeping the cloth pad in place was difficult as one of my legs is thin and the muscles don't have much power. Cloth pads are thicker and do not fall out easily or shift fast".

Ritual practices performed at the onset of menstruation vary between the different castes, but generally include seclusion so as to minimize contact with males whom they could be seen as polluting (Bhattacharya, 1980). The practice of and adherence to these rituals varies from family to family depending not only on caste, but also on family type and location of the family and the degree of disability. Mild-to-moderately disabled girls from rural areas from the lower castes and those from upper castes in urban areas found the rituals more strictly enforced in their lives, as they were equally applicable for all the women of the family. In families that follow rigorous ritual observances at the onset of a girl's menstrual cycle, disabled girls were treated like the other daughters and had to undergo the same ritualistic practices. These practices include separate confinement during the first cycle, taking a bath to purify oneself at the end of the period and undergoing ritualistic *puja* at the end of it. Girls are confined to a separate room during their first menstrual cycle for fear of their sexuality and its polluting nature, and they are directed to have minimal contact with men. Asha was told, "If you see men during that period, then they will die soon". Rituals of purification included bathing and washing of the hair and discarding all the clothes used during the 4–5-day confinement. For Manju, the first cleansing bath and ritualistic *puja* was held on the *ghats* of the river Hooghly, which was both scary and embarrassing for her. "There was a big *puja* held at the *ghat* and everyone came to know that I had started my periods and become a woman. It was so embarrassing. For me, getting into the *Ganga* with my callipers also was quite difficult. My mother told me to take them off and I was scared I would slip and break my leg on the *ghat*. Later I was also embarrassed by the fact that I had to sit on the crowded *ghat* and lift my dress up to my thighs to take off and wear the calliper. But my mother was adamant about the rituals for me too".

The sociocultural practices with regard to menstruation and the menstrual period decrees that women have to undergo and maintain strict observances, the most common restriction being on touching the *thakurer asan* (seat of the gods) while having periods. Mita's family was the strictest in terms of ritual observances during the menses. All the sisters would be strictly confined in a particular room when they had their menstrual cycle every month, and all the articles of daily use by them would be kept separate to avoid all contact with the rest of the family. They would sleep on separate beds and rooms for those few days, and when the monthly periods ended, all the clothes, bed sheets, covers, pillow covers and even the mosquito nets used would be thoroughly washed. They were not allowed to touch the *bhater hari* (pot of rice and other food items) and the *thakur ghar* was absolutely banned to them. However, they were allowed to do some of the household tasks such as cleaning the rooms, washing clothes, cleaning utensils. Over the years, Mita has been able to relax some of the proscriptions and although she still has to sleep in a separate bed and wash all the bed linen and clothes after the periods are over, now they are allowed to enter the kitchen. At Aparna's home, her *ma* enforced only the ritual observance of not touching the *thakurer asan* (seat of the family gods) and barred all the sisters from doing the *sondhye arati* (evening ritual of lighting lamp in front of the seat of the gods and then taking to all other rooms of the house).

For some of the severely disabled girls, living mostly in Kolkata, the proscriptions associated with menstruation were difficult to follow. A certain subversion of the gendered rules surrounding pubertal changes and menstrual avoidance can be seen, probably because of the negation or freezing of the sexuality of disabled women. Dora's father was forced to inform her about and assist her with the process of menstruation, as her mother had left them when she was a baby. He had been worried about the fact that her periods had been delayed and used to ask her openly about it. "I don't have a mother, so my daddy had to be my mummy also. Once when I was staying with him, he gave me a homeopathic medicine and my periods started soon after. Daddy went and bought sanitary napkins for me". Chobi, severely disabled and requiring help in all personal care tasks, recalls that although her mother used to help her during her periods, her father used to help her clean up and also change the sanitary pads. "Initially I used to feel shy but what could I do? I never felt any shame with Baba maybe because he had always been bathing me and taking me to the toilet". This transgression of norms is probably due to the fact that these girls are seen as frozen in childhood and devoid of sexuality, even though they may be undergoing bodily processes that point to their being a woman.

Girls having orthopaedic disabilities have been experiencing early menopausal symptoms, and are worried about their bodies and health even though some term it as a "special blessing from God" to lessen their difficulties. Both Asha and Sandhya feel blessed that their periods are so minimal that they are not affected by it at all. Asha says that gods must have felt pity on her for being disabled and said "let her have fewer problems in life". Sandhya, who never went to a doctor for irregular menstrual cycles, feels that for disabled girls menstruation is a pain. "I believe that god has blessed me, as with my disability managing during those days would have been so difficult. God has seen to it that I am rid of those problems and associated aches and pains. Also, it reduces chances of pregnancy just in case".

8.3.5 Desirability and Denial

Sociocultural ideologies construct disabled women as unsuitable for marriage, and from their adolescence girls are given subtle messages and come to accept the impossibility of the idea of their marriage. While families rarely tell the girl directly, silences convey the message that she is not considered marriageable, equally loudly. Asha recalls that at her home, no one ever talked of her marriage even though she was the oldest of the sisters. Asha's grandmother would tell her, "You stay in this house like a son. Other girls will get married and leave but you will stay here always. My mother also says I am like her son as I will never leave home". Subtle messages are used to condition the young disabled girl to accept her "fate" by comparing her to the sons of the family who never have to leave their natal home. The de-sexing of girls is evident in the analogy of the disabled girl being like a son, denying her femininity and sexuality and at the same time underlining the fact that she would never be married off like her other sisters. Manju's female relatives used to commiserate with her mother, "they would all tell *ma* 'you will never have a younger son-in-law'". Rita recalls that the women in their neighbourhood would repeat, "'*bhalo*' (non-disabled) girls can expect a lot of things and have lots of *sokh* (desires), which is not allowed for disabled girls".

The notion of the *bhalo meye*, a woman who is physically unimpaired, beautiful and capable of physical labour, plays an important role in the representation of disabled women as unmarriageable. The association of marriage for a woman with the ability to engage in household work was foremost in the minds of people in the neighbourhood, who used to ask Asha's father "Who will marry her? She cannot walk, how will she manage the household work?" Families, people in the community and the girls themselves, accept that the nature of their impairments would make it impossible for them to assume responsibility for an entire family and perform all the tasks expected of a married woman. For girls with impairments, functional capacity becomes one of the primary reasons for not being considered as fit for marriage. Inability to cope with household work and caring for the affinal family are the most common reasons cited for the lack of marriage prospects for disabled women. Sandhya's sister elaborated, "Which boy will feed her if she is not able to contribute to the *sansarer kaaj* (household work)? *Ke boshiye khawabe* (who will feed her just like that, without doing any work)? How will she be able to do the *sansarer kaaj*?"

However, aspirations regarding marriage vary with age as well as severity of disability. From her adolescence, Sandhya has always known that marriage was an impossible proposition for her. "How could they (parents) have even dared to think of my marriage?" Asha felt that, "they (parents) knew it was of no use thinking about my marriage. I have no legs (meaning that she cannot walk). How could I get married?" As they grow older, girls with moderate-to-severe disabilities reconcile themselves to the fact of remaining single throughout their lives. Older girls express fears of being deserted by men after marriage, especially if they were persuaded with the promise of dowry. Asha feels that men may agree to marry her in return for a huge *pon*, but knows that there is no guarantee that he would stay with her. Younger girls are still struggling against societal and familial ideologies that deem that they cannot get married. Sulekha's older and younger sisters have been married off by her parents, who are now looking for a suitable match for their son. Sulekha's mother justified their actions, "my other daughters were growing up so fast that I did not dare to keep them in my house". Sulekha feels a bit disappointed that her parents are not thinking of her marriage at all. "If I could walk like other girls, then my marriage would be considered before my brother's or sister's marriage".

Media images of desirable, perfect and marriageable women relegate disabled women to the realms of women not fit for consideration for marriage, as is illustrated by the matrimonial advertisements in the newspapers. Agatha says that from an early age, she had been looking at those advertisements, which look for "tall, fair, beautiful girls", and over the years, came to realize and accept that she would never fall into the category of a "beautiful" girl. "I have learnt that men always look for someone who is perfect. They will not look at girls like me who are less than perfect or who are not 'normal'. It's not that I am imperfect, but I am not what most men think of as perfect". Notions of social acceptability and the public ramifications dominate the minds of disabled girls when it comes to marriage. Asha felt that if she were married, she would always be conscious of her husband's embarrassment whenever they went outside the home. "Like when there is some social function either at our home or other place, he may like me to go with him. How will he take me? Will he walk there and I will crawl beside him? Will he carry me on his shoulders? People would stare and pass comments. Will any man like to have a wife like me?" Fears regarding their capacity to bear and rear children also dominate the minds of disabled women and their mothers. "If I have children, the child may want his/her mother to go around with him/her, carry him/her. I cannot fulfil those wishes. I can take him/her on my lap but will not be able to soothe him/her or rock him/her by pacing up and down".

Proposals for marriage were received only by the girls with mild-to-moderate disabilities, with the precondition that the groom should be a disabled man himself, as he would probably be the only one willing to marry such a woman. Mita says that for a long time she too felt and accepted such ideas, as she "felt that adjustment would be better as we would understand each other's flaws". When she was 14 years old, Aparna's parents received a proposal for her from the family of a young man with speech and hearing impairment, who felt that it would be a good match as both were disabled even though Aparna was "dark and ordinary to look at". Aparna's mother was very happy with the proposal as she felt that a "good" boy would ask for a huge dowry for marrying a disabled girl. With four other daughters to marry off, she felt that this was a good match, but her father refused to marry off his disabled daughter to a disabled man. Aparna's mother had argued with him, "Where will you get a prince to marry your lame daughter?"

Disabled girls feel that, judged against the imaginary norm of femininity and the ideal *bhalo meye*, they are found wanting in all relationships that allow women to express their sexuality. Ideologies of feminine attractiveness represent impaired bodies and disabled women as undesirable, unfit for attracting the attention of possible partners and incapable of entering relationships that require women to assume roles of wife, mother and carer for the family members. The encounters that these women have had with men in the public sphere have reaffirmed these beliefs and representations, with rejection and negation of their femininity being the primary responses. Marriage, as an option, was one of the last considerations for disabled girls and proposals, solicited at later ages compared to their sisters, were received mainly from disabled men, reinforcing notions of devaluation as women.

Disabled girls also fear both the reputation of a loose woman as well as the shame associated with a disabled woman having sexual urges. This kind of fear of social shame and ostracism, however, was more visible in girls living in rural areas, as these are relatively closed communities, where every action is noticed and commented upon. Sandhya revealed that she has consciously never allowed any man to get close to her. Although she talks to other men in the neighbourhood or in the village, she maintains a distance so that people around them will never get a chance to gossip about her. "How can I? Just imagine, people would say, 'she is like that and look, how she is flirting with boys'". Asha confirmed that she felt scared whenever she talked with men and boys, because rumours about her liaisons with men would ruin her reputation in the village. The onus of maintaining their reputation as *bhalo meye* in the moral sense is doubly important for disabled women, as they feel that they already have lost status as a physically and functionally perfect woman. Despite the denial of their sexuality, disabled women fear repercussions, both physical and social, over any sexual attention that they might receive.

8.4 Impaired Bodies in Public Domains

The social valuation of perfect bodies not only accentuates visible differences but coupled with teasing comments and taunts gives rise to feelings of inferiority and devaluation. In the public domain, girls are more openly confronted with dominant ideas regarding femininity and ability and stereotypical representations that cast them as dependent, incapable and weak. Girls, who are unable to walk, feel a sense of shame because of the way in which they move, either by crawling or by dragging their hips, which makes them the object of ridicule and pity in public. These feelings get crystallized during adolescence and are manifested in diverse ways of dealing with the shame, one of which is to lead a reclusive existence. Asha started feeling ashamed of herself and the way in which she moved after she came back from the rehabilitation centre during her early teenage years. "Everyone around me would be walking and I would be crawling along. I was ashamed of going out like this, as people would stare at me all the time. So I stopped going out of the house". Chobi started feeling ashamed of being carried to different places, especially in public spaces and going out thus became a source of continuous shame and a reinforcement of her incapability. "I used to feel like an animal in a zoo. Everyone would stare at me, as if I was someone from another world, an extraordinary thing, something people had never seen before".

Seeing them in the public domain amounts to transgression of norms of acceptability, which is both gendered and ability centred. The degree of disability or the visual impact of one's impairment determines the kind of attention one gets, feels Sulekha, who has been aware all her life that people stare at her. "But if I go out of the house crawling, instead of with the callipers, more people would stare at me". When she is walking with her callipers, she feels that people stare at her but there is less pity in their eyes than when she is crawling along the road. In the public spaces, girls also have to reckon with the way in which people react to them and use derogatory language to refer to them. Dora, who has been in a wheelchair all her life, used to feel demeaned every time she went to public places, as people around her would always be commenting about her. "Some people even said, what is the use of her living?" Living and dealing with pity and ridicule on a daily basis makes the girls more aware of their differences with other women, and the fact that compared to non-disabled women they are found to be wanting. Whenever Asha goes out in public transport, people make her feel as if there is nothing as worse as a disabled woman. "People say, 'oh what a sad thing to happen, if only god had not taken away both legs, if only she could walk, what a punishment for such a beautiful girl.' It was as if all my beauty would now be wasted as I cannot walk". The "gaze" for disabled girls is constituted not just by the way men look at and objectify women, but also by the way in which the non-disabled world looks at disabled people. Hence, these girls simultaneously feel the pressure of feminine and able-bodied bodily norms especially in varied social situations, where they feel the gaze constantly assessing and demeaning them.

The realization of difference, of being distinctive so as to become the cynosure of all eyes in the public domain and of debasement, has been the general experience of disabled girls whenever they have ventured out into the public sphere. The degree of disability or the visual impact of one's impairment determines the kind of attention one gets, feels Sulekha, who has been aware all her life that people stare at her. "But if I go out of the house crawling, instead of with the callipers, more people would stare at me". When she is walking with her callipers, she feels that people stare at her but there is less pity in their eyes than when she is crawling along the road. Agatha has developed a thick skin and different strategies of ignoring unwanted attention and processes of objectification in public spaces. Initially, she used to stare back at them, but over the years she has realized that they stare because they have not seen many disabled people in the public arena.

Prevalent ideologies posit them as "incomplete" women, who do not need any form of ornamentation or dressing up as against "normal" women, who have to adhere to acceptable notions of femininity. Manju recalls that when she was in college, if she dressed up and went out, boys would invariably taunt her, "*hatte cholte pare na abar sejeche dekho. Jeno amader sajar kono icche hote pare na. Amar o mone hote laglo je seje ki korbo?* ". (She can't walk properly yet see how she dresses up. As if disabled girls have no right to dress up. So I also started feeling that I shouldn't dress up or put on make-up to make myself pretty.) Disabled women, considered to be unfeminine and unattractive, are relegated to the sidelines of femininity and hence need not attempt to beautify themselves as objects of male pleasure. Krishna, who travels regularly by bus, often has to hear derogatory comments about being "overdressed". "One day, in a crowded bus, when I got a seat, I bent down to release the knee-lock of my calliper. I like to wear long dangling earrings and these were jangling as I struggled with the task. One man said to the other, '*Pa kharap ar sajer bahar dekh*!' (Look at her, disabled and she is so dressed up!)".

Krishna feels male-centric society defines notions of femininity and acceptability according to conventional ideas of beauty. According to her, men stare at her and pass comments not only because she is disabled, but also because despite being disabled, she wears unconventional or non-traditional trendy clothes like jeans and blouses. "I feel if I conformed in dress code and did not wear jewellery or ostentatious makeup, people would find it easier to accept my disability. People want disabled women to be conformist. Maybe if I wore a *saree* then I would receive lesser comments". Sandhya has been made to accept over the years that village people do not prefer to see her "all dressed up". "*Gramer dike lokera amader sokh ahlad dekhte chaye na. Ektu sajle porei lokera bolte shuru korbe*, '*dekh khora meye abar heroine seje ghurche.*' *onek dhorroner katha bole jemon* '*dekh orokom abar sokh koto*'". (People in the village do not want to see a disabled girl dressed up and if I wear good clothes or jewellery they will say, "see the disabled girl, dressed up like a heroine". They say many things like, "see how she is and so much of desire to dress up".)

Disabled women face both a denial of their sexuality as well as sexual abuse in the public domain. Men in public spaces often treat these women as available for not only ridicule and pity but also for sexual favours. The ideology that deems these women as sexually unattractive works in the favour of men who treat disabled women as objects of pleasure without fear of repercussions, as "who would ever think of doing anything to a girl like her?" Anita feels sad when her sexuality is denied by men who deem her unfit for marriage, while making sexually suggestive comments when they meet her in social situations. Even some of her *gyati* (blood-kin) men and brothers-in-law tease her with sexually loaded comments and invite her alone to watch movies or go out for a pleasure trip. "Don't I know what they want? I have to be very careful, because I am a woman". Anita feels they think that because she is short, she also must be less intelligent. "Some jokingly offer to marry me, and others refer to me as their '*choto bou*' (younger wife with the connotation of short or small wife). I feel sad, because I know they would never dare to crack such jokes with other women, yet they laugh loudly at me". Anita knows that if she complains, very few people would believe that she had been treated as a sexual object while others would feel that she invited the comments in some way.

Thus, women, growing up with a disability, come to accept and negotiate their bodies in accordance with the notions they internalize about their femininity, and experience their embodiment in specifically different ways in comparison to other women. While the ability to and the manner in which they move affects the way in which they present a feminine self and participate in the activities labelled as feminine, girls themselves seek to express their femininity through the ways in which they dress and behave. While trying to merge the demands of an impaired body with the imperatives of a normative femininity, women adapt and redefine notions of femininity, which is seen as unavailable to them as their sexuality is considered to be frozen at adolescence and feminine practices, which they modify to suit their needs when they participate in such rituals.

8.5 Conclusion

The cultural meanings attributed to different bodies have a great impact on formation of identities that are gendered yet coloured by abilist ideologies. For women with disabilities, the body becomes the sole point of both similarity and difference between them and other women and determines the ways in which they perceive and experience the difference in everyday lives. In Bengali culture, a "*bhalo meye*" refers to a good girl, which is common parlance refers to a morally upright girl with all the positive feminine attributes, one who is the pivot of an ideal family. A *bhalo meye* symbolizes a girl, with a unimpaired body and capabilities, one who is seen as potentially capable of taking on increasing amount of responsibility to cater to the needs of her natal and affinal families, one whose productive and reproductive capacities blossom and develop from adolescence to adulthood. A *bhalo meye* is one who gets married and adheres to the cultural stereotype of being a wife and mother. For disabled girls, the situation is specifically different because they are not expected to get married due to the sociocultural constructions of marriageability for women. Disabled girls, located beyond definitions of sexuality, desirability and marriageability, live in the liminal space of being not being a *bhalo meye* and yet not being a "*baje meye*" (bad girl).

An embodiment that is shaped by an impaired female body coupled with the sociocultural valuation of a disabled person as well as of the different social roles a woman plays greatly influences the way in which disabled femininity is constructed, nurtured and contested. For many women with disabilities, an "ideal" body may be difficult to attain because it implies certain basic features such as being of an appropriate height or having two ordinarily functioning arms and legs. However, the internalization of dominant ideas of female subordination by disabled women themselves as well as their subjection to medical interventions together colludes towards the normalization of the imperfect female body (Meekosha, 1998). The creation of differences, based on the material reality of their impairment as well as assumed preconceptions about their capabilities leads them to accept their impaired bodies as something which is devalued and "wanting" as compared to other women. Disabled women in Bengal strive to adhere, as far as possible, to the socially acceptable ideas about a *bhalo meye* through different strategies of presenting a feminine self, in gait and bearing, in dress and comportment and through activities and practices. Normative femininity is accepted and endorsed, and negotiated with the ramifications of their impairments. The process of negation and denial of the sexuality of disabled women proceeds from suppression within the household to encounters in the public sphere that serve to reinforce the ideologies and lead to withdrawal of disabled women, sometimes reluctantly, from the arena of sexuality. But this process varies according to the degree of disability as well as the family contexts in which the girls are located and the aspirations they are allowed to harbour from adolescence into adulthood. Yet these women also redefine the ideal of a *bhalo meye* in the different domains of their daily lives, whether in the private realms of their homes and personal processes or in the public sphere. In day-to-day practice, the impaired body engages in and manages almost all of the activities and practices that govern daily lives of these women, although this may vary according to the degree of disability.

References

Bagchi, J. (1990). Representing nationalism: Ideology of motherhood in Colonial Bengal. *Economic and Political Weekly, 25*(42–3), 65–71.

Bagchi, J. (1993). Socializing the girl child in Colonial Bengal. *Economic and Political Weekly, 28* (41), 2214–2219.

Bagchi, J. (Ed.). (1995). *Indian women: Myth and reality*. Kolkata: Sangam Books.

Bannerji, H. (1994). Textile prison: Discourse on shame (*lajja*) in the attire of the gentlewoman (*Bhadramahila*) in colonial Bengal. *Canadian Journal of Sociology, 19*(2), 169–193.

Bannerji, H. (2002). Re-generation: Mothers and daughters in Bengal's literary space. In S. Chaudhuri & M. Sajni (Eds.), *Literature and Gender*. Hyderabad: Orient Longman.
Bartky, S. L. (1992). Foucault, femininity and the modernisation of patriarchal power. In J. Kourany, J. P. Sterba, & R. Tong (Eds.), *Feminist philosophies*. New Jersey: Prentice Hall.
Bhattacharya, N. N. (1980). *Indian puberty rites*. Delhi: Munshiram Manoharlal Publishers Pvt. Limited.
Begum, N. (1992). Disabled women and the feminist agenda. *Feminist Review, 40*, 70–84.
Bordo, S. (1993). Feminism, Foucault and the politics of the body. In C. Ramazanoglu (Ed.), *Up against Foucault*. London: Routledge.
Bordo, S. (1996). Anorexia Nervosa. In A. Garry & M. Pearsall (Eds.), *Women, knowledge and reality. Explorations in feminist philosophy*. New York: Routledge.
Campling, J. (1983). *Social work with disabled people*. Hong Kong: Macmillan.
Chakraborty, S. (1998). *Andare antare: Unnish satake bangali bhadramahila*. Kolkata: Stree.
Chatterjee, P. (1993). *The Nation and its fragments: Colonial and post colonial histories', in the partha chatterjee omnibus*. Delhi: OUP.
Cormack, M. (1953). *The hindu woman*. New York: Columbia University Press.
Davis, K. (1997). Embodying theory: Beyond modernist and post-modernist readings of the body. In K. Davis (Ed.), *Embodied practices*. London: Sage.
Das, V. (1989). Femininity and the orientation to the body. In C. Karuna (Ed.), *Socialization, education and women: Explorations in gender identity*. New Delhi: Orient Longman.
Dube, L. (1985). Introduction. In L. Dube, E. Leacock, & S. Ardener (Eds.), *Visibility and power —Essays on women in society and development*. Delhi: Oxford University Press.
Engels, D. (1996). *Beyond purdah? women in Bengal 1890–1939*. Delhi: OUP.
Garland-Thomson, R. (1994). Redrawing the boundaries of feminist disability studies. *Feminist Studies, 20*(3), 583–597.
Garland-Thomson, R. (2002). Integrating disability, transforming feminist theory. *NWSA Journal, 14*(3), 1–32.
Hillyer, B. (1993). *Feminism and disability*. Norman, OK: University of Oklahoma Press.
Mazumdar, S. (1994). Moving away from a secular vision? Women, nation and the cultural construction of hindu India. In V.M. Moghadam (Ed.), *Identity, politics and women: Cultural reassertions and feminisms in international perspective*. Boulder: Westview Press.
Meekosha, H. (1998). Body battles: Bodies, gender and disability. In T. Shakespeare (Ed.), *The disability studies reader: Social science perspectives*. London: Cassell.
Mookerjea-Leonard, D. (2005). Jyotirmoyee devi: Writing history, making citizens. *Indian Journal of Gender Studies, 12*(1).
Rimassa, P. (1997). Women with disabilities. In A. Leitinger (Ed.), *The Costa Rican women's movement: A reader*. Pittsburgh: University of Pittsburgh Press.
Roy, M. (1972). *Bengali women*. Chicago and London: University of Chicago Press.
Tharu, S. & Lalitha, K. (1991). *Women writing in India: Vol. 1: 600 B.C. to early twentieth century*. New York: Feminist Press.
Tighe, C. A. (2001). 'Working at disability': A qualitative study of the meaning of health and disability for women with physical impairments. *Disability and Society, 16*(4), 511–529.
Wadley, S. (1999). Women and the hindu tradition. In J. Doranne & S. Wadley (Eds.), *Women in India: Two perspectives*. Delhi: Manohar.
Wendell, S. (1996). *The rejected body: Feminist philosophical reflections on disability*. New York: Routledge.

Chapter 9
Women and Men at Work: Livelihood Experiences of Persons with Disabilities (PwD) in West Bengal

Ipsita Sapra

Abstract Narratives of inactivity and dependence surrounding the persons with disability (PwD) often undermine the barriers erected by institutions mandated to support them. Whether educational or administrative, institutional failures at several levels prevent the PwDs from optimizing capabilities. Based on PhD research by the author on livelihoods of PwDs in Mandirbazar, a rural block in South 24 Parganas district of West Bengal, the present piece attributes the limited range and quality of livelihood choices of PwDs to institutional failures at several levels. This also challenges an individualistic understanding of disability. Documenting the work lives of the PwDs and illustrating their struggle to secure an economic foothold through a range of paid and unpaid work, the piece subjects the notion of "dependence" to greater scrutiny and argues that an overwhelming engagement with this narrative takes attention away from the fundamental issue institutional accountability. This chapter emphasizes that understanding livelihoods of PwDs requires deeper engagement with them and developing understanding of opportunities and barriers through their lens.

Keywords Disability · Work lives · Experiences · Policies · Dependence

9.1 Introduction

Popular response to the idea of living with disabilities often vacillates between extremes. On the one hand, a handful of heroes who overcome seemingly insurmountable constraints of their bodies and achieve great feats are celebrated through such mediums as cinema and literature. On the other hand, the rest, struggling with a range of constraints and their interaction with the physical and social environment surrounding them, are largely ignored. While acknowledging the contributions of the "heroes" in providing inspirational role models, this piece primarily engages

I. Sapra (✉)
School of Livelihoods and Development, Tata Institute of Social Sciences, Hyderabad, India
e-mail: ipsita.sapra@tiss.edu

N. Ghosh (ed.), *Interrogating Disability in India*,
Dynamics of Asian Development, DOI 10.1007/978-81-322-3595-8_9

with the everyday ordinariness of lives of persons with disabilities (PwDs). Given that such ordinariness characterizes the lives of the bulk of the PwDs, "ordinary people doing ordinary things" (Oliver, 1990a, b: 91) are the foci of the study.

Despite significant strides made in the understanding of disability as impairments that interact with various barriers to hinder participation (Article 1, UNCRPD), the predominant ideology concerning the PwD confers a passive and dependent status to their existence—physically, socially and financially. In the domain of livelihoods, such notions about dependence get exacerbated with presumptions around "inactivity" being taken as given. Existing data also reinforce such understanding. NSS indicates that only 36 % of the men and 10 % of women with disabilities are employed (NSSO, 2002, cited in MoSPI 2011). Such low levels of economic engagement are unquestioningly accepted and attributed to the functional limitations of impairment. Moreover, so powerful is the narrative of dependence that the PwDs themselves internalize it. Seeking individualistic explanation for their condition they engage in self-pity over their impaired bodies is somewhat akin to the Marxian notion of "false consciousness" (Shakespeare, 2009).

Based on doctoral research by the author on livelihoods of PwDs in Mandirbazar, a rural block in South 24 Parganas of West Bengal, the present chapter is intended to question and challenge this understanding, subjecting it to greater scrutiny. Specifically, it emphasizes the need to shift the gaze from the individual to the institutional, which, it believes, illustrates the inadequacies and failures that curtail pathways to economic engagements for the PwDs. In addition, documenting the work lives of the PwDs and illustrating their struggle to secure an economic foothold, the study presents the picture of dynamic and diverse economic engagements, critiquing the ideology of passivity and dependence.

9.2 Methodology and Theoretical Underpinnings

The present study is based on an ethnographic account of livelihood experiences of PwDs in a rural context carried across seven villages and institutions around them. This study targeted an age group of 24–35 years as it comprised a section most proactively seeking livelihood opportunities and had some experience to reflect on. Through the narratives about their experiences, it reconstructed their pathways to livelihoods, specifically through their experiences of interface with institutions: educational, those imparting vocational training, and institutions mandated to support livelihood opportunities. This not only illustrates the inadequate institutional response but also the unequal relationships in which the PwDs find themselves with regard to the institutions. In doing so, this study engaged with a range of institutional stakeholders such as schools, vocational training institutions and administrative offices. This study also interacted with the family members to understand their perceptions about such efforts and their outcomes. In addition, multiple stakeholders—government and non-government agencies—members of the Panchayati Raj Institutions, research and academic bodies and representatives of the nodal training agencies were interviewed and the institutional performance for livelihood promotion was assessed through review of secondary data such as annual reports.

The arguments in this piece are theoretically anchored in the social model of disability (Oliver, 1996) that rejects a "personal tragedy" approach, locating disability within society (Oliver, 1990a, b, 1996). Premised within this overarching framework, this chapter interrogates the commonplace reasoning that attributes low levels of employability of those with disabilities to their biological attributes. In the process, it steers the gaze towards institutional inadequacies that place enormous constraints on the PwDs illustrating the social arrangements that are disabling (Oliver, 1996). The model also questions the policies and programs developed by establishment that institutionalize discrimination and call attention to address "conditions" that make social and economic participation difficult for those with disabilities (Oliver, 1990a, b).

However, this study differs from the social model in acknowledging the constraints that the body imposes and the need to include the same in the narrative. It also finds the model inadequate in terms of accounting for the multiple levels of marginalization that PwDs experience especially in an Indian context where the intersection of disability with such factors as caste, religious affiliations, plays an important role in defining vulnerability. While being alert to the criticism of the social model for its denial of the embodied experiences, this chapter highlights the enormity of a range of disabling environments. So while bodily constraints exist, a preoccupation with the same diverts attention from the more important constraints that the state and the society creates, sustains and yet conveniently undermines.

This chapter also borrows essential components of the capabilities approach developed by Sen (1980, 1985, 2004) and Nussbaum (2000, 2003, 2006). Specifically, it uses the following key ideas: *functioning* or the actual achievements; *capabilities,* the effective opportunities to achieve these functioning; and *conversion handicaps*, the barriers to convert opportunities into functioning (Robeyns, 2006).

Using the idea of "capabilities" to refer to the gamut of resources and opportunities ostensibly available to the PwD, it illustrates the "conversion handicap" that impedes realization of these opportunities into "functioning" livelihood outcomes. These three key concepts of the capability approach lend themselves to provide theoretical underpinning to the chapter. This chapter demonstrates that across stages of their lives, as the PwDs try to access education and later vocational training, despite resources in terms of schools and institutes, they face constraints that are institutional rather than individual. These constraints act as conversion handicaps that place unsurmountable barriers for the PwDs. From the schools that offer no provisions for special education in terms of teachers and infrastructure to training institutes that are city-based and far removed from the villages, the existing opportunities are unrealisable for most PwDs. Despite capabilities, poorly resourced and badly designed programmes act as conversion handicaps that thwart functioning, in this case, attempts by PwDs to engage in education and later work.

The agility of the capabilities approach, especially the model proposed by Sen as a normative lens for conceptualization, enables its import to the disability discourse.

It is also possible to take a step back and question the idea of what comprises "work" that is here taken to represent livelihoods. Barnes, (2003) identifies the root of disproportionate representation of PwDs in work in the way labour market is organized. The profit maximization objectives of the modern economies foster excessive competition between individuals that, in effect, disadvantage not just the PwDs but indeed all those who are perceived to have some types of functional limitations. While this proclivity towards intense competition with employment opportunities tuned to take only those who "fit the bill" completely appears to be obvious, historical evidence points otherwise. Giving the example of the UK, Barnes talks about the Second World War period when the country had brought women and PwDs into the labour force as a part of human resource mobilization efforts for the war. There are similar examples from the USA as well, reinforcing the idea that just as disability is often socially constructed, the meaning of "work" and the way it is organized is also a social construct and therefore amenable to change (Barnes, 2003). This is relevant because not just does it lead to greater interrogation of the ideas surrounding work, narrowly used as livelihood in this chapter, but also it actually reiterates the postulates of social model in terms of debunking the constructed nature of what we take for given.

Finally, this chapter emphasizes that understanding lives and livelihoods of PwDs can be developed only through deeper engagement and greater appreciation of opportunities and barriers through their lens. This would not only facilitate a better understanding of their situation but also provide a greater insight on institutional response. While the study draws from case study to present narratives of efforts, successes and failures of the PwDs, it is important to note that these are just not anecdotal accounts. These vignettes of experiences are important "exemplars" (Robert Kuhn, 1987, cited by Flyvbjerg, 2006) and are illustrative of a wider situation. It facilitates the scientific process of "falsification" (Popper, 1959 cited in Flyvbjerg, 2006) wherein just one observation to the contrary is sufficient to challenge the proposition.

While the PhD research covers a wide spectrum of issues concerning livelihoods, this chapter specifically interrogates the institutions. Scrutinizing aspects that support livelihoods, education and vocational training, it looks at capabilities or existing opportunities, efforts by the PwDs to utilize these and the institutional response that act as handicaps impeding their conversion into livelihood outcomes. This chapter also points out the policy bias towards formal sector employment despite the engagement of a miniscule section of the PwDs in the formal sector, while others cope with challenges in informal set-ups. It also brings forth the culture of class-based distancing that institutions practise with regard to the PwDs leading to their apathetic disposition towards PwDs, especially the poor. The piece argues that this not only leads to continued exclusion of PwDs but also significantly compromises the ability of the institutions to be of relevance for most of the PwDs. Finally, it borrows "exemplars" from the PhD research to demonstrate and uphold the dynamic work lives of the PwDs and their varied livelihood pursuits. Thus, the chapter is categorized into the following sections:

I. Thwarted efforts to access education, the fundamental pathway to livelihood;
II. Vocational training and skill development: The weak link to livelihood;
III. Formal sector policy bias and the exclusion from state support programs;
IV. Unequal encounters: The experience of the young persons with disabilities with the governmental institutions;
V. A glimpse of the actual work lives.

The sections take a closer look at the aspects mentioned above to challenge the dominant individualistic ideology that attributes poor livelihood circumstances to PwDs and their functional limitations. It does so by exposing conversion handicaps in institutional thought and action on livelihood. Across the sections, there is a continuous cross-referencing between the field-level reality and the insights from existing literature or data from secondary sources to reinforce and reiterate the pervasive nature of the problem.

9.2.1 Thwarted Efforts to Access Education, the Fundamental Pathway to Livelihood

Education is widely recognized as a major step towards a stable and secure livelihood. The study also noted people's demonstrable interest in education, often an outcome of the perception that education and the access it creates to livelihood opportunities form an important vehicle to move out of poverty. Equally important is the realization that once educated, PwDs can take advantages of affirmative action in the form of job reservations. Yet, access to education remains elusive for most children with disabilities (CwD).

Existing studies indicate an overall low level of educational participation among CwDs. Findings of a recent report suggest that only 10 % of the CwDs are in school and that one-third of the 77 million (6–11-year of age) children currently out of school have a disability (UNESCO, 2007 cited in Miles and Singal, 2010). According to the District Information System for Education (DISE), Government of India, data on elementary education, CwDs comprise only 0.87 % of the total enrolments at the primary level which gets further reduced to 0.79 % at the upper primary level. Within this, the girls have further lower rates of enrolment across both the levels (DISE, 2013–2014). Poor access to education implies that the most effective capability in the form of a pathway to employment is blocked. While it is convenient to attribute exclusion to their impairment, a closer look would steer attention to a range of institutional failures and non-committal policies that have not only just allowed but arguably perpetuated such exclusion.

Based on the research, the following subsections describe the issues surrounding access to education in the rural setting where it was undertaken.

9.2.1.1 For the CwD, Access to Education is "Type" Dependent

While disability is a generic term, attention to the complex heterogeneity it presents is crucial for a complete account of its impact on access to education. Subsuming under a homogenized category of "disability" undermines the specific challenges that children with various types of impairment face. Among those covered in the study, education had been available mainly to those with orthopaedic impairments, a pattern not restricted to the study area. According to the state-level figures, the bulk of the enrolment figures of CwD is actually skewed. While children with orthopaedic impairments comprise the bulk of those in schools, children with vision-, hearing- and speech-related impairments are hugely under-represented among children with impairments in school. Thus, while those with orthopaedic impairment comprise about 92 % of CwDs, blind and children with low vision comprise 1.8 % and children with hearing and speech impairment comprise 2.6 % of all CwDs enrolled in schools (WBCDSW, 2011).

This scenario is explained by the simple fact that the children with orthopaedic impairment demanded least adjustment by the schools, pedagogically and physically. Minor adjustments such as shifting classes to lower levels (ground floor) were all that was required. Also, the parents had been proactive in taking the children to the school, in several cases, physically carrying them to the schools. Pedagogically, no changes were required in teaching–learning methods. Once the accessibility issues (a major deterrent) were addressed, there was no other major difference with regard to acquiring education. In addition, Sarva Siksha Abhiyan (SSA) and the Right to Education (RTE) had contributed to making schools more accessible by funding physical infrastructure. In West Bengal, ramps with handrail were constructed in more than 51,000 schools and more than 200 schools had barrier-free toilets (WBWCDSW, 2011).

However, while important, these are not sufficient for ensuring educational access (Singal and Rogers, 2009) as a large number of CwDs, especially those with impairments other than orthopaedic, do not adequately benefit from ramps and therefore continue to be excluded. It has been argued that creation of physical infrastructure can be a misleading indicator of accessibility as it can work to create an impression of access while catering to only a section and undermining the needs of children with other types of impairments (Thomas, 2006 cited by Singal, 2007). As Thomas, 2006 cited by Singal, 2009 says,

> "the significant financial resources allocated to the SSA programme were actually a problem,… there is great pressure on education staff to spend, and be seen to be spending, their budgets. The result is that money is thrown at very visible and easy areas. Shiny new ramps and rails are a suitable quick fix." (Thomas, 2006 cited by Singal, 2007: 23).

This preoccupation with "demonstrable impact" takes attention away from less demonstrable aspects as curriculum, pedagogy and classroom interactions (Singal and Rogers, 2009) that act as powerful conversion handicaps for those with other types of impairments.

Access to education also needs to be understood in a contextual manner. In the study area, much before the Right to Education Act, the local schools enrolled all children, including those with impairments. However, this open access was not accompanied by any strategic effort towards creating opportunities for learning outcomes of the students with disabilities. None of the schools were equipped to handle their heterogeneous needs: they neither had trained teachers skilled to teach such children nor facilities such as Braille or sign language. Children were just herded together, and those with disabilities were expected to drop out, "in the natural course" as a result of *their* inability to follow the school curriculum. Despite the presence of capabilities in the form of schools, "casual integration" (Miles cited in Singal, 2007) acted as a conversion handicap resulting in little learning outcomes for the CwDs.

9.2.1.2 Teacher Training: Inadequate and Incomplete

Only a handful of teachers received comprehensive in-service training and orientation on special education. Identifying selective teachers for training in special education and entrusting them with the responsibility of teaching CwDs created enormous logistical demand and supply gap. West Bengal, for example, had only 2150 teachers for children with special needs, a shortfall of 4350 (WBDCDSW, 2010). In the study area, there were only two trained special educators who were expected to discharge their duties by travelling across 62 primary schools and 15 upper primary schools in the block. Needless to say, this was not adequate to meet the needs of the children studying across these schools.

This is reflective of a broader systemic problem with regard to teachers training for addressing the special needs of the CwDs. While the SSA has provisions for teachers training for children with disabilities, most of the teachers receive at the most 3–6 days of training in inclusive education which is more of an orientation rather than training and cannot be expected to build skills in teaching children with different types of needs. Less than 0.2 % of teachers covered under Sarva Siksha Abhiyaan (SSA) had been through the programme that provided 45–90 days of training in inclusive education that is comprehensive and can actually enable teachers to evolve pedagogies that can facilitate inclusive education (World Bank, 2007, cited by Singal, 2007). There is also an option of 1–2 days of training in inclusive education. These are of little use in terms of skill building to engage in inclusive education.

Significantly, the approach perpetuates an individualistic approach to disability although studies demonstrate that teaching–learning methods used for CwDs contribute towards improving the quality of education (Singal, 2007). In spirit, it absolves other teachers of any responsibility towards CwDs. However, popular perceptions do not engage with the devil in detail. It is far more convenient to join the bandwagon of people attributing the "plight" of such children to "tragedy" of functional limitations rather than questioning established institutions and their systems.

Interactions undertaken with the headmasters of the local schools also indicated the attitudinal issues that underlined exclusion. They maintained that by enrolling CwDs to schools, they had fulfilled their responsibilities towards such children. The commitment towards helping children attain educational outcomes that can eventually help them secure livelihoods was clearly not on the agenda. The school had no role to play in their achievements, making it a rather passive institution. Such thoughts reflected a very individualistic understanding, absolving institutions of any responsibilities towards expanding capability sets and making commitments towards outcomes. Finally, the schools felt that the children who were able to do well despite these problems were "extraordinary" or were well supported by their parents.

9.2.1.3 Teachers' Attitudes and Academic Expectations

Interaction with the teachers highlighted that an acceptance that CwDs would eventually drop out was deeply entrenched. This notion had set out low teacher expectations that arguably impacted the students. This was indicated by the young persons with disabilities covered under the study. All of them felt that teacher expectations from them in terms of educational performances were lower and that they were treated with sympathy rather than sensitivity, hurting their self-confidence. Studies have indicated that being caring does not automatically translate into believing in the capacity of the children with disabilities to learn and achieve as others (Boersma FJ and Chapman JW (1982), and McGrew KS and Evans J (2003) both cited in WHO, 2011). The research demonstrated that the interface with the teachers reinforced their "impaired" status, and over the years, this attitude resulted in a lack of self-esteem as they experienced a feeling that their impairment compromised their learning abilities. The study noted deep internalization of negative self-perceptions in the psyche of most of the young persons. Despite practical opportunities or capabilities, teachers' attitude worked as a covert but powerful conversion handicap that eroded the faith of the students in their abilities disabling students from making the best of the available opportunities.

While the study cannot generalize beyond those covered, these indicated that despite progressive changes at the policy level, the front end of the education system remains unchanged and as exclusive as ever. In the process of study, there were several instances of teachers and headmasters taking active personal interest in creating access of children to disability scholarship and other forms of state support. However, pedagogical support that was of critical importance was the most difficult and least forthcoming for the children. Inability of the local schools to create appropriate teaching–learning opportunities for the children with disabilities erected covert conversion barriers that were far more difficult to overcome than visible physical barriers. These pedagogical challenges that actually reflect a continued influence of an individualistic understanding of disability greatly compromised the access of CwDs to education and eventually to livelihoods.

In the context of local schools ill-equipped to handle children with impairments other than orthopaedic, the only possible alternatives were the special schools. Among those studied, only one individual from a prosperous family was able to pursue education in such a school. However, most others found it unaffordable. It did not help that the school was located in the city.

Most special schools across the country are run by NGOs and located in and around the cities. Such education also involves financial cost of residential arrangements, special equipment and often software packages, making these inaccessible for the rural poor with disabilities. The ambivalent approach of the state to special education makes it further inaccessible to the rural poor.

9.2.1.4 Gender Roles and Early Withdrawal of Girls from Education

While the gender–disability intersection is a vast area of study beyond the scope of this research, any discussion on disability remains incomplete without reflecting intersections involved and the socio-cultural positioning of women with disabilities. Importantly, while institutional responsibilities might not appear very apparent, the apathy and indifference of the schools is widespread. All the young women covered in the study, other than those who acquired impairment after marriage, narrated that there was urgency on the part of the families to get them married at the earliest. This often entailed withdrawing them from the schools irrespective of their interest or performance and marrying them off to ensure that the enormously difficult responsibility of getting a daughter with impairment married was undertaken at the earliest. This "eased the burden" of the girl's family as she became the responsibility of another family. The schools remained silent on the issue that their marriage was prioritized over their education and their educational opportunities were curtailed. The schools overlooked the gendered phenomenon of exclusion of girls with disability as the girls with impairment experienced pressures of an "early adulthood" which compromised their educational pursuits also, in a way, limiting their livelihood choices.

Thus, education, both formal and special, remained out of the reach of the CwDs more due to institutional rather than individual reasons. There appeared to be little reconceptualization of education in a scenario of diverse needs of the students. While a whole range of research indicates this, the concerns remain confined to academic writing, making inroads neither into policies nor into the collective conscience. The dominant ideology persists with the tragedy saga placing the children at the receiving end of sympathy for their impairment, rather than holding the institutions accountable for creating and sustaining conversion handicaps in the form of inadequate skills and infrastructure. Institutions and people, in this case, the schools and the teachers, continue to "disable" children who they fail to teach and hold impairment responsible for such failure. Given that it fits well into the dominant ideology, the institutional fault lines that accentuate disabilities and create barriers to education are overlooked.

9.2.2 *Vocational Training and Skill Development: The Weak Link to Livelihood*

In a scenario of limited access to education, PwDs realized that skill development could be important route to livelihoods. As such, most of those covered in the study engaged in some form of vocational training programmes. Vocational training opportunities available to the PwDs could broadly be classified into three categories: formal training programmes through centralized government institutions (e.g. the Vocational Rehabilitation Centres [VRCs] or Industrial Training Institutes for the Physically Handicapped [ITIPH]); Formal training programmes organized locally by the government or NGOs; and Informal training acquired by people through their own social networks. This section examines the state of the vocational training programmes, livelihoods these create and the way these add to the narrative of incapacity of the PwDs.

9.2.2.1 Centralized Formal Training Institutes

Set up with expensive, state of the art and specially designed machines for the PwDs, centralized formal training institutes have high-cost infrastructure and are well resourced with counsellors to offer flexible and aptitude-based skill development programmes. However, none of those covered in the study had any idea about the existence of these institutions or the facilities they offered, and as such, these institutions had little relevance for them.

The reasons were not difficult to understand. These centres were located in cities (in this case, the city of Kolkata) with non-existent or poor outreach mechanisms. That this lack of information was not restricted to the studied respondents was evident from the fact that ITIPH reported lack of enough students with disabilities interested in taking up their courses. This lack of demand was despite the fact that these courses were linked to employment opportunities in the formal sector. Surely, the scenario points not to a demand–supply gap but to poor dissemination and outreach about the institution. The VRCs on the other hand provided residential courses with good facilities for young persons to stay and learn. However, the location made it largely inaccessible for those in the rural areas, where most of those with disabilities lived. Also, in terms of the quality of skills, at least some of the skills imparted by the VRCs such as bookbinding, stenography and typing were rather outdated.

The VRC in Kolkata had only two established rural extension centres located in two districts. For the rest, the institution responded when approached by NGOs. However, at the time when the research was conducted, the number of NGOs working on disability was significantly lower in rural areas than in cities, a situation that still persists. In West Bengal, there were 139 such NGOs located in Kolkata while in the districts (barring South 24 Parganas), there were only 10–12 organizations on an average (Sphuran, 2010). Naturally, such demands were not forthcoming. Given the scenario, the institution had very limited outreach for the PwDs in the rural areas.

9.2.2.2 Trade-Based Livelihood Opportunities

Building on the vocational training received, there are also institutional support mechanisms to engage in trade-based activities. National Handicapped Finance and Development Corporation (NHFDC) is one of the most important institutions set up by the government of India with the mandate of providing financial assistance for such activities. It has the potential to promote livelihood through the process of financial asset building of the PwDs through a wide range of income-generating activities (NFHDC website).

However, the PwDs covered in the study were mostly unaware of the institution. Those who knew had either unsuccessfully attempted to secure assistance or were deterred by the obstacles to secure loans. As in most of the government schemes, the institution had "conditions" for support that were difficult to meet. In order to secure financial support or loans, the agency needed the assurance of a "guaranteer", a financially well-settled individual who would agree to be responsible for debt or performance under a contract. However, the vulnerability context of economic class meant that most of the young persons with disabilities had limited social network that included such individuals. As such, meeting this criterion was extremely difficult and it acted as a conversion handicap.

This also curtailed the capabilities of the institution. As per the records of the State Channeling Agency through which the NHFDC disbursed its funds, in a period of ten years from 2001 up to 30 November 2010, the National Handicapped Finance and Development Commission had supported 83 individuals in the entire district of 24 Parganas (S) of which only four were in Mandirbazar Block (West Bengal Women's Development Corporation, State Channeling Agency for NHFDC 2011). So while there were institutions and schemes that supported livelihood enhancement through self-employment, the access of the persons covered in the study was found to be low. While this is partly attributable to their lack of awareness, more importantly, the conditional nature of the support did not take into account the vulnerability context of the PwDs in the rural areas. Also, NHFDC focused exclusively on finances without adequate entrepreneurial support, addressing only one part of the entire business cycle.

While the observations made above are based on research that is limited in its scope, there are reasons to believe that these point to certain generic institutional failures specifically pertaining to the bureaucratic processes involved in accessing livelihood support that acts as barriers (Hiranandani and Sonpal, 2010). Existing studies also point to the poor performance of the institution. Not only was the coverage extremely limited, but also an overwhelming number of those supported were men with locomotor impairment (Mitra and Sambamoorthi, 2006).

While there are not many comprehensive evaluation of the existing vocational training programmes, in introducing a new approach to skill development for the PwD, the Government of India has recognized the inadequacies in the training programmes currently being offered, saying that these are "non-homogenous, lacks quality and is low on employability" (pp. 3). It also admits that very few of these training programmes are available in the rural areas, where most of those with disability live (GoI, 2015). Existing reports also indicate lack of support towards acquiring entrepreneurial skills that can enable people to develop and implement business plans. Despite programmes on paper, there is a lack of access to financial resources and proper handling support required to initiate and sustain businesses (Society for Disability and Rehabilitation Studies, SDRS, 2008). A National Action Plan for Skilling the Persons with Disabilities has been prepared by the Department of Persons with Disabilities (DEPwDs) in 2015–2016. However, it is too early to comment on its efficacy.

Finally, the reach and efficacy of such efforts can be assessed by an estimate that put together all interventions that directly facilitated access to employment for PwDs (special employment exchanges, NHFDC, VRCs) and calculated the outreach to be about 0.2 % of this potential labour force (Mitra and Sambamoorthi, 2006). However, this gets hidden under the overwhelming narrative of failure of PwDs and the functional limitations of their impairment.

Ranjana, orthopedically impaired, had enrolled in a machine knitting programme undertaken by an NGO facility, about 10 kms from her village. For one year, she attended the course negotiating a range of constraints. She often did not have enough money for transport. She also went without food on some days to be able to complete the course.

However, when Ranjana tried to utilize her skills, she realized that she had little support to procure wool, no guidance on designing and finally no way to market the products. Her skills remained unutilized, and she joined subsistence-level piece rate work.

9.2.2.3 Locally Organized Formal Training Programs

The study also captured the efforts of PwDs to develop skills through engaging in an array of locally organized skill development programmes. Contrary to the narrative of dependence and passivity, most of the PwDs covered in the study had attended training programmes locally organized by government agencies and NGOs, to help themselves engage in skill-based livelihood. However, while they made considerable efforts to acquire skills through formal training programmes, these programmes were so ill-conceived and short-sighted that they failed to support the PwDs. Focusing exclusively on skills, these addressed only a few aspects of enterprise development. Insulated from the realities of the market situation, such programmes neglected the crucial steps involved in translating a skill into a livelihood outcome by excluding inputs on functions such as market assessment, access to credit, procurement of raw materials, production and marketing remained outside the purview. In the process, they failed to close the loop that is required to set up a skill-based enterprise/employment venture. Also, the programmes remained confined to those with orthopaedic impairment since there were no special arrangements for those with hearing and speech or visual impairment.

The study documented that the PwDs had engaged in 15 different types of vocational training programmes including food processing (jam, jelly, fruit squashes) training, first aid, woollen garments making, mushroom cultivation, tailoring and bookbinding. This demonstrates not just the available range of options but also indicates their efforts to acquire skills to engage in livelihoods. However, none of those trained could use these for livelihood generation demonstrating the ineffectiveness of such programmes, given their emphasis on skill development per se without clear mechanisms to convert skills into livelihoods.

Finally, livelihood options based on self-enterprise were complicated and a majority of those with disabilities were risk averse. Without a commitment to a start-to-end-approach, expecting livelihood creation through such programmes is largely flawed. However, rather than focusing on the inherent flaws in the institutional efforts, livelihood failures were invariably attributed to and signalled individual failures.

9.2.2.4 Informal Training

In addition to formal training initiatives, several PwDs covered in the study, engaged in informal skill acquisition using their social networks. The advantage of informal training was that it was already an integral part of an established business and the new recruits just joined the supply chain. In the study area, weaving fishing nets, zari work or theromocole flower making fell in this category of work. Most of those who picked up skills informally were better assimilated into work. However, such work, involving low levels of skill, was usually low paying and did not support individuals' exit from poverty.

To summarize, the state of the available vocational education was inadequate for the livelihood needs of the PwDs. To a large extent, this highlighted the lacuna of a top-down approach to vocational training that runs with predecided programmes without linking those to wider livelihoods of the area. Existing literature point to the failure of such vocational training programmes on two accounts: (1) in creating access of PwDs to the courses and (2) in follow-up to ascertain whether the skills imparted could be used for livelihood generation (World Bank, 2007; WHO, 2011). Studies also suggest that often these programmes are high on costs, low in terms of creating employment-relevant skills and fail to reach a significant proportion of their target recipients (WHO, 2011). However, given that the dominant ideology is so apt at locating the "flaws" with the individual, design, content and implementation, flaws of the institutions and policies are completely overlooked.

9.2.3 Formal Sector Policy Bias and the Exclusion from State Support Programmes

Most of those covered in the study were engaged in livelihood opportunities in the informal sector, reflective of a wider scenario. The study highlighted that the state support mechanism for livelihood of this enormous section was extremely limited. The only entitlement was of Rs. 1000 for undertaking income generation programme and that was also difficult to access for those covered.

The informal sector of the economy that engaged 92 % of the working force (NCEUS, 2009) also provided livelihood to most of the PwDs. However, the disability policies on creating employment opportunities seemed to be heavily focused on the formal sector. Most of the provisions under the PwD Act 1995 pertained to formal sector employment. The formal sector bias percolated to the state government level: of the 13 government support schemes listed, only three schemes, economic assistance of Rs 1000 each to PwDs from poor economic background, support under microcredit programme and financial assistance under NHFDC, could be used for livelihood promotion outside the formal public sector (Office of the Commissioner of Disability, West Bengal, 2010). This emphasis on formal sector and extremely inadequate engagement with the informal sector led to the exclusion of most of the PwDs. Neglect of the informal sector that employs most of the PwDs compromised the ability of the existing policy to expand livelihood capabilities for the PwDs. A policy bias combined with curtailed opportunities to access education was one of the important reasons for a systemic exclusion and invisibility of PwDs in formal sector employment.

9.2.3.1 Exclusion from State Programmes on Poverty and Livelihood

Existing studies describe that negotiating complex official process for accessing support under policy framework remains an overwhelming challenge for the PwDs (World Bank, 2007). The research reinforces similar constraints experienced by the respondents as they described their inability to secure state support due to procedural barriers erected by the institutions. The very first step towards receiving support, getting a disability card, was cumbersome. Multiple visits required to get the disability card led to loss of wages and that acted as a major deterrent. Again, this is reflective of a wider situation. In West Bengal, by 2010–2011, only 39 % of the PwDs had a disability card (WBWCDSW, 2011).

In addition, the performance of some of the livelihood based poverty alleviation programmes with stipulations for the inclusion of PwDs has been very poor.

The National Centre for Promotion of Employment for Disabled People (NCPEDP) in India in its publication titled "People with Disabilities in Rural India, 2009" evaluates the performance of the various government programmes that have been designed to support the PwDs. A summary of the same is provided below that amply demonstrates the failure of the programmes to include/benefit the PwDs.

- In the Swarnjayanti Gram Swarozgar Yojana (SGSY) that addressed poverty by organizing social mobilization into self-help groups (SHGs), capacity building and provision of income-generating assets, the PwDs comprised just 1.81 % of those assisted. Financial inclusion of PwDs across all programmes has been limited due to questions about their "credit-worthiness" (Handicap International, 2006).
- Sector-wise analysis of the special projects sanctioned under Swarnjayanti Gram Swarozgar Yojana (SGSY) since its inception in 1999 demonstrates that out of the total 236 projects sanctioned, only 7 projects were sanctioned under the disability sector.
- In Indira Awas Yojana that provides housing to the poor, only 1.76 % of the total dwelling units were allotted in the name of PwDs.
- In the Sampoorna Grameen Rozgar Yojana (SGRY) that provides wage employment in the rural areas along with food security, creation of durable community, social and economic infrastructure in the rural areas, only 0.17 % works were reported to have benefited the PwDs (NCPEDP, 2009).

In addition, in the flagship rural employment guarantee programme MGNREGA that provides 100 days of assured employment to a member of every rural household for unskilled manual work, only 84,550 PwDs have found work in West Bengal and 357,700 in India. Calculated against the total figures for employment provided to 4.48 crore households, across India PwDs comprise just about 0.79 % of the total beneficiaries till December 2013 (compiled from GoI, 2013).

The abysmal figures here draw a picture of systemic exclusion of the PwDs from all important state interventions and the way in which these curtail effective opportunities and possibilities of outcomes. Yet, there is little questioning of these institutions and policies.

It might be pertinent to note that the Indira Kraft Patham model, initiated in the erstwhile united Andhra Pradesh, offers important insights into a large-scale programme that has worked to support livelihoods for the PwDs. Undertaken as a part of the state effort to collectivize the poor as a means to promote their access to financial resources, the programme extended the self-help group (SHG) model to women with disabilities. An important part of skill development actually included skilling them in mobilizing themselves and initiating savings and credit activities. There was practical support towards linking these to banks and financial institutions. The programme also connected young persons with disabilities to formal training institutions in the NGO sector. Special provisions were made within existing programmes such as MGNREGA to include the PwDs and were closely followed up to ensure inclusion. The Andhra Pradesh example stands out as an important exception to a largely grim situation of islands of excellence amidst oceans of failures with regard to livelihoods for the PwDs (UNDP, 2012).

9.3 Unequal Encounters: The Experience of Young Persons with Disabilities in Governmental Institutions

Finally, one of the most distinctive facets about living with disabilities is perhaps the unequal relationship that the PwDs find themselves in with regard to the institutions that are created to support them. This relationship between the service providers and the service recipients can be described using binaries—of power and powerlessness and of authority and subordination. PwDs remain, largely, in a relationship of subservience to the institutions and their representatives.

Despite his postgraduate degree, Padmalochan, visually impaired, faced enormous resistance from the school administration when he was placed as a teacher under "general" quota. His protest angered the representatives of the Department of Education who responded: "Why aspire to become a teacher? Go and beg on local trains, like all blind persons should do". Padmalochan believes that underneath superficial civility, the dominant ideology remains highly exclusive and discriminatory.

In the study, individuals across the divides of gender, class, type of impairment and educational qualifications echoed that state institutions, whether educational or administrative, remained largely unapproachable. Being in a disadvantaged condition such as being poor or a woman or from a rural background exacerbated such subservience and made them vulnerable to greater apathy and insensitivity. This indifference acted as a major conversion barrier impeding access to the little state support that PwDs were entitled to. From getting a disability card to claiming their pension or state assistance towards self-employment, the PwD encountered resistance and mistrust, often thwarting their efforts at leading a life of dignity through engaging in livelihood.

"Don't touch anything here. This is a gentlemen's (bhadralok) place. If they see you touching their things, they will call us thieves and throw us out of this office".

- *An elderly woman to her grandson who had come to collect her pension from the Panchayat office.*

Perplexing as they are, experiences of institutional apathy are not extraordinary. Across the world, the poor and the disadvantaged, encounter similar classist discrimination with institutions that are primarily established to serve them. Distancing is the common response that the poor experience from the non-poor. Lott (2002) argues that this is manifested at an institutional level as classism erects barriers and maintains inequities. These were recurrently reflected in the study as the PwDs recounted their experiences. Perceived to be "non-entities, expendable or undeserving" (Opotow, 1990 cited in Lott, 2002: 1), their access to state resources was hugely curtailed with such perceptions acting as conversion handicaps.

Interactions with the front-line government officials undertaken as a part of the research revealed deep contempt towards the poor, the PwDs included. Their suspicion about "false claims" to access state benefits resulting in pilferages exacerbated the importance of "evidence"—a range of documents that further complicated procedures to access benefits. In real terms, these acted as deterrents that prevented the PwDs from approaching institutions for support. To summarize, the institutions vested with the responsibilities to channelize livelihood, social protection and development schemes were largely unresponsive and apathetic to the needs of the PwDs. The pervasive nature of this attitude acted as conversion handicaps compromising both their intent and their effectiveness to enhance capability set for livelihoods. However, dominant ideology exempts institutions and locates the problems with PwDs and their bodily "imperfections".

9.4 Glimpses into the Work Lives of PwDs

Despite an overarching preoccupation with the incapacities of PwDs and institutions often working against their interests, the reality of work lives of the PwDs studied was remarkably different. Those covered engaged in a range of paid and unpaid work (see Box 9.1). This included most PwDs, including those with severe forms of impairment, except those who were completely immobile. While the PwDs recounted the functional limitations of the body and experiences of difficulties in performing certain tasks, the range of work they were involved in was indicative not just of their efforts but also of the range of responsibilities they actually shouldered. Arguably, most of those covered were too poor not to work and engaged in a range of activities to sustain themselves.

Box 9. 1

Rupali, orthopaedically impaired, made paper packets and theromocole flowers. She also worked as a cook for the mid-day meal programme of a local school. During agricultural season she husked, boiled and dried grains. All these, in addition to household chores and childcare responsibilities.

(Sapra, unpublished PhD thesis, 2013)

Unpaid work, largely carried out by women with disabilities covered under the study, included domestic chores such as cooking, cleaning and childcare responsibilities. It also included agricultural activities such as husking, boiling and drying grains during agricultural seasons. Women were also engaged in a range of low paying piece rate activities to supplement family incomes.

Significantly, several women with disabilities covered under the study supported other women in the family with childcare responsibilities, freeing them to pursue paid work. While this role is seldom acknowledged, it made a major contribution and enhanced livelihood capabilities or opportunities at the household level.

Men covered under the study also had a diverse livelihood portfolio. Excepting a handful of those who engaged in formal sector employment, most of the others were engaged in available opportunities in the area. They tried all possible options and exhausted all possibilities, including, in some cases, work that was in direct conflict with the nature of their impairment or compromised their safety (see Box 9.2).

While the study was rooted in the social model of disability, it also documented the frustration of the PwDs with their functional limitations that impeded their pursuits. The blind saree seller, who failed to understand the non-verbal communication of his clients or respond to their choice of colours and patterns, and the deaf young person, who found it difficult to adjust to the phonetic rhythm of the manual work under MGNREGA, provided important insights of impairment infringing on livelihood pursuits. It also provided the nuanced understanding that the narrative of livelihood of the PwDs would be incomplete without an acceptance of the reality of certain functional limitations. However, this chapter emphasizes the need to look beyond the limitations and focus both on the contributions and capabilities of the PwDs, while holding institutions accountable for their non-performance towards addressing removable barriers in the physical environment.

Box 9.2

Kausar, visually impaired, is engaged in a range of activities based on the time of the year: Saree selling during Durga Puja, wall painting during Eid, fruit and vegetable vending in the local trains in the winters and trading in waste during other times of the year. Given the poor state of village roads, he has had his share of accidents, falling in ponds and ditches. However, that has not deterred him from optimizing his opportunities.

(*Sapra, unpublished PhD thesis 2013*)

It is important to note that notwithstanding broad commonalities, livelihood experiences of PwDs were also deeply contingent on the intersections of vectors. In addition to the most obvious, the type and severity of impairment that produce differential livelihood capabilities and outcomes, factors such as gender, caste, class and rural location played an important role (Ghai, 2009; Pal, 2011; DFID, 2000). The study also highlighted an often unexplored dimension—the vulnerabilities experienced by the minorities with disabilities as they negotiated multiple disadvantages. These intersections of vulnerabilities are powerful "conversion handicaps" in terms of the limitations they impose on the range and quality of opportunities that PwDs experience and to the actualization of such opportunities. However, these remain inadequately understood and articulated leading to a homogenization of the narrative that deprives it of the complexity.

9.5 Conclusion

Based on an understanding of disability drawn from the United Nations Convention of the Rights of the Person with Disabilities (UNCRPD), the ability of PwDs to engage in livelihoods can be understood as an outcome of an interaction of their impairment with the wider socio-institutional environment. This chapter demonstrates that livelihood insecurities that PwDs experience are, to a lesser extent, outcomes of their impairment. The limited choice and options are often reflective of institutional failures. These inadequacies create a situation where the PwDs experience very few capabilities or effective opportunities and where opportunities exist, and a range of conversion handicaps impede possibilities of converting these into livelihood outcomes.

Touching upon three important pathways out of poverty for PwDs, education, vocational training and state supported livelihood opportunities, this chapter demonstrates the challenges faced by the PwDs in their interface with the institutions. At the same time, based on ethnographic engagement, it elicits the dynamic and diversified work lives of PwDs. However, the dominant ideology that persistently conceives disability as an individual trait not only undermines the contribution of the PwDs, but also overlooks institutional failures. It is, therefore, imperative to develop frameworks that sufficiently engage with the range of capabilities, functioning and conversion handicaps that dot the experiences of PwDs in their pursuit for livelihood. An important part of such frameworks needs to engage with institutional accountability.

Finally, it is important to recognize PwDs as contributing members who proactively seek and engage in work, both paid and unpaid. However, this recognition is contingent on an understanding of livelihood that emanates from a deeper engagement with the PwDs. Such engagements and understanding also need to be based on the centrality of the PwDs and their experiences at the core of the process of inquiry. This would facilitate bringing the biological together with the social, opening up possibilities of securing preventive and rehabilitative interventions while comprehensively addressing the institutional inadequacies.

Finally, writing about PwDs and their livelihoods needs to look beyond dominant ideologies and perceptions for a greater reality check. This would ensure a change of narrative from one that is largely oriented around deprivation and dependence to one that speaks the language of actualizing their entitlements and ensuring institutional accountability.

References

Barnes (2003), Work is a four letter word Disability, Work and Welfare Colin Barnes, Invited Presentation, Working Futures: Policy, Practice and Disabled People's Employment University of Sunderland. http://disability-studies.leeds.ac.uk/files/library/Barnes-work-2.pdf. Accessed May 12th 2015.

DFID. (2000). Disability, poverty and development. Available from: www.livelihoods.org/static/dfid_N163.html. Accessed October 12, 2010.

Flyvbjerg, B. (2006). Five misunderstandings about case-study research. *Qualitative Inquiry, 12*(2), 219–245.

Government of India. (2008). Ministry of rural development. Annual Report 2007–08. Available from: http://rural.nic.in/sites/downloads/annual-report/anualreport0708_eng.pdf. Accessed June 30, 2011.

Government of West Bengal. (2010). Sphuran Office of the Commissioner of Disability, Government of West Bengal.

Government of West Bengal. (2011). *Annual report, 2011*. Department of Women and Child Development and Social Welfare, West Bengal (WBWCDSW).

Government of India. (2013–2014). District information system on education (DISE) Available from: http://dise.in/Downloads/Elementary-STRC-2013-14/All-India.pdf. Accessed May 17, 2015.

Government of India. (2013). MGNREGA briefing book. Available from: http://nrega.nic.in/Netnrega/WriteReaddata/Circulars/Briefing_booklet13.pdf. Accessed May 19, 2015.

Government of India. (2015). The scheme of financial assistance for skill training of persons with disabilities. National Institute for Empowerment of Persons with Multiple Disabilities, Ministry of Social Justice and Empowerment, Department of Empowerment of Persons with Disabilities. Available from: http://niepmd.tn.nic.in/documents/skill-0715.pdf. Accessed April 16, 2016.

Ghai, A. (2009). Disabled women: An excluded agenda of Indian feminism. *Hypatia, 17*(3), 49–66 [Feminism and Disability, Part 2 (Summer, 2002)].

Handicap International. (2006). *Good practices for the economic inclusion of people with disabilities in developing countries: funding mechanisms for self-employment*. Handicap International.

Hiranandani, V., & Sonpal, D. (2010). Disability, economic globalization and privatization: A case study of India. *Disability Studies Quarterly, 30*(3/4).

Lott, B. (2002). Cognitive and behavioral distancing from the poor. *American Psychologist, 57*(2), 100–110.

Mitra, S., & Sambamoorthi, U. (2006). Government programs to promote employment among persons with disabilities in India. *Indian Journal of Social Development, 6*(2), 195–213.

Miles, S., & Singal, N. (2010). The education for all and inclusive education debate: Conflict, contradiction or opportunity? *International Journal of Inclusive Education, 141*, 1–15.

National Sample Survey Organization (NSSO). (2002) Disability in India. Statistical data. Available at http://mospi.nic.in/Mospi_New/upload/disablity_india_statistical_data_11mar2011/Chapter%202%20-Overview.pdf. Accessed April 19, 2011.

National Centre for Promotion of Employment for Disabled People (NCPEDP) (2009) In people with disabilities in rural India: Base line Report

National Commission for Enterprises in the Unorganized Sector (NCEUS). (2009). *The challenge of employment in India: An informal economy perspective* (Vol. I).

Nussbaum, M. (2000). *Women and human development: The capabilities approach*. Cambridge: Cambridge University Press.

Nussbaum, M. (2003). Capabilities as fundamental entitlements: Sen and social justice. *Feminist Economics, 9*(2/3), 33–59.

Nussbaum, M. (2006). Poverty and human functioning: Capabilities as fundamental entitlements. In B. David, Grusky & R. Kanbur (Eds.), *Poverty and inequality*. Stanford UP.

Oliver, M. (1990a). The individual and social models of disability. Paper presented at Joint Workshop of the Living Options Group and the Research Unit of the Royal College of Physicians on People With Established Locomotor Disabilities in Hospitals. Available from: http://www.leeds.ac.uk/disability-studies/archiveuk/Oliver/in%20soc%20dis.pdf. Accessed March 23, 2010.

Oliver, M. (1990b). *The politics of disablement: A sociological approach*. New York: St Martin's Press.

Oliver, M. (1996). *Understanding disability: From theory to practice*. Basingstoke: Macmillan.

Pal, G. C. (2011). Disability. *Intersectionality and deprivation: An excluded agenda, psychology developing societies, 23*(2), 159–176.

Robeyns, I. (2006). The capability approach in practice. *Journal of Political Philosophy, 14*(3), 351–376.

Sen, A. (1980). Equality of what? In S. McMurrin (Ed.), *The Tanner lectures on human values*. Salt Lake City: University of Utah Press.

Sen, A. (1985). *Commodities and capabilities*. Amsterdam: North Holland.

Sen, A. (1999). *Development as freedom*. New York: Knopf.

Sen, A. (2004). Capabilities, lists, and public reason: Continuing the conversation. *Feminist Economics, 10*, 77–80.

Shakespeare, T. (2009). Disability: A complex interaction. In H. Daniels, H. Lauder, & J. Porter (Eds.) Knowledge, values and education policy: A critical perspective. London: Routledge.

Singal, N. (2007). Conceptualising disability and education in the south: Challenges for research. *RECOUP* Working Paper 10, University of Cambridge.

Singal, S., & Rogers, J. (2009). Transitions to adulthood for young people with disabilities in India: Current status and emerging prospects. *Asia Pacific Disability Rehabilitation Journal, 20*(1). Available from: http://www.aifo.it/english/resources/online/apdrj/selread100/full_document.pdfAccessedon10-2-2012. Accessed June 30, 2011.

Society for Disability and Rehabilitation Studies (SDRS). (2008). *Employment of persons with disabilities in public sectors in India emerging issues and trends*—An Evaluation Study with Special Reference to Persons with Disabilities Act (1995) Commissioned by Planning Commission, Government of India. Available at https://wadhwani-foundation.org/wp-content/uploads/2014/12/2008-Planning-commission-report-on-PwD-Employment.pdf. Accessed March 28, 2016.

United Nations Development Programme. (2012). Livelihood opportunities for persons with disabilities. Available from: http://www.undp.org/content/dam/india/docs/pub-povertyr-eduction/livelihood-opportunities-for-persons-with-disabilities.pdf. Accessed June 30, 2011.

WBDCDSW. (2010). Annual Report. Department of women and child development and social welfare. Government of West Bengal.

WBCDSW. (2011). Annual Report. Department of women and child development and social welfare. Government of West Bengal.

WHO. (2011). *World report on disability*. World Health Organization and the World Bank.

World Bank. (2007). *People with disabilities in India: From commitments to outcomes*. Human Development Unit, South Asia Region. Available from: http://siteresources.worldbank.org/INDIAEXTN/Resources/295583-1171456325808/Chapter07.pdf. Accessed November 27, 2010.

Chapter 10
The Disability Rights Movement in India: Its Origin, Methods of Advocacy, Issues and Trends

Jagdish Chander

Abstract A number of social movements took place during the second half of the 20th century in India. These included the women's movement, environmental movement, *Dalit* movement, etc. One such movement was the disability rights movement which originated during the late 1980s. This chapter discusses the emerging trends and issues covered as a part of the disability rights movement as well as the methods of advocacy adopted by the activists of this movement following the Persons with Disabilities Act, India (1995). This chapter includes a brief comparative analysis of the disability rights movement in India by situating it in the context of the broader disability rights movement at the international level in the post–Americans with Disabilities Act period.

Keywords Disability · Rights · Movement · India

India underwent many social and political changes after gaining independence from British rule in 1947 (Rudolph and Rudolph, 1987: 66). The *Dalit* (anti-untouchability) movement (Omvedt, 2001), the socialist movement led by Jai Prakash Narayan and Ram Manohar Lohia (Limaye, 1984; Mohan, 1984), and the Naxalite (radical communist) movement (Vanaik, 1990: 182) all led to tremendous political upheavals and social changes. However, it is only recently, beginning in the 1990s, that India has witnessed the emergence out of the shadows of previously silent groups like women and the disabled.

The late 1980s and early 1990s witnessed certain developments in India which were supported by an international atmosphere that legitimized the advocacy approach in the field of disability. These developments provided an impetus to the movement led by the National Federation of the Blind (NFB), the largest and most powerful advocacy organization of the blind in India for demanding enactment of a comprehensive disability rights legislation. This resulted in the passing of the Persons with Disabilities (equal opportunities, protection of rights and full participation) Act,

J. Chander (✉)
Department of Political Science, Hindu College, University of Delhi, New Delhi, India
e-mail: jagdish100@gmail.com

N. Ghosh (ed.), *Interrogating Disability in India*,
Dynamics of Asian Development, DOI 10.1007/978-81-322-3595-8_10

1995, which became a law in 1996 after it received the assent of the then President Dr. Shankar Dayal Sharma on 7 February 1996 (Bhambhani, 2004: 28). This law is popularly known as the "PwD Act" (NHRC, 2005: 245) or the "disability law" (Baquer and Sharma, 1997: v). The passage of this law is an example of the success of the disability rights movement.

This chapter analyses the origin of the disability rights movement in India, methods of advocacy used applied in this movement as well as trends and issues characterizing this movement in the post-1995 period in the aftermath of the enactment of the PwD Act. However, it needs to be emphasized that the ground for the origin of the disability rights movement was prepared by the self-advocacy movement of the blind during 1970s and 1980s. It is, therefore, important to first engage in a brief discussion of the origin and growth of the self-advocacy movement of blind India during those two decades in order to understand the background of disability rights movement which, as elaborated further, began in the late 1980s when the NFB focused its attention on the movement demanding the enactment of the disability rights law.

10.1 Self-advocacy Movement of the Blind

Like their counterparts in the United States, the blind were among the first disability groups in India to wage a vigorous struggle for their rights, beginning in the early 1970s. The self-advocacy movement of the blind, which is described as the "movement of the organized blind" in India (Chander, 2011: 9), formally began at the national level in 1970 with the founding of the National Federation of the Blind Graduates, the membership of which was initially restricted to college graduates. However, in 1972, its membership was made open to all blind people and the word "graduates" was dropped from its name to be changed to the National Federation of the Blind (NFB), popularly called the "Federation" (Chander, 2011: 9). This movement of the organized blind in India preceded the larger disability rights movement. While the attention of the leadership during the initial phase of the movement of the organized blind during the 1970s was basically devoted to organization building and the initiation of some service delivery projects, it was through the use of the forum of the Federation that, as early as 1973, blind people came to the streets for the first time to demand jobs, citing their right to be employed as qualified candidates (Chander, 2011: 150–154).

Through this radical advocacy movement, the organized blind in India began to challenge the hegemony of service agencies for the blind like the National Association for the Blind that were predominantly led by sighted philanthropists who primarily adhered to a charity-based approach (pp. 122–125). This marked the beginning of a shift from the charity-based approach to self-advocacy.

The development of consciousness in the approach of the blind activists regarding their rights inspired them to press their claim for affirmative action, referred to as "positive discrimination", and enshrined in the Constitution of India under the

Fundamental Right to Equality.[1] This recognition of the need to press for their claim for equal rights was also buttressed to some extent by the issuance of the Office Memorandum of 1977, which recognized the rightful claim of the disabled to be covered under the concept of affirmative action on the basis of positive discrimination. Through this Office Memorandum of 1977, a quota for 3 % of jobs in the third and fourth categories of positions, described as "C" and "D" categories of jobs, respectively, was introduced for the disabled in Central Government Services and Public Undertakings (Mani, 1988: 60–62; Pandey and Advani, 1995: 100–102). This included 1 % each for the blind, physically impaired, and the deaf (Mani, 1988: 60–62; Pandey and Advani, 1995: 100–102).

The issuance of the Office Memorandum of 1977 was notable, in that it represented for the first time a concrete action to ensure the right of the disabled to employment. It had far-reaching implications for triggering the struggle for the right of the disabled, particularly the right to employment for blind people, as it was instrumental in raising the expectations of the activists. This was the first time that the Indian State recognized the rightful claim of the disabled to employment by way of legally protecting this right through the quota system. It strongly influenced the launching of the struggle for employment and provided momentum for the movement. As a result of this provision, the educated unemployed blind youth gained confidence to continue the movement, as they believed that they had the required qualification for the jobs and at the same time their right to employment was legally protected through this Memorandum.

As is the case with most of the legal provisions in India, this provision was only enforced when pressure was exerted for its implementation. Courts were not highly active in the late 1970s and early 1980s. Also, it is worth mentioning that the 1970s had witnessed a wave of movements, such as the anti-emergency rule movement as well as socialist movements in various parts of north India. So, there was also a strong culture of democratic and socialist movements in North India at that time. Therefore, the most effective method of advocacy to get the Office Memorandum of 1977 regarding the quota of the disabled in certain categories of Central Government jobs implemented or the disability law enacted was through what Barnartt and Scotch (2001) called 'contentious political action' or 'contentious political activity'. This method of contentious political action or contentious political activity in the context of Indian situation included: *dharnas* (picketing), hunger strikes, rallies, disruption of rail, and road traffic. These were the methods of advocacy in addition to representation and persuasion that were adopted by the activists of any kind of advocacy movement during 1970s and 1980s. Therefore, the activists of the movement of the organized blind too adopted these methods as a means of demanding the implementation of the provisions of this Memorandum throughout the decade of 1980s (Chander, 2011: 199–247). However, once the PwD Act was enacted, the activists altered their tactics and became focused largely on getting the provisions of this law implemented through lobbying as well as litigation and appeals before the Chief Commissioner on

[1]*Constitution of India*. (2004). (2nd pocket ed., pp. 7–9). Government of India: New Delhi.

persons with disabilities (a quasi-judicial body mandated under the provisions of the PwD Act), in addition to occasionally still resorting to the traditional methods of contentious political action or contentious political activities. A detailed discussion of this change in the method of advocacy and certain other developments in the field of disability rights movement follows later in this chapter, but it is first useful to briefly discuss the developments that led to the origin of disability rights movement.

10.2 Origin of Disability Rights Movement

One major concern of the activists engaged in the movement of the organized blind was that the Office Memorandum of 1977 did not address the issue of employment of the blind in an adequate manner. Its implementation was not considered to be as effective as the implementation of a duly enacted law would have been as the government always lacked the political will to actually implement the Memorandum and employ the blind. At the same time, the organized blind were quite conscious of the fact that this Memorandum merely covered the issue of employment in highly restricted categories of jobs and did not cover rights in other areas such as education, housing and social security. They, therefore, felt that if a comprehensive disability rights law was passed by the Parliament, it would be easier to address the issue of employment as well as other issues concerning the rights of the disabled. Along with this realization on the part of the blind activists, the time was right by late 1980s for the Federation to focus on the demand for the enactment of the disability rights law which as mentioned earlier, is also popularly referred to as "disability law" or "disability legislation".

There were broadly two identifiable developments that took place during the late 1980s, leading to a change in the focus from employment of blind people in the government sector to the demand for enactment of the disability law by the NFB. These were (1) a special recruitment drive to employ a sizable number of eligible unemployed blind people in 1987 and (2) submission of the Justice Baharul Islam Committee Report in 1988 strongly recommending the enactment of a disability law. The special recruitment drive in 1987 led to the employment of 239 blind people by early 1988 (Chander, 2011: 301). The success of this recruitment drive also boosted the morale of the leadership and revitalized its strength. Also, once that recruitment drive was completed and a good number of qualified blind were absorbed in different jobs, the Federation was relatively free to focus its attention on the struggle for the enactment of disability rights legislation.

A draft disability law was prepared during the International Year of the Disabled Persons in 1981 (Mani, 1988: 56–58). But it was rejected by a senior bureaucrat of the Ministry of Social Welfare, now called the Ministry of Social Justice and Empowerment, the ministry that deals with disability-related issues.[2] However, the

[2]L. Advani, personal interview, 21 January 2005, cited in Chander (2011: 301).

most important development in relation to the introduction of disability law was the formation of a committee under the chairmanship of a former judge of the Supreme Court, Justice Baharul Islam, in 1986 (Bhambhani, 2004: 17). This step was taken by the regime of Prime Minister Rajiv Gandhi. The Justice Baharul Islam Committee submitted its report in early 1988 (p. 17). The committee was headed by a senior legal expert who was highly respected by those in power within the government. The committee's strong recommendations for the introduction of disability legislation proved to be a watershed development leading towards the introduction of such legislation. Similar to the recruitment drive mentioned above, the committee's recommendations were a great morale booster for the leadership of NFB to make this issue a priority. Hence, following these two major developments—the special recruitment drive of 1987 and the submission of the report by the Bahrul Islam Committee recommending the need for the introduction of a disability law—it was an ideal time to launch a movement for the enactment of such a law starting from 1988 onwards.

Santosh Kumar Rungta, who had been successful in mobilizing the blind activists since late 1970s and who succeeded in carrying out a sustained movement for the most part of the decade of 1980s to get the Office Memorandum of 1977 for 3 % quota for the disabled in (C) and (D) categories of jobs in Public Undertakings in Central Government Services, was re-elected as the general secretary of the Federation during its biannual Convention in September 1988 (Chander, 2011: 302). The team of leaders who were elected or re-elected made it clear that the demand for enactment of the disability law would be their highest priority and raised this demand through a press statement after they resumed their office ("The Bill for the Disabled is in Flux", 1988; "Anguish on Delay in Making Law for the Disabled", 1988). This group of board members, led by Rungta, organized a rally in early December 1988. During that rally, they vehemently criticized the government for not making sincere efforts to enact the law by implementing the recommendations of the Justice Baharul Islam Committee, which had submitted its report during the early part of the year ("Blind Protest against Govt's Apathy", 1988). As elaborated further in the following press coverage, the primary focus of that rally was on the demand for enactment of the disability law in addition to the quota in government jobs:

> The blind marched from Paharganj to place their long pending demands. Among their major demands are the reservation in the government jobs and a comprehensive legislation to protect the interest of the disabled persons. The blind men also staged demonstrations outside various government offices on Thursday ("Members of National Federation of the Blind Marching towards Boat Club", 1988).

This rally marked the beginning of a series of advocacy activities leading to a strong movement by the Federation in 1989 primarily to lobby for enactment of the disability law. This in a way can be regarded to be the beginning of the disability rights movement in India (Chander, 2011: 353–359). A sustained movement was carried out by the Federation demanding the enactment of disability rights law in the ensuing years with some brief intervals till the enactment of the PwD Act.

A detailed discussion of this movement demanding the disability law carried out by the Federation from 1988 to 1995 can be found elsewhere (pp. 296–331). It is beyond the scope of this chapter to engage into a detailed discussion of this movement; it must, however, be mentioned that the disability rights movement in India began in 1988 when the Federation launched a sustained movement demanding the disability rights law. Although there was little participation in the advocacy movement by cross-disability groups until the early 1990s, the fact cannot be denied that the movement of the organized blind encompassed cross-disability advocacy in the fight for and enactment of the disability law. Thus, the scope of the agenda of the struggle by the blind was expanded to advocate for the rights of other categories of the disabled as well, in addition to the rights of the blind through the enactment of comprehensive disability rights legislation. The enactment of the PwD Act of 1995, ensuring the rights of a broader group of disabled and not just the blind, was thus the result of this struggle carried out primarily by the Federation from 1988 onwards (Chander, 2011: 296–331). Therefore, even if the movement for the disability law for ensuring rights of different disability groups was predominantly led by the organized blind, this should be regarded as the beginning of the disability rights movement because of the focus of its agenda. Prior to this, the movement was not only led primarily by blind activists; it rather remained an impairment-specific movement because of its narrow focus. Thus, it can be safely concluded that the period from 1988 onwards marks the beginning of the disability rights movement in India. It may, however, be acknowledged that this movement was significantly enhanced by the increasing participation of various disability groups, and there is a coexistence of a cross-disability rights movement as well as impairment-specific movement in the post-1995 period. However, the struggle did not end with the passage of the PwD Act in 1995; rather it now continues in courts and streets for its implementation. What follows next is, therefore, a discussion of the struggle for the implementation of the PwD Act and the changes in the methods of advocacy in the post-1995 period.

10.3 Struggle from the Streets to Courts, Quasi-Judicial Bodies and the Use of Internet

The existence of the PwD Act enabled the disabled activists to have a strong basis for engaging in a struggle to press for the realization of their rights in various spheres of life through implementation of its provisions. As mandated in chapter XII of this law (PwD Act, section 57, chapter XII) the Chief Commissioner for persons with disabilities (CCPD), a quasi-judicial body, was established in 1998 to look into complaints regarding violations of the provisions contained in this law (Case Law Reporter, 2008: 1). Subsequently, comparable counterparts were also established in various states (2008: 1). Similarly, the PwD Act was also used by advocates to approach the courts in India to seek the realization of the rights of the disabled in accordance with its provisions (NHRC, 2005). At the same time, access to the Internet enabled the English-educated disabled activists to connect with each other and lobby for implementation of the law in a unified manner. Thus, prior to the passing of the PwD Act the disabled activists (particularly the blind activists as the movement then was predominantly led by the blind), primarily relied on traditional methods of advocacy involving contentious political action. However, the post-1995 period witnessed the continuation of struggle through new means of court cases, filing complaints in the offices of the State Commissioners and Chief Commissioner for persons with disabilities, and use of the Internet.

As elaborated in the next section, a number of lawsuits were filed by disability rights organizations as well as individual disabled people in various high courts and the Supreme Court of India in the post-1995 period. This is not to say that the disabled did not approach the courts in the past for their rights. There were a few lawsuits relating to the issue of disabled people's right to employment filed under the general principle of right to equality enshrined in the Constitution of India (see footnote 1, pp. 7–8) before the PwD Act was passed.[3]

To sum up, it may be concluded that prior to passage of the PwD Act, it was only in rare situations that the activists approached the courts to deal with the issue of discrimination and they primarily relied on contentious political action to advocate for their rights. It may, however, be emphasized that while the post-1995 period witnessed the emergence of these new methods of advocacy, it does not mean that the traditional methods of advocacy involving contentious political action became redundant during this period. Rather, as elaborated in the next section dealing with the enrichment of the movement encompassing cross-disability groups participation, there was a coexistence of both the traditional as well as new methods of advocacy during this period, and traditional methods of advocacy involving contentious political action were used quite often by an organization like the Disability Rights Group and even the NFB. However, before moving to the next section, it is worth mentioning that in addition to the use of law as an instrument for the realization of the rights of the disabled in the post-1995 period, it is worth noting that another important development which took place during this period in India, particularly since the first decade of the twenty-first century, is the proliferation of Internet services and their usage by disabled people, particularly the blind activists.

The advent of Internet services brought great change around the world; in particular, in India, it has helped the English-educated disabled to be informed of developments at the international level and promoted interaction among the disabled activists and their allies. Access to the World Wide Web and use of e-mail have been immensely influential in promoting the mobilization of the disabled in

[3]A few lawsuits filed before the PwD Act came into force included: Daya Ram Tripathi versus State of U.P. and Ors (1986, cited in Pandy et al., 2005: 163), Narendra Kumar Chandla versus State of Haryana and Ors (1994, cited in Pandy et al., 2005: 106), Lance Dafadar Joginder Singh versus Union of India and Ors (1995, cited in Pandy et al., 2005: 106), and Nandkumar Narayanrao Ghodmare versus State of Maharashtra and Ors (1995, cited in Pandy et al., 2005: 106).

the United States in the process of the struggle for their rights (Barnartt and Scotch, 2001: 214).

One of the e-mail groups worth mentioning is the Disability Studies India Google Group,[4] which has been operational since 2010. It was initially started to promote interaction among the disability studies scholars and researchers to exchange ideas and research with each other. Its scope has also, however, increased drastically over a period of time and it has been joined by various activists as well. Over a period of time its membership has grown in size and variety, which comprise primarily, the scholars, researchers, and students engaged in disability studies as well as activists and rehabilitation professionals engaged in the field of disability.[5] These members of this group have constantly been engaged in a discussion related to wide range of issues which are of interests for scholars and educated middle-class activists involved in the field of disability, and the group serves as a forum of discussion and sharing information on various academic and political issues in this field.

Additionally, use of the Internet has particularly enabled blind activists in India to exchange their ideas through e-mails and to gain access to a wealth of information in electronic format through the use of screen reading software. Several e-mail groups have been established by blind people in India to exchange ideas with each other related to specific areas of interest. One such group is the Access India Yahoo Group; it was originally created on 4 January 2001 for blind computer users to discuss computer-related issues.[6] But over a period of time, the scope of discussion has expanded significantly. The group has a very wide membership which has connected a big group of blind people as well as their allies as it has now been joined by a large number of subscribers who regularly exchange their ideas and share relevant information among themselves. It has now become a forum for blind people as well as sighted allies working in the field of blindness from different parts of the country to exchange ideas on numerous issues including the issues of employment discrimination, obstacles to education, and the like. It has helped blind people and their allies join forces in order to deal with discrimination on the basis of blindness and implementation of the provisions of PwD Act, as well as initiating discussion of issues relating to the rights of the disabled not covered in this Act.

The availability of e-mail groups like the Access India Yahoo Group and Disability Studies India Google Group as well as other electronic mailing groups has enabled disabled activists to exchange legal documents and to work collaboratively on the filing of lawsuits in various high courts and the Supreme Court in India as well as on complaints to be registered in the offices of the Chief Commissioner for persons with disabilities and the State Commissioners for

---

[4]Retrieved on 1 September 2015 from the link: https://groups.google.com/forum/feed/disability-studies-india/msgs/atom.xml?num=15.

[5]https://groups.google.com/forum/feed/disability-studies-india/msgs/atom.xml?num=15.

[6]Retrieved on 1 September 2015 from Access India information page from the link: http://accessindia.org.in/mailman/listinfo/accessindia_accessindia.org.in.

persons with disabilities. The access to e-mail has also facilitated their correspondence with government authorities. Hence, access to the Internet has in a number of ways enhanced the advocacy efforts of the disabled in India.

In addition to the beginning of new methods of advocacy, the post-1995 period also witnessed a change in the nature of the disability rights movement in India. There are discernable trends and issues that are distinguishable from trends in the earlier phases of this movement. The most important identifiable trend that distinguishes the nature of the disability right movement during the post-1995 period from the pre-1995 period is the broadening of the agenda of struggle and cross-disability participation. Since the PwD Act ensured a wide range of rights of the disabled in India, the disabled people have now been getting a wide range of rights realized through implementation of the Act. It is, therefore, now important to analyse the recent trends in the disability rights movement in the post-1995 period due to the broadening of the agenda of struggle and the increasing participation of cross-disability rights groups. It is followed by a brief analysis of the change in the attitude of the non-governmental organizations towards advocacy.

10.4 Broadening the Agenda of the Struggle for Rights and Emergence of a Cross-Disability Character of the Movement

While there was always some sort of overlapping of issues for which struggle was carried out in the pre-1995 period, the focus was basically on a specific demand and the movement was led by an impairment-specific group, particularly the blind activists. The founders of the self-advocacy movement of the blind were primarily focused on organization building and engaged in mild forms of advocacy during the 1970s. On the other hand, the struggle for right to employment and the enactment of a disability law became the focal points of the advocacy agenda of this movement led by blind activists during the 1980s and early 1990s, respectively. However, while the predominant agenda of the struggle carried out by the National Federation of the Blind, particularly through contentious political action, was the implementation of Section 33 of the PwD Act, which mandated 3 % reservation for the disabled in public employment, the struggle carried out by the NFB as well as the other disabled people in their individual capacity and through advocacy organizations in the post-1995 period was very wide in scope. It also involved several lawsuits filed in courts and complaints registered in the offices of various state commissioners for persons with disabilities, as well as the CCPD. These lawsuits and complaints have been related to a very wide range of issues including the right to housing, access to social security, and the right to education, among others (Pandy et al., 2005; NHRC, 2005; Case Law Reporter, 2008). However, it needs to be acknowledged that the majority of the lawsuits were still related to the issue of right to employment.[7]

It is true that the struggle led by the organized blind since the late 1980s to 1995 aimed at accomplishing an agenda that is considered to be common to the interests of different categories of disability groups, namely the passage of a comprehensive disability rights law. However, the major limitation of the self-advocacy movement of the blind prior to the passage of the PwD Act was that it lacked cross-disability participation. In contrast to this, the post-1995 period witnessed the beginning of participation of diverse disability groups in the struggle for their rights; this has contributed significantly to the enrichment of the disability rights movement.

A cross-disability rights group called the Disability Rights Group (DRG) was established in Delhi in March 1994 (Bhambhani, 2004). This marked the beginning of a cross-disability rights alliance in the capital city. Since the DRG came to play a very effective role in advocacy for a broader group of the disabled including the blind, the issues of promotion and protection of rights of blind people also were included in that process. While the NFB continues as a leading advocacy organization addressing issues regarding the rights of blind people, increased participation of diverse disability groups, particularly the DRG, has made a significant contribution in strengthening this movement.

The contribution of the DRG is particularly crucial in two ways: First, the DRG succeeded in widening the scope of issues concerning various categories of disabled as it actively advocated for the rights of cross-disability groups instead of focusing on the rights of any disability-specific group. Second, despite the fact that over time, DRG began to be essentially a one-person organization, dominated by Javed Abidi who claimed to speak on behalf of all disabled people and who made unilateral decisions; it must be acknowledged that this was for the first time that disabled activists with different types of disabilities had come together to advocate for their rights (Ray, 2001). Some of the common issues addressed by DRG through contentious political action included:

[7]Some of these include: Ashok M. Shrimali and Ors. versus State Bank of India and Ors., (2001, cited in NHRC, 2005: 134); Baljeet Singh versus Delhi Transport Corporation, (2000, cited in Pandy et al., 2005: 163–164); Delhi Transport Corporation versus Sh. Harpal Singh and Anr., (2003, cited in Pandy et al., 2005: 111); Government of NCT of Delhi versus Bharat Lal Meena and Surinder Singh, (2002, cited in Pandy et al., 2005: 152); Jaswant Singh and Anr. versus State of Punjab, (1996, cited in Pandy et al., 2005: 107); Kunal Singh versus Union of India, (2003, cited in Pandy et al., 2005: 110–111); LIC of India versus Chief Commissioner for Disabilities and Anr., (2003, cited in Pandy et al., 2005: 111); Pushkar Singh and Ors. versus University of Delhi and Ors., (2001, cited in Pandy et al., 2005: 108–109); Ravi Kumar Arora versus Union of India and Anr., (2004, cited in Pandy et al., 2005: 113); Shall Kumar versus Bharat Petroleum Corporation, (2004, cited in Pandy et al., 2005: 113); Smt. Shruti Kalra versus University of Delhi and Ors., (2001, cited in Pandy et al., 2005: 109); University of Rajasthan versus Surendra Kumar Goyal, (2003, cited in Pandy et al., 2005: 112–113); and I. S. Uppala Venkat versus South Central Railway and Ors., (2003, cited in Pandy et al., 2005: 100).

- appointment of the Chief Commissioner on Disability in 1997 (Bhambhani, 2004: 45);
- inclusion of the disabled in the 2001 census (Menon, 2000);
- raising the limit of the income tax exemption for disabled people and parents of disabled children (The Indian Express, 2002);
- exemption of customs/excise duties on aids and appliances used by the disabled (The Hindu, 2003);
- right to accessible voting (The Hindu, 2004; Disability News and Information Service, 2004a, b);
- Opposition to appointment of able-bodied professionals as the head of the apex level institutions in the field of disability like the CCPD, the Rehabilitation Council of India, and the National Trust for Welfare of Persons with Autism, Cerebral Palsy, Mental Retardation, and Multiple Disabilities (Bhambhani, 2004: 50–52).

Similarly, the issues taken up by the DRG through court cases included: right to vote and expansion of the definition of disability under the PwD Act to include dyslexia as one of the types of learning disabilities for the purpose of granting admission under the quota for disabled students at the college level. Earlier, Javed Abidi, the leader of the DRG, had also filed a lawsuit against Indian Airlines to provide discounts for wheelchair users and ensure accessible airports. The verdict in this trial was identifiably the first victory by and for disabled persons in India under the PwD Act of 1995 (Bhambhani, 2004).

Before concluding this section, it is worth mentioning that there has been a marked changed in the attitude of the middle-class professionals which is evident through the example of composition of the DRG at the time of its formation as IT reflected the change in the approach of the middle-class disabled members as well as the non-governmental organizations (NGOs) engaged in promoting rehabilitation measures in the field of disability. One of the leading members of DRG at the time of its founding in March 1994 was Javed Abidi who happened to be a wheelchair user. Abidi was then heading the Disability Division of the Rajiv Gandhi Foundation, a foundation established by the family of the former Prime Minister of India in 1991 to carry out philanthropic work.[8] Yet another leading member at the time of its founding was Lal Advani who had spearheaded the process of rehabilitation in the field of disability in India as a civil servant (Chander and Baquer, 2005: 4). The other core group members of DRG at the time of its founding included Sarvjit Singh, a wheelchair user, who was then serving as a high-level civil servant in the Ministry of Railways, Ali Baquer who was heading an NGO engaged in the field of intellectual disabilities, and Jagdish Chander, a blind professor in the University of Delhi (Chander, 2011: 386). This composition of the core group of DRG at the time of its founding in 1994 reflects the fact that there was beginning to be a degree of acceptance of the advocacy-based approach by middle-class disabled members of

[8]Retrieved on 7 January 2011 from the home page of Rajiv Gandhi Foundation from the link: http://www.rgfindia.com/index.htm.

the society as well as professionals working in the field of disability. It is symbolic of a significant change in the approach of middle-class professionals engaged in the NGOs working in the field of disability, in contrast to their traditional approach of disregard for the contentious political action adopted by radical advocacy organizations like the NFB. Following this brief overview of the beginning of cross-disability advocacy in the post-1995 period, what follows next is a brief mention of another trend that emerged during the recent years, i.e. the acceptance of the rights-based approach by the NGOs engaged in the disability sector, particularly the ones engaged in the field of blindness.

10.5 Acceptance of a Rights-Based Approach by NGOs in the Field of Disability

The self-advocacy movement of the blind had gained momentum in India by the beginning of the 1980s, but it was not until the early 1990s that the advocacy-oriented approach was accepted by the service delivery organizations engaged in the field of disability. These organizations were highly dependent on the state and charitable or philanthropic institutions or individuals for funding during the second half of the last century (Mohanty and Singh, 2001). Neither the State nor the generous private funders endorsed the advocacy approach adopted by the disabled. These NGOs, therefore, had no choice but to avoid association with organizations practicing an advocacy-oriented approach based on a radical disability rights perspective and involving methods of contentious political action as they were not in a position to displease their funders. However, in recent years, this situation has been changing because of various international developments. One of the most crucial of these is the emergence of the philosophy of self-advocacy within the field of disability. This has led to an acceptance of the advocacy approach by NGOs working in the field of disability including those involved in the field of blindness in India. As a result, there has been a marked shift in their approach from significant opposition to any kind of advocacy to its acceptance.

It is well established that most NGOs in the field of disability in India have been run by able-bodied individuals and have had very limited participation of the disabled in their decision-making processes. As noted in 2005 by the National Human Rights Commission in its manual on disability:

> Majority of the voluntary organizations working in the area of disability in India are dominated by able-bodied, philanthropic individuals and professionals. They view people with disabilities as unfit to carry out day-to-day affairs of their lives. Such an approach is characteristic of the biocentric model, which presupposes the inability of people with disability to take charge of their own situation. … There were over 3,000 such service-delivery NGOs engaged in the field of disability in India in the year 2005 (NHRC, 2005: 35).

However, despite such a preponderance of NGOs dominated by able-bodied philanthropists and professionals which continue to adhere to a traditional, paternalistic approach towards the disabled, there is a beginning of acceptance of a rights-based approach by the leading NGOs in the field of disability.

In recent years, the disabled have not been allowing able-bodied professionals to speak on behalf of them and, instead, have themselves been leading the movement for their rights. Thus, there has been an emergence and acceptance of the philosophy of self-advocacy symbolized by the slogan "Nothing about us, without us" (Charlton, 1998). Activism in the field of disability leading to a disability rights movement in various parts of the world provided a greater legitimacy to advocacy in the field of disability at the international level. This, in turn, influenced the civil societies as well as the states internationally. The movement for enactment of the Americans with Disabilities Act (ADA) in the United States and similar movements led by disabled people in different parts of the world led to an increased participation of disabled people in the process of advocacy for their rights. For example, the Disabled People's International (DPI), which is a leading international organization of disabled people, was founded on the bases of philosophy of self-advocacy. DPI soon acquired widespread support from international organizations working in the field of disability.[9] Even international organizations that are not focused solely on disability have begun to support a disability rights perspective; for example, World Bank hired Judy Heumann who has been a pioneer of the Independent Living Movement and leader of the disability rights movement in the United States (Disability World, 2002) and lately, she was hired to work in the Obama administration as special advisor for international disability rights, under the US State Department.[10] This illustrates a change in the attitude towards advocacy leading to a rights-based approach at the international level.

In an era of globalization and the Internet, India has been an active participant in international affairs and so it is logical that its civil society organizations as well as government authorities would be considerably influenced by international developments. Emergence of an approach based on the philosophy of self-advocacy was thus bound to influence the ideology of the service delivery organizations in the field of disability. These organizations could no longer be oblivious to this newly emerging advocacy-oriented approach after it acquired legitimacy at the international level. At the same time, the change in the approach towards advocacy at the international level also influenced the government, private funding bodies, and individual donors in India. Hence, the fear of alienating funders through adoption of an advocacy-oriented approach has also been decreasing, which is proving to be a very important factor in prompting the NGOs engaged in the disability field to change their attitude towards advocacy. The change reflected in the attitude of All India Confederation of the Blind (AICB) which was established after a split in the

[9]Retrieved from the home page of Disabled Peoples' International on 7 January 2011 from the link: http://www.dpi.org/.

[10]Judith E. Heumann's biography, retrieved on 7 February 2012 from the US State website's link at: http://www.state.gov/r/pa/ei/biog/144458.htm.

NFB in 1978 is illustrative of the acceptance of advocacy approach by the NGOs engaged in the field of disability.

From the time of the formation of AICB in 1978, its prominent leader, Jawahar Lal Kaul, and his close associates actively opposed the advocacy-based approach adopted by NFB for about a decade. However, by the late 1980s, the leadership of AICB gradually began to accept this approach. Similarly, its involvement in contentious political action as well as advocacy through the use of legal forums to get the provisions of the PwD Act implemented was clearly noticed in the post-1995 period. For instance, AICB was the co-organizer with the NFB of a joint rally in August 2005 demanding the implementation of some of the provisions of the PwD Act, particularly its Section 33, seeking amendments to the law and replacement of a sighted director of NIVH with a blind individual (The Tribune, 2005).

In addition to involvement in certain advocacy activities involving contentious political action, the AICB has regularly engaged in advocacy through registering complaints before the CCPD. For example, the AICB filed a complaint with the CCPD in 1999 relating to the issue of denial of promotion of blind employees selected under the reserved quota system for the blind in a leading government run bank (Chander, 2011: 350). Similarly, citing Section 33 of the PwD Act, the chief functionary of AICB took the matter of promotion of blind employees in higher levels of jobs through the forum of the Central Administrative Tribunal, which deals with issues of the rights of Central Government employees. At the same time, the AICB has also been knocking on the doors of the court from time to time to get the provisions of the PwD Act implemented.

Prominent lawsuits filed by the AICB in the Supreme Court of India included one under which it demanded that it is the responsibility of the government to provide school level text books in Braille (All India Confederation of Blind and Anr versus Union of India and Anr, 1998, cited in NHRC, 2005: 94–95). Similarly, another very crucial issue was related to the relaxation of qualifying grades for the test conducted by the University Grants Commission (the apex level body which sets standards for higher level education) for eligibility for teaching positions at the higher education level (All India Confederation of the Blind versus Union of India, 2002, cited in Pandy et al., 2005: 470). Hence, the approach of the AICB towards advocacy started changing slightly by the late 1980s, but its leadership began to clearly adhere to the advocacy-oriented approach in the post-1995 period.

10.6 Conclusion

Blind activists were pioneers among the disabled activists to launch their self-advocacy movement during the 1970s. This disability-specific movement led by the blind was converted into a broad disability rights movement when the NFB-led movement was focused on the demand for the enactment of a broader disability rights legislation from 1988 onwards, which ultimately, led to the passage of the PwD Act. Disabled activists along with their allies started to make frequent use of this law both on an individual basis as well as through advocacy organizations. Hence, in the post-1995 period, law has become an instrument that can be used by any disabled person covered under it to seek the realization of his or her rights. While contentious political action such as rallies and picketing took place sporadically, filing of lawsuits in the courts of India and complaints in the offices of various quasi-judicial bodies, namely the State Commissioners for persons with disabilities, the CCPD, and the National Human Rights Commission, were adopted as important means of advocacy. Therefore, the post-1995 period was characterized by the use of a combination of methods of advocacy ranging from traditional contentious political action to legal approaches through an increase in use of courts to litigate rights and file complaints in the quasi-judicial bodies. This period has also been marked by a beginning of participation of different disability groups as well as advocacy for an expanding horizon of issues relating to the rights of the disabled. At the same time, this period also witnessed a drastic change in the attitude of NGOs operating in the field of disability towards the advocacy-oriented approach.

Thus, the rights-based perspective is now widely embraced by the current generation of disability rights activists from cross sections of disability and the non-governmental organizations. This perspective has evolved as a well-established and internalized approach that dominates the thinking of the disabled activists. It is likely to strengthen over time as it crystallizes at the national and international levels. Disabled people are, therefore, no longer going to be passive recipients of services. Rather, they are active advocates for their rights and will emerge as the masters of their destiny.

References

Baquer, A., & Sharma, A. (1997). *Disability: Challenges vs. responses*. Concerned Action Now: New Delhi.

Barnartt, S., & Scotch, R. (2001). *Disability protests: Contentious politics 1970–1999*. Washington, DC: Gallaudet University.

Bhambhani, M. (2004). *From charity to self-advocacy: The emergence of disability rights movement in India*. Unpublished master's thesis, University of Illinois at Chicago.

Case Law Reporter. (2008). Vol. 1, (1999–2002). Office of the Chief Commissioner for Persons with Disabilities: New Delhi.

Chander, J. (2011). *Movement of the Organized Blind in India: From Passive Recipients of Services to Active Advocates of Their Rights. Cultural Foundations of Education—Dissertations.* Paper 50. Syracuse University, Syracuse, New York. Retrieved on 5 August 2015 from: http://surface.syr.edu/cfe_etd/50

Chander, J., & Baquer, A. (2005). *Lal Advani: The torch bearer*. Delhi: Indian Association for Special Education and Rehabilitation: Delhi.

Charlton, J. I. (1998). *Nothing about us without us: Disability, oppression and empowerment*. Berkeley: University of California Press.

Disability News and Information Service. (2004a). Protest outside EC office: several activists detained. 2(9), 1 May. Retrieved on 4 July 2009 from: http://www.dnis.org/index-2.php?issue_id=9&volume_id=2

Disability News and Information Service. (2004b). Dharna moves Election Commission to action, 2(19), 1 October. Retrieved on 4 July 2009 from: http://www.dnis.org/index-2.php?issue_id=19&volume_id=2

Disability World. (2002). World Bank Appoints Judy Heumann to New Disability Adviser Post. Issue 13, April–May. Retrieved on 7 January 2011 from: http://www.disabilityworld.org/index.htm

Limaye, M. (1984). Socialist movement in the early years of independence. In G. K. C. Reddy (Ed.), *Fifty years of socialist movement in India: Retrospect and prospects* (pp. 38–53). New Delhi: Samata Era Publication.

Mani, D. R. (1988). *The physically handicapped in India: Policy and programmes*. Delhi: Ashish Publishing House.

Menon, S. (2000). Disability rights group to strike over Census issue. *The Indian Express*, 19 April. Retrieved on 30 June 2009 from: http://www.indianexpress.com/ie/daily/20000419/ina19045.html

Mohan, S. (1984). The turbulent years: 1952–55. In G. K. C. Reddy (Ed.). (1984). *Fifty years of socialist movement in India: Retrospect and prospects* (pp. 54–60). New Delhi: Samata Era Publication.

Mohanty, M., & Singh, A. K. (2001). *Voluntarism and government policy, programme and assistance*. New Delhi: Voluntary Action Network India.

National Human Rights Commission (NHRC). (2005). *Disability manual*. New Delhi: NHRC.

Omvedt, G. (2001). Ambedkar and after: The dalit movement in India. In G. Shah (Ed.), *Dalit identity and politics: Cultural subordination and the dalit challenge* (Vol. 2, pp. 143–159). London: Sage Publications.

Pandey, R. S., & Advani, L. (1995). *Perspectives on disability and rehabilitation*. Delhi: Vikas Publishing House.

Pandy, S., Chirimar, P., & Desouza, D. (2005). *Disability and the law*. New Delhi: National Human Rights Law Network.

Ray, A. (2001). Giving visibility to the disabled in India. *Changemakers.net Journal*. January 2001. Retrieved on 28 June 2009 from: http://proxied.changemakers.net/journal/01january/ray.cfm

Rudolph, R. I., & Rudolph, S. H. (1987). *In pursuit of Lakshmi: The political economy of the Indian state*. Chicago: University of Chicago Press

The Hindu. (2003). Rally to make govt. see reason. 17 February. Retrieved on 28 June 2009 from: http://www.hinduonnet.com/2003/02/17/stories/2003021707080400.htm

The Hindu. (2004). Abidi to fast unto death over EC's attitude, 14 April. Retrieved on 3 July 2009 from: http://www.hinduonnet.com/2004/04/14/stories/2004041409260400.htm

The Indian Express. (2002). Disabled rights activists rally to awaken Centre, 7 May. Retrieved on 30 June 2009 from: http://cities.expressindia.com/fullstory.php?newsid=16875

The Tribune. (2005). Visually impaired take out rally, 17 August. Retrieved on 1 July 2009 from: http://www.tribuneindia.com/2005/20050817/delhi.htm

Vanaik, A. (1990). *The painful transition: Bourgeois democracy in India*. New York: Verso.

Chapter 11
Disabled People's Organizations in India: Assertions and Angsts

Nandini Ghosh

Abstract Social movements are conscious, collective, concerted and sustained efforts by broad social alliances of people connected through their shared interest in affecting social change. Over the past few years, alliances of persons with disabilities, termed Disabled People's Organizations (DPOs), are being forged at local levels in order to initiate localized disability advocacy struggles in various parts of India, and also in order to bring about a perceptible change in the status of disabled people. Such DPOs are formed on the basis of a collective identity for all persons with disability and are organized on the lines of self-help groups (SHGs) by local NGOs, either working on disability-specific issues or on general community issues. This chapter explores the formation and genesis of such DPOs in different parts of India and the processes whereby these groups have engaged with the goals they were set up for. The chapter attempts to assess the extent to which these groups have been able to achieve a movement for change of social attitudes at the grass-roots level and the resultant effect it has on their identities. The engagement with social movement processes has also revealed and crystallized divisions within the DPOs themselves, with internal power struggles and dynamics influencing the outcomes of their achievements.

Keywords Disabled people's organizations · Social movement · Identity · Advocacy · Social change

Social movements are conscious, collective, organized, concerted and sustained efforts by ordinary people to challenge and change cultural beliefs and social practices or the attitudes of the authorities or power holders (Goodwin and Jasper, 2009). The relationship between power and identity becomes crucial for individuals and groups who are experiencing institutionalized forms of inequality and discrimination. Participants in these new movements seek to regain control over their personal and collective sense of identity. The personal becomes political.

N. Ghosh (✉)
Institute of Development Studies Kolkata, Kolkata, India
e-mail: nandinighosh@gmail.com

N. Ghosh (ed.), *Interrogating Disability in India*,
Dynamics of Asian Development, DOI 10.1007/978-81-322-3595-8_11

Freire (1970) maintained that social transformation and the liberation of oppressed, marginalized groups in any society can only be realized when such groups come together to reflect on their situation (past and present) and collectively plan for change. Barnes and Mercer (2010) argue that the disabled people's movement can be defined as a new social movement because it is marginal to conventional politics which is demonstrated by the fact that most organizations run by disabled people have been peripheral to conventional political structures. The disabled people's movement offers critical evaluation of society and systematic oppression of disabled people. The barriers are embedded in policies and practices based on individualistic medical approach to disability. Consequently, the removal of such barriers requires a fundamental reappraisal of the meaning and medicalization of disability and a recognition that multiple deprivations experienced by disabled people are the outcome of hostile physical and social environments and the way in which society is organized (Barton, 1993). The disability movement has focused on developing collective organization for the benefit of all disabled people (Campbell and Oliver, 1996).

Disability movements in Western, developed countries have focused on the improvement of the quality of life of persons with disabilities by confronting the disadvantages and discrimination people with disabilities face in society. In India, disability activism started in the 1990s; however, the complexity and diversity entailed in disability did not allow the unification for the foremost reason that disabled people are a diverse group cut across by race, caste, class divisions (Mehrotra, 2011). In India, the emergence of a disability rights movement has practically started post the 1995 landmark legislation which, for the first time, ensured some basic rights for disabled people. However, before this period, visually impaired people had begun organized self-advocacy movements in the 1970s and 1980s, to ensure rights of blind people to education and work (Chandar 2012). In 1994, a cross-disability coalition was formed in New Delhi in order to deliberate on the new legislation that was being formulated in India due to international pressure and advocacy efforts of some powerful disabled people with contacts in the right places. The Disability Rights Group (DRG) was a group of like-minded people, mainly persons with different categories of disabilities: it was probably for the first time in India, persons having different disabilities joined hands to fight for a larger cause, ignoring their individual differences. Alongside the DRG, a National Disability Network (NDN) has also emerged which seeks to build a strong cross-disability rights movement in India by linking disability groups around the country so that they can all share ideas and participate in the decision-making process. This national network aims to act as a pressure group to influence meaningful policies at various levels—village, block, district, state, and national—regarding persons with disabilities. These local-level disability advocacy groups are being promoted and facilitated by funding agencies and NGOs to mobilize locally for access to government schemes and facilities and to create role models in society which they hope will promote inclusion.

Thus, political consciousness regarding disability identity has been a post-legislation development in India. A political consciousness does not in itself constitute a social movement, as people may be aware of their own identity marker but not be able to posit a similarity in the conditions of oppression faced by them and other people with disabilities. There is need for building awareness about the commonness of the situation of people with disabilities as disability is not a homogeneous category—people with a varied range of impairments are grouped together in a category, and the difficulties and responses to being disabled are influenced by class, race, gender and age factors, which cushion or compound the experience of discrimination and oppression. The identity of disabled people is sought to be built on the daily realities of discriminatory experiences, in order to develop a sense of self-worth and resistance based on an alternative set of values and interpretations. Thus, the struggle of disabled people is for a positive self-identity, empowerment and full participation in society.

The politics of disability in India has followed a different trajectory in India as the national-level leadership of disabled people was unable to reach out to the people living at grass-roots level. This void was filled by NGOs and funding agencies, who had a stake in developing collectives of persons with disabilities at local level, who would then be able to rally against the oppression faced by them on a daily basis at the local level. One of the main reasons funding agencies took up the cause of stimulating a movement of disabled people was that international funding was increasingly being made available not for support towards rehabilitation but for enabling people to exert pressure on governments to respond to the needs or rights of disabled people. International agencies, fuelled by the emerging definitions of disability and international politics, sought to utilize the people's power to pressurize governments to deliver—this was part of their strategy of ensuring sustainability of service delivery by making the state more responsible. Working through different NGOs, funding agencies sought to organize disabled people into collectives. The movement kicked off in the southern states of India and in some parts of north-western India, namely Gujarat. It has now taken off in most of the eastern states of India, the north-eastern states and the central belt. The vision of action taken up was to bring together people with different impairments, to help them to identify themselves as disabled persons, and to understand the ways in which they experience oppression.

This chapter is based on the study of 19 groups or federations of persons with disabilities from 7 different states (Andhra Pradesh, Karnataka, Tamil Nadu, Odisha, West Bengal, Jharkhand and Nagaland) and 1 union territory (Pondicherry) in the eastern, north-eastern and southern regions. Members in the groups vary from 5 members (which is the minimum size for forming a group) to 15–18 members with all types of disabilities. Amongst the Disabled People's Organizations (DPOs) visited, some have been formed around recently while others have been working for a decade or so. Most of the DPOs have been mentored in accordance with the norms of the Swarnajayanti Gram Swarozgar Yojana (SGSY) groups in India, which receives support from local governments. Usually, the leaders of the group are selected by voice vote but in some large federations in South India, elections are held for different posts of the office bearers. Most groups also have developed some norms of functioning, which are written in monthly meeting registers, but there are few DPOs that have been formalized through laws or statutes. It is only in the lager federations and mostly in South India that written codes of conduct and memorandum of association are seen.

11.1 Disability Politics in India

Disabled people's collectives have achieved much success in terms of generating awareness amongst disabled people regarding their rights and entitlements, developing self-confidence amongst members and changing attitudes at the community level. The first impediment to developing such collectives was the fact that having a disability does not itself ensure participation in collective political action with others who have disabilities (Scotch, 1988). Other movements by oppressed people have relied on physical proximity and shared interests to mobilize them to initiate and sustain a movement. However, for disabled people both these factors influence their mobilization for movement. Persons with disabilities are spread spatially and demographically across the general population, although many disabilities may be concentrated amongst those with the least economic, social and political resources in their societies. This means that to gather them together, given the exigencies of their impairments is a major challenge. Added to this is the task of creating unity amongst disunity—people with different types and degrees of impairments have differing experiences of the social world and their "oppression". Thus, the concept of oppression has to be manufactured in order to posit a unity based on their differing experiences, some of which might be related to infrastructural barriers, others to attitudinal and still others to exclusionary practices. The differing nature of their impairments is also a major barrier for most persons with disabilities identifying with each other. The main reason for this is that different impairments have different needs for support and management and as these vary largely between those with gross physical impairments to people with intellectual disabilities the identification of similar experiences across disabilities is difficult. Thus, for persons with disabilities to form groups and lobby for their rights is an exercise that is made difficult not only by the nature of their impairments but also because of the sociocultural ideologies within which these people are located.

Forming of cross-disability groups is also a challenge not only because the issues of people with different impairments is different, but also because of the sociocultural ideologies within which these people are located. The task of uniting persons with disabilities and forging a common identity based on the experience of impairment and discrimination in India has been taken up by grass-roots-level NGOs. Unlike other marginal identity groups, and somewhat similar to the gay population, disabled people live scattered all over the villages or locality and are not acquainted with one another as most of them hardly step out of their homes. Their physical and social isolation enforced by combination of their impairments, the social and infrastructural barriers they encounter both inside and outside their homes and the resultant low self-esteem most of them have, influences the joining of groups by persons with disabilities. Notions of incompetence and dependence influence their daily lives where these people are seen as incapable of performing any productive role in family or society. Lack of proximity becomes a major factor in their coming together as a group and poses a challenge for mentoring NGOs in grouping them into functional units. For disabled people who have never been out of the homes, let alone their village, even the thought of going to meet other disabled people initially is a challenge. "I thought how can I go? Who will take me? Will anyone have time? What can we discuss there? What can I contribute?" says Nagamani of the Mashal Federation Odisha. For most others, the terrain, lack of roads and proper transport, lack of people to help them on the way, etc., all become a barrier to attending group meetings. Karuppaiah from Visthar Federation felt, "How can I expect people to carry me all the way to the other end of the village for the meeting? It is also damaging for my self-esteem".

The disabled people's groups are dominated by men, and the representation of women is less, with the male–female ratio being roughly 60:40 in the groups. However, while 80 % of the men attend the meetings regularly, only 40 % of the women are able to come to the meetings on a regular basis. Thus, issues that are concerned specifically with gender are often overlooked as the disability oppression is the primary focus. Because of the nature of their impairments and the voice that they have, most of the DPOs are dominated by persons with mild to moderate locomotor and visual impairments. The severely disabled people, persons with sensory impairments and mental challenges remain marginalized within the groups even though the groups purport to represent all categories of persons with disabilities. Members who are mentally challenged hardly attend the meetings and are represented by their caregivers. There is very minimal presence of persons with mental health issues and their caregivers in most of the groups, except in some pockets in the south where NGO-driven programmes have ensured inclusion of persons with mental illness in the groups. What was interesting in the south is that the other markers of identity are quite steady—most of the people belong to the poorer section and to the lower castes. On the other hand, in Bengal and Jharkhand, while the DPOs claim to have members from all caste backgrounds unified on the basis that all are poor and hence oppressed, there were hardly any member of the upper castes in the DPOs. While the selection of issues for action did not display any caste dimension, what came up as a finding was that the leadership positions were assumed by people of the dominant caste, with disabled members voting along caste lines.

Participation in the activities and meetings of the DPOs is determined by the local history and culture of people's movements in the region. In the southern states where there is long history of people's struggles against hegemony, most of the disabled adults themselves attend the meetings of the groups with a few parents or caregivers of persons with intellectual impairments and mental illness also attending. On the other hand, in the eastern and north-eastern parts of the country, the meetings are attended mostly by the parents of disabled people, with very few disabled adults participating in the meetings. While one of the reasons for this may be the fact the DPOs in the south have been working for the last 5–7 years while the others are relatively newly formed, the major reason seems to be cultural, where the creation of a disability identity was spurred on by disabled adults themselves acting as animators of the NGOs and DPOs were started as movement for adult people. In the east and north-east, DPOs have a lot of children as members, whose parents represent them in the groups. As a result when the child grows into an adult, parents still represent their adult wards in the meetings instead of handing over the responsibility to the disabled person. Even when the disabled person is an adult, there is a tendency in eastern and north-eastern part of the country for the parents to represent them in DPO meetings.

11.2 The Collectives: Vision and Activities

As almost all of the disabled persons belong to the poorest families in the community, there is great divergence in the reasons given for forming collectives. This varies regionally and also depending on the participation of disabled people in the groups as well as on the age of the DPO. In the east and north-east where parents dominate the groups, the major concern behind forming the DPO was to ensure the care and protection for their mentally challenged children or young adults. In Disability Welfare Association of Nagaland, mothers of adult persons with intellectual impairments clearly stated, "We are worried about the future when we will no longer be there. Their siblings may take care of them and they will have a place to stay. But who will care for them? What will happen then?" The parents felt that the group as a whole could take responsibility for ensuring that the disabled people have a good life after the parents are dead. In the north-east because of community spirit amongst Christian-dominated tribal villages, most of the DPOs talk in terms of helping each other and extending support in times of stress.

However, one of the major stimulating factors towards mobilization into groups has also been to seek improved or increased income—an overwhelming need of almost all persons with disabilities. For many of the village-level disabled people who become members of DPOs, the first and foremost concern is of financial security, which savings credit ensures to a limited extent. Members of the Deep Viklang Samity in Jharkhand who came to the federation meeting all claimed that they call their group SHGs: "We do not think there is any difference between DPO and SHG. This language helps us to access grant from the state". Moreover, groups interested in livelihood activities either individually or even as a group feel that advocacy for inclusion and equal rights is better achieved once they can secure their daily existence. In Tamil Nadu, in 2004, when the state government decided to provide a sum of Rs. 10,000 to all SHGs in the state, in Tiruvallur for the first time disabled people came forward to form their own SHGs in order to claim the revolving fund. Most of the work done by the DPOs and the Federation in Icchak and Hazaribagh blocks of Jharkhand has been to consolidate and engage persons with disabilities in income-generating activities. "The main focus of our work has been to ensure the livelihood options for our disabled members".

Most of the DPOs have savings and credit as one of their primary activities, where each member saves a fixed amount of money on a monthly basis, which are then deposited in bank accounts opened in the name of the DPO. While almost all the groups save money, it is more an imperative in the northern and north-eastern states where the general standard of living is worse than in South India. Moreover, in the southern states almost all disabled people receive disability pensions, which serve to fulfil immediate needs. In South India where almost all members receive pensions, members' contributions are as high as Rs. 50 per month per person but in most of the rural areas of West Bengal and Odisha, where there is no provision of pension or income contributions per month per member varies between Rs. 10 and Rs. 20. Members take loans for various reasons ranging from running petty shop, buying books, school uniforms and paying fees for the children, medical expenses, etc. These savings and credit activities have helped the members of DPOs to become self-dependent and earning members of the family and community. Most of the disabled people with little skill training and few resources, financial or otherwise, to take up income generation activities have actually been able to use the funds generated by the savings activities to either initiate new income generation activities or augment their already existing family businesses. These loans have helped disabled people to start income-generating work, ranging from setting up petty shops, to rearing livestock, to hiring out essential commodities to local workers. In Odisha, the DPO members have taken internal loans from the group and invested in *sawai* grass business. In Jharkhand, DPOs have concentrated mainly on improvement of livelihood chances of their members, through tailoring, poultry, piggery and petty shops. However, the focus of such activities has remained the disabled people who are able to access such facilities—the locomotor disabled and the visually impaired. "Disabled people having their own income have changed attitudes to some extent. What it has also done is give us confidence to start our own small business".

As economic empowerment remains one of the main thrusts, the DPOs have undertaken a lot of advocacy work on livelihood issues. Economic empowerment is ensured by tapping government financial schemes and other provisions like NABARD loans and bank loans with the help of NGOs. Disabled People's Sangha in Tamil Nadu has worked hard for getting bank loans which is important for them to earn a livelihood. However, one of the major challenges most groups have faced with regard to savings and credit is with the opening of the banks account. Most banks still refuse to open savings accounts for such DPOs. Most banks open bank accounts for SHGs, on the principle of homogeneity, whether it is women, farmers, etc. When the disabled people's groups approached banks for opening an account, most banks refuse for two reasons. One is the lack of homogeneity amongst the members, which may also include persons with intellectual and severe disabilities. These groups of people are not allowed as signatories to the bank and even their membership in the group is frowned upon. Often the issue is resolved by parents taking the place of these members as signatories, which is violation of rights and assumptions regarding minimal capacities of persons of disabilities. The second reason is more cultural—most banking institutions do not consider disabled people as a good proposition and are afraid that the account may not be continued over a period of time. From Mashal Odisha, one member said:

> The bank officials ignored us when we went to open an account. They looked at us, the way in which we were dressed and moved, and then asked us to wait. After a long time, they came and said that we could not open an account there.

In the south, however, refusal by banks merits strong action by the DPOs. Suraksha Federation (to preserve anonymity.....have done with some of the others ...missed some) working in Pondicherry and Tamil Nadu filed a complaint with the district collector against a bank manager who spoke rudely to group members and did not sanction loan. Action was taken against the manager, and they also got the loan amount sanctioned.

One of the main issues that have been chosen for advocacy most groups is livelihood. Armed with the stipulation in the PwD Act that disabled people are entitled to 3 % reservation in all poverty alleviation schemes, the DPOs have been clamouring for inclusion in the National Rural Employment Guarantee Schemes (NREGS) being implemented in rural areas. These efforts have, however, met with limited success, depending on the people in charge of the programme in different districts. In the south, successful advocacy has meant that several states have passed exemplary legislation and framed inclusive rules to ensure disabled people enjoy the right to work. Under the NREGS in Andhra Pradesh, the work allotted is for 150 days for person with disabilities. So instead of paying equal wage for less pay or paying lesser wages, the strategy has been to provide more work to benefit persons with disabilities and their families. After becoming organized, DPOs are now helping members to access work. In the Baripada district of Odisha, Nagamani got work under the NREGS. "The work given to a general labourer is soil work. I had done 7 days of work but the contractor wrote 12 days in my job card. So I demanded the wage of 12 days as it is written in the card and got it". In Nagaland, most of the job cards of people registered under the NREGS is in the hands of the Village Development Board members. In Modesty Group, Nagaland, the Village Development Board gave work to 2 disabled people for 1 day each only. The DPO had requested for work as a group and worked for 1 day but no payment was made as the Village Development Board said that there was no money sanctioned separately for disabled people in 2009. "They said what work can the disabled person do? The persons with hearing impairment works anyway as daily labourer".

11.3 Advocacy for Rights

For most of the disabled people who become members of DPOs, the group is a means to do something for disabled people. Most of the members of the groups/federations speak in terms of forming a group to realize their rights—the understanding of rights is varied and connected mainly to their basic needs.

> Rights are what should be provided to us by the government – food, house and shelter. Government has to take responsibility for our needs. Visthar Federation, Tamil Nadu.

> Government has a duty to protect and provide for us and that is why they have made different schemes. We are claiming these schemes as our right – these are for us. Mashal, Odisha.

> Rights are available from the Panchayat and the block – it is their duty to deliver the schemes to us which is our right to receive. Viklang Samity, Andhra Pradesh.

The human rights jargon has percolated down to the grass-roots level without proper understanding of what it entails in terms of rights holders and duty bearers and their corresponding obligations. For most group members, their entire life has been characterized by poverty and thus rights are interpreted as entitlements and schemes framed by either central or state government for persons with disabilities. Disabled people have analysed their situation and realize that people who benefit from different schemes are those who are proximate to people in positions of power, while such schemes remain unreachable for the vast majority of people, who are poor and more in need of such provisions. Finding comfort in group or common identity helps disabled people to rally together to demand for their rights and entitlements. Karuppaiah from Tamil Nadu said, "For each individual it is very difficult to get the rights individually, but through *sangha*s (groups), together they can make the change". Disabled members of a *sangha* in Themmavoor in Tamil Nadu said that they came together for unity and oneness. "If a group of persons together ask for any scheme/benefits then there is a possibility of getting it". Members of Mashal Odisha echoed the same thought: "When we go alone to ask for something, the government does not listen to us. This is the reason we have decided to go together as a group to present our demands to the existing government set up".

Disabled people's organizations in India have been formed around the issue of social and economic rights, with the major focus being on the access to different government entitlements ranging from scholarships, to mobility aids and appliances to loans and pensions as these are the easiest to lobby for and access. The interpretation of rights has been in terms of access to facilities which the governments are bound to provide for persons with disabilities as they have "suffered" certain disadvantages in life. Most of the disabled people were denied benefits because of more systemic reasons before they became members of the group. "We didn't have any disability certificates, bus pass, rail concession etc. We got no other benefits". Most of the efforts of almost all the DPOs have been concentrated in ensuring all members have disability certificates. As Livingston, President of the Visthar Federation declared, "Yes every member should possess ID card. If any disabled member without ID card asks for help they are also included in the group but are encouraged to get the card as soon as possible". The identity card, which is based on the principles of the medical model, is then used to access the entitlements from the government. The relevance of the social model and increasing realization about oppression have been translated into compensatory actions by the governments, whose duty is seen as protection of rights of people with disabilities. As a member of Samiksha Odisha explained:

> At the GP (gram panchayat/local government) level, we tried to influence the panchayat and worked on issues like documents which have to be acquired from the panchayat—residence certificate, bus pass etc., job cards—getting work under NREGS (national rural employment generation scheme), entitlements like pensions. We have focused mainly on disability certificate, aids and appliances, job cards, pensions etc. – helping each other in the group to get these benefits.

Disabled people who are members of DPOs have also started to participate in *gram sabha* meetings with panchayats, which means getting involved in community development and politics at the grass-roots level.

Yet, advocacy efforts, especially in the north and north-east, have remained focused around welfare and social security schemes such as scholarships and pensions, which do not instil empowerment or independence but rather create a sense of dependency amongst the disabled people. In the south almost all disabled people have access to disability pensions and scholarships for disabled children going to school. Thus, issues chosen for advocacy vary from group to group depending on their concerns, but vary regionally as well. The age and maturity of the DPO also decides the range of advocacy activities that are taken up by them. The DPOs in the southern states have been advocating for different issues over a long period of time and have moved from basic survival issues to more systemic issues for advocacy. In the northern states, most of the efforts are concentrated on advocating for inclusion of disabled people in the below poverty line (BPL) list and issuing of ration card to the families of disabled people, so that they can benefit from the schemes meant for the poor. In the north-eastern states, however, advocacy efforts are still at the most basic level not only because these groups are newly formed but also because the awareness of rights and the voice to speak are still to develop.

Part of the newness of disability politics is the use of different tactics to achieve change. Some of the advocacy strategies used by these groups include information sharing, awareness raising discussions, petitions, rallies, *dharna*s (protests). Groups in South India have achieved a reasonable amount of success in engaging government systems and non-governmental bodies to respond to their demands, especially with regard to access to entitlements and financial processes, mainly writing petitions, taking out rallies and staging *dharna*s to influence people in power in their favour. In the northern states, groups in the formation stage are more passive and non-confrontational and thus petition governments to grant them their rights. Groups in Odisha and Jharkhand spoke about the petitions they have submitted to different government departments for inclusion in schools, inclusion in NREGS work, and for special privileges like concessions in road transport. Nagamani of Mashal Odisha elaborated on how the joint efforts of the groups in the area led to change in the practice of the transport operators:

> The concession in the private and government buses came about as we all went together in a rally to the BDO (block development officer) and the district collector and gave them a petition. We had filed an RTI (right to information) application and found that the government rules mention that if concession is not given the licence of the bus can be cancelled. Then, the district collector issued an order to all transport operators in Baripada about the concessions to be given to disabled passengers.

However, groups have started moving beyond individual disability concerns to focusing on concerns of the community. One DPO in one of the villages wanted to get the *anganwadi* centre (local primary health centre) to work better so that their disabled children could benefit from preschool education. Their children had to go to an *anganwadi* centre, which was quite far away from their village, so the group decided to start a mini *anganwadi* centre in their area. They have built a house and have approached the government to take over by recruiting staff.

In the south, groups have advocated more aggressively on a range of issues which has helped many of their disabled members. Members of the Sandhya in Cuddalore came to know about the government's tsunami relief fund and tried to mobilize this fund for persons with disabilities in the area, but were told that they would need a national ID card to claim the fund. The disability ID card was seen as insufficient to access this relief fund. The doctors in the area declined to issue ID cards to the disabled people, which led to a protest by the federation in the form of a road blockade.

> Ten members sat on the road in protest and all were beaten by police. The government doctor was called by the police and out of 250 people with disabilities, 50 % got the tsunami relief fund. The government doctor signed the national ID card and each person with disability got Rs. 10,000 through the tsunami relief fund.

Some of the DPOs, especially in South India, that have been working for more than 5 years have taken up community-level activities like awareness programmes for teachers in village primary schools about inclusion of disabled children within the classroom. Besides including disabled children in the school, they help other non-disabled dropouts and motivate them to go to school. Sasikumar said that in his group Ismail, a disabled boy studying in Class X, was dismissed from school. He had low vision with 75 % disability. The group took this up as an issue and spoke with the management and principal and enabled Ismail to take the public examinations. The Differently Abled Group, Tamil Nadu, has ensured that two of their members who are mentally ill receive free medicine from the government primary health centre (PHC) and that regular follow-up is done.

With regard to selection of issues for advocacy within the groups, there is a clear trend of domination by certain groups of disabled people. Most of the benefits to date have been monopolized by the people of these two categories, while people with other disabilities are placated with pensions and the like. Disability wise, the representation of issues within the DPO as well as actions taken up by them represents the core concerns of the dominant groups, while the concerns of the other groups of disabled people and sometimes that of parents receive less importance. Representation of persons with hearing impairments is minimal as communication is difficult, while parents of people with intellectual impairments are assigned a peripheral role within the groups. The concerns of people with severe disabilities are sidelined because most of these people do not attend the meetings and their representatives also attend only occasionally. In one of the groups in Tamil Nadu, when asked to reflect on what else could the group have taken up for addressing, one parent of a girl with mental retardation spoke aloud that probably the group should start thinking of long-term living arrangements for people like his daughter —a statement that reflected that such needs had not been discussed before in the group. What was interesting was that the idea was immediately shot down by the other, more vocal, members, mostly the visually impaired and locomotor challenged. One thing that needs to be mentioned here is that these DPOs seem to be disconnected from parents' groups, which have been formed under the umbrella of Parivaar or National Trust. As in the West, there is an ongoing debate whether parents or other family members of disabled individuals should be seen as part of the disability community and allowed to represent the community in political forums.

11.4 Implications for Movements

Involvement in social movements leads to changes in the participants themselves, especially in terms of their self-awareness and identity. What has emerged is the construction of a marginalized identity based on the experiences of discrimination that these disabled people have faced at different points of time in their lives. The efforts for advocacy and working together as a group have given confidence to the persons with disabilities, mostly from poor rural households, to press for their rights. Members from Mother Teresa Trust elaborated: "People thought that persons with disabilities can do nothing, we thought of doing things for ourselves. And we have done many things". Awareness about rights and their success in advocacy efforts has also developed their capacities to publicly deal with government officials to assert their rights. This has been particularly successful in the south where most of the groups have been working for the last 8–10 years. "When we go to the BDO office, we ask the government officials about the provisions available for disabled people. If they say that there are no provisions we ask them to give in writing. On the basis of such a document we can fight further for our rights", says Luther, Visthar Federation, Tamil Nadu. Members of ADT also are able to identify the changes that have occurred in the attitudes of people, especially government officials. Podu of ADT in Tamil Nadu said, "Initially, the government officials looked at us differently and made us feel uneasy. Initially the people were unable to judge the officials' reaction. Before they ignored the disabled person's rights, but now their attitude has changed".

Being part of DPOs has led to the capacity-building of persons with disabilities who rarely used to go out of their homes. Most of the disabled people and especially the leaders have become well versed in group management, like the framing of rules and procedures, printing of stationery and having a seal, conducting meetings and communicating with both group members and government and other officials. This building of capacities has enhanced the self-confidence of the group members. Being leaders of the DPO has also brought recognition. Nagamani of Mashal Odisha said, "Now all of us are known to all in the GP. Though I belong to another village, the people of this GP are proposing my name for the *sarpanch* (leader of local government) election".

Being part of the groups has helped to foster solidarity amongst the members and this is most widely felt in the north-east. Members of the self-reliance group in Nagaland feel that this feeling of solidarity has also helped them to work together as a group. In Nagaland, groups had demanded for the issue of disability medical certificates and identity cards to all members. However, this process was stalled due to the lack of availability of printed booklets that serve as identity cards, as booklets were exhausted and the relevant department showed no interest in printing fresh ones. When the Dimapur office of the social welfare department located 2–3 such booklets, the group refused to take the identity cards, insisting that the cards must be issued to all the members at the same time.

Despite the fact that most of the DPOs had been working for more than one year at the time of research, there is a lack of understanding of all the issues concerning all persons with disabilities. As has been pointed out, there are power groups amongst these DPOs based on the dimensions of disability, caste, class and privilege. Within the group, issues are dominated by the locomotor disabled and the visually impaired and the issues of people with other disabilities are sidelined, especially persons with hearing impairment, mental retardation and multiple disability. This is the scenario not only in the new groups, where solidarity may not have been reached as yet, but also in the older groups. In ADT, when the group members were asked to reflect on how they could help the more severely disabled members, most of them could only talk of pensions and other benefits like the Indira Awaas Yojana and Total Sanitation programme. In the end, it was the father of two girls with mental retardation in Tamil Nadu, who burst out, "Who will take care of my children when I am no longer there? Who will assume responsibility for them?" The group members were not able to think of or envisage a community care system for these girls, so that the girls are able to live within the community and in familiar surroundings. The DPO as a unit does not deem such issues as its responsibility but rather passes it on to the government, saying it is the duty of the government to provide to protect and fulfil the rights of these disabled girls.

For some of the older groups, there is the possibility of stagnancy. DPOs such as Visthar Federation in Tamil Nadu and Mashal Federation in Odisha report a slowdown in their activities and in the enthusiasm of the members after the first spurt of activity and lobbying that resulted in most of the members claiming some entitlement or other.

> We were all together when we were mobilizing for benefits like disability certificate, scholarships and pensions etc. Once most of the members had received all the benefits they could receive, people's interest in the group went down.

DPOs are based on the principle of common activities that bind them together and hence, when restricted to lobbying for access to entitlements, most DPOs face the risk of fading out once the entitlements have been realized.

The ADT has been expanding its activities to newer GPs and forming fresh groups along with extending their own activities to more varied services like vocational training. Visthar Federation has moved to looking at mainstream policies and initiating advocacy to ensure disabled people are included in these programmes, while extending support services to any new disabled people in the area who approach them. Both these federations dream of becoming NGOs themselves, with staff and funding to carry on their activities. One of the reasons for this is that the role model they follow is the NGO that mentored them and hence their aspiration is to be as structured as them. On the other hand, Mashal Federation in Odisha was carefully steered by their NGO mentor towards looking not only at entitlements, but also towards solidarity, group feelings and cooperation. "We were asked to discuss on how many issues like health education livelihood affect our lives including those of disabled people".

11.5 Conclusion

Disability politics is about changing government responses, changing relations at an interpersonal level and changing identities at a personal level. The growth of DPOs can be viewed basically as the consequence of exclusion and discriminatory practices towards disabled people. The disability movement links the personal cultural realm to the political by raising issues that are often dismissed or ignored. Thus, while the initial impetus was to encourage disabled people "to solve their problems themselves and not have them solved" by others, there was also a further aim which was "to identify the needs of the membership as a whole and articulate them, both to statutory agencies and political parties at both a local and a national level" (Oliver and Hasler, 1987). DPOs are usually seen as social (human rights) movements, though a genuine review of lots of community-based DPOs will indicate that many of them are in fact SHGs, trying to promote usually some income-generating activities for their members. Sometimes, SHGs may form federations, which can be observed in a number of states in India. Such federations have a stronger voice; they foster active citizenship and together or under a national umbrella organization they may be very successful in combating injustices in society. It was in South India for instance that the joint effort of SHGs helped to successfully fight corruption at the pension payout points. However, the spirit of being a SHG, which was initially based on the values of concern for one another and helping themselves and other group members, has not developed overtly, mainly as a result of the stress placed on rights and advocacy. What could have been, as in the West, a source of personal support and encouragement has remained mired in self-interest and individual development.

Regional variations in successes achieved amongst the DPOs reflect a whole range of factors that influence their development and efforts. One of the foremost reasons is the role played by the mentoring agencies or the NGOs that have stimulated the development of these groups. NGOs working solely with disability issues have ensured that the mentoring process is more thorough and empowering, whereas if they are grass-roots-level community development agencies, the vision and goal adopted by the DPOs are limited and are hardly focussed on independence from the mentoring agency. Newer groups are still stuck in the notions of personal gain through group action, while older and more mature groups have moved towards advocacy or larger issues and are more inclusive. Almost always, the age and maturity of the group is reflected in the systematic procedures involved in running, maintenance and advocacy strategies adopted.

The second major reason for successful DPOs is their location within a larger framework of people's struggles. In the south where the *Dalit* movement (anti-untouchability and anti-upper caste movement) has been very strong, the groups have found it easier to internalize and rally using an identity marker with which they had not identified previously as a group. In Odisha, too, the association with the land rights movement and farmers' struggles that have taken place in the area has helped DPOs to benefit from their experience and strategies in successfully lobbying for their rights. People in the area have a prior exposure to struggles and negotiations, which people in many other areas do not have and this predisposes them to take initiative on their own. On the other hand, in the north-east, disabled people are so isolated within their own communities because of the hilly terrain of the region that they have not been able to capitalize on the experiences of the militant groups operating in the regions, especially so in Nagaland.

In India, the grass-roots-level DPOs have put to use a wide variety of strategies for advocacy to lay claim to their political rights, but most of these have been peaceful and placatory towards the people in positions of power. The DPOs have mostly adopted a collaborative stance with the state in order to access state resources rather than challenging policies and programmes. Thus, most of the DPOs have remained at the periphery of all social activities within the community, mainly because the disabled members themselves doubt their own revolutionary potential. These groups and their disabled members, though united on the basis of identity, have not been able to develop a group pride in identity as in the West and in the case of other marginalized group movements. DPOs themselves have rarely broadened their vision to move towards mainstreaming or inclusive societies.

There are also tensions and contradictions within the dominant ideology of disability rights—the subtle difference between the minority group model and the social model. Most of the DPOs have followed the minority group strategy in claiming a disadvantaged status and thus benefits that will improve the economic and social condition of persons with disabilities and their families. Although this has benefitted disabled people who are members of the groups, there have been few efforts at community advocacy for greater inclusion in everyday life and community participation, which is at the heart of the social model. This is radically different from the West, as most of the political activity has been directed towards increasing the scope or level of government benefits, not towards the goals of equal access, community integration and independent living. However, the age and the maturity of the DPO and the cultural contexts also act as a decisive factor in determining the advocacy efforts of the DPOs.

Representation is typically concerned with relations of power, dominance and subordination. One important political task facing the disabled people's movement in India, as any other oppressed social group, is to gain control over the way their situation is described and defined. The challenge is how best to uphold the common features of disability as a form of social oppression and to promote a common identity amongst disabled people as a group, while weaving in physical, intellectual, mental and sensory dimensions of disability along with other major social divisions such as class, gender, race, nationality, ethnicity, age, language, sexual orientation, and religion.

References

Barnes, C., & Mercer, G. (2010). *Exploring disability*. Cambridge: Polity.

Barton, L. (1993). *Disability, difference and the politics of definition*. Inaugural lecture, University of Sheffield. Source http://disability-studies.leeds.ac.uk/files/library/Barton-inaugral-lecture-barton.pdf. Accessed on August 19, 2010.

Campbell, J., & Oliver, M. (1996). *Disability politics: Understanding our past, changing our future*. London: Routledge.

Chander, J. (2012). *The disability rights movement and defining disability under the persons with disabilities act in India*. Paper presented at the Annual Meeting of the Eighth Annual Congress of Qualitative Inquiry, University of Illinois at Urbana-Champaign, Urbana, Illinois, May 16.

Freire, P. (1970). *Pedagogy of the oppressed*. New York: Seabury Press.

Goodwin, J., & Jasper, J. M. (2009). Introduction. In J. Goodwin & J. M. Jasper (Eds.), *The social movements reader: Cases and concepts*. Sussex, UK: Wiley Blackwell Publishing.

Mehrotra, N. (2011). Disability rights movements in India: Politics and practice. *Economic and Political Weekly, XLVI*(6), 65–72.

Oliver, M., & Hasler, F. (1987). Disability and self-help: A case study of the Spinal Injuries Association. *Disability & Society, 2*(2), 113–125.

Scotch, R. (1988). Disability as the basis for a social movement: Advocacy and the politics of definition. *Journal of Social Issues, 44*(1), 159–172.

Printed in Australia
AUOC02n0649271016
279994AU00001B/2/P

9 788132 235934